Pentaho 8 Reporting for Java Developers

Create pixel-perfect analytical reports using reporting tools

Francesco Corti

BIRMINGHAM - MUMBAI

Pentaho 8 Reporting for Java Developers

First published: September 2017

Production reference: 1120917

Published by Packt Publishing Ltd.
Livery Place
35 Livery Street
Birmingham
B3 2PB, UK.
ISBN 978-1-78829-899-5

www.packtpub.com

Credits

Author
Francesco Corti

Reviewers
Ruben Oliva Ramos
Juan Tomas Oliva Ramos

Commissioning Editor
Amey Varangaonkar

Acquisition Editor
Viraj Madhav

Content Development Editor
Cheryl Dsa

Technical Editor
Dinesh Pawar

Copy Editor
Safis Editing

Project Coordinator
Nidhi Joshi

Proofreader
Safis Editing

Indexer
Tejal Daruwale Soni

Graphics
Tania Dutta

Production Coordinator
Arvindkumar Gupta

About the Author

Francesco Corti is an enthusiastic consultant in software solutions and loves working in developer, sales, and customers teams. Proud of the role of a software engineer, he is often involved in pre-sales presentations, public speaking, and IT courses. Developing software, designing architectures, and defining solutions in ECM/BPM and BI are his favorite areas of interest. He has completed dozens of projects, from very small ones to more complex ones, in almost 20 years of experience.

A product evangelist at Alfresco, Francesco represents the famous open source ECM in the developer community. In addition to helping developers adopt Alfresco technologies, he often helps Alfresco to improve the developer experience through talks, articles, blogging, user demonstrations, recorded demonstrations, or the creation of sample projects.
He is the inventor and principal developer of Alflytics (previously named Alfresco Audit Analytics and Reporting), the main business intelligence solution over Alfresco ECM, entirely based on the Pentaho suite. He authored the Pentaho Reporting video course with more than 40 videos and courses on the Pentaho Reporting Designer and SDK.
Francesco has specialty and principal experiences in enterprise content management solutions with Alfresco ECM and Hyland OnBase (he is an OnBase certified installer); business process management solutions with Activiti, JBPM, and Hyland OnBase; data capture solutions with Ephesoft, Hyland OnBase, and custom software; record management solutions with O'Neil software and custom software (using Alfresco ECM and Hyland OnBase); and portal and collaboration with Liferay and MS SharePoint.

About the Reviewers

Ruben Oliva Ramos is a computer systems engineer from Tecnologico de Leon Institute, with a master's degree in computer and electronic systems engineering, teleinformatics, and networking specialization from the University of Salle Bajio in Leon, Guanajuato, Mexico. He has more than 5 years of experience in developing web applications to control and monitor devices connected with Arduino and Raspberry Pi using web frameworks and cloud services to build the Internet of Things applications.

He is a mechatronics teacher at the University of Salle Bajio and teaches students of the master's degree in design and engineering of mechatronics systems. Ruben also works at Centro de Bachillerato Tecnologico Industrial 225 in Leon, Guanajuato, Mexico, teaching subjects such as electronics, robotics and control, automation, and microcontrollers at Mechatronics Technician Career; he is a consultant and developer for projects in areas such as monitoring systems and datalogger data using technologies (such as Android, iOS, Windows Phone, HTML5, PHP, CSS, Ajax, JavaScript, Angular, and ASP.NET), databases (such as SQlite, MongoDB, and MySQL), web servers (such as Node.js and IIS), hardware programming (such as Arduino, Raspberry pi, Ethernet Shield, GPS, and GSM/GPRS, ESP8266), and control and monitor systems for data acquisition and programming.

He has authored the book *Internet of Things Programming with JavaScript* by Packt Publishing. He is also involved in monitoring, controlling, and the acquisition of data with Arduino and Visual Basic .NET for Alfaomega.

I would like to thank my savior and lord, Jesus Christ, for giving me the strength and courage to pursue this project; my dearest wife, Mayte; our two lovely sons, Ruben and Dario; my dear father, Ruben; my dearest mom, Rosalia; my brother, Juan Tomas; and my sister, Rosalia, whom I love, for all their support while reviewing this book, for allowing me to pursue my dream, and tolerating not being with them after my busy day job.

Juan Tomas Oliva Ramos is an environmental engineer from the university of Guanajuato, with a master's degree in administrative engineering and quality. He has more than 5 years of experience in management and development of patents, technological innovation projects, and development of technological solutions through statistical control of processes. He is a teacher of statistics, entrepreneurship, and technological development of projects since 2011. He has always maintained an interest for the improvement and the innovation in the processes through the technology. He became an entrepreneurship mentor and technology management consultant and started a new department of technology management and entrepreneurship at Instituto Tecnologico Superior de Purisima del Rincon.

He has worked on the book *Wearable Designs for Smart Watches, Smart TVs and Android Mobile Devices*.

He has developed prototypes through programming and automation technologies for the improvement of operations, which have been registered for patents.

I want to thank God for giving me the wisdom and humility to review this book. I want to thank Ruben, for inviting me to collaborate on this adventure. I also thank my wife, Brenda, our two magic princesses, Regina and Renata, and our next member, Tadeo. All of you are my strengths and happiness, and my desire is to be for the best for you.

www.PacktPub.com

For support files and downloads related to your book, please visit www.PacktPub.com. Did you know that Packt offers eBook versions of every book published, with PDF and ePub files available? You can upgrade to the eBook version at www.PacktPub.comand as a print book customer, you are entitled to a discount on the eBook copy.

Get in touch with us at service@packtpub.com for more details. At www.PacktPub.com, you can also read a collection of free technical articles, sign up for a range of free newsletters and receive exclusive discounts and offers on Packt books and eBooks.

https://www.packtpub.com/mapt

Get the most in-demand software skills with Mapt. Mapt gives you full access to all Packt books and video courses, as well as industry-leading tools to help you plan your personal development and advance your career.

Why subscribe?

- Fully searchable across every book published by Packt
- Copy and paste, print, and bookmark content
- On demand and accessible via a web browser

Customer Feedback

Thanks for purchasing this Packt book. At Packt, quality is at the heart of our editorial process. To help us improve, please leave us an honest review on this book's Amazon page at https://www.amazon.com/dp/1788298993.

If you'd like to join our team of regular reviewers, you can email us at customerreviews@packtpub.com. We award our regular reviewers with free eBooks and videos in exchange for their valuable feedback. Help us be relentless in improving our products!

Dedicated to my wife, Natalija

Table of Contents

[ ]

Preface

How many times you have been asked to develop appealing reports with the most up-to-date technology in a few days (or probably less) in various different formats using a web-based solution or a custom Java project? If this is the case, this book will enable you to reach that goal using the dedicated tool of the Pentaho suite, named Pentaho Reporting.

This book is a definitive guide for Java developers and information technologists about the open source reporting tool, allowing you to create pixel-perfect reports of your data in PDF, Excel, HTML, text, RTF, XML, and CSV, based on a wide range of data sources, using a visual design environment and the SDK to embed the Pentaho Reporting Engine into your applications.

The book is written when Pentaho Version 8 were about to be officially released, and it is mainly based on this version. The description of the features, tips and tricks and best practices is done using a learning-by-example approach. To better guide you through the different topics and the definition of a learning path, the book is organized into four main parts:

- Introduction and basics of Pentaho Reporting
- Core concepts and advanced features of Report Designer
- All about the Reporting SDK
- Additional Pentaho Reporting topics

What this book covers

Chapter 1, *Introduction to Pentaho Reporting*, covers the typical uses, history, and origins of Pentaho Reporting, along with a more detailed overview of the reporting functionality that Pentaho Reporting provides.

Chapter 2, *Getting Started with Report Designer*, is focused on getting up and running with Pentaho Reporting. It'll begin by setting up an environment for building and embedding reports. From there, the reader will walk through creating a report using the wizard and will finish the chapter learning how to save the report into the filesystem.

Chapter 3, *Getting Started with Reporting SDK*, is about the Pentaho Reporting SDK. The reader will walk through embedding an existing report into a generic Java application.

Chapter 4, *Creating a Report with Report Designer*, goes one step further, covering the most commonly used features for creating a report from scratch instead of using the wizard. The core concepts, such as customizing the report, saving it in the Pentaho repository, and previewing the content, will be detailed step by step.

Chapter 5, *Design and Layout in Report Designer*, dives deep into all the concepts and functionality of Pentaho's Report Designer related to design and layout. The reader will explore in depth the ins and outs of design and layout of reports using the Pentaho Report Designer.

Chapter 6, *Configuring JDBC and Other Data Sources*, teaches you the configuration of the data sources in all the ways Pentaho Reporting is able to connect in. The data source definition will be shown using Pentaho Reporting Designer.

Chapter 7, *Including Graphics and Charts in Reports*, shows how to incorporate charts and graphics into Pentaho reports. You will learn about the different types of charts supported and how to configure them in Pentaho Report Designer. This chapter will also help you to populate a chart with various types of data.

Chapter 8, *Parameterization, Functions, Variables, and Formulas*, starts off by learning how to parameterize a report. This chapter covers all the predefined functions and expressions available for use within a report. It will help readers learn about Pentaho Reporting's formula capabilities, including the correct syntax and available formula methods.

Chapter 9, *Internationalization and Localization*, shows the details of internationalizing and localizing a report.

Chapter 10, *Subreports and Cross Tabs*, covers building from scratch some examples of subreports and cross tabs, exploring the capabilities offered by Pentaho Reporting. We will build a multi-page subreport that demonstrates the use of the sticky flag available for managing page headers and also build a subreport with a summary chart.

Chapter 11, *The PRPT Format and the Java API to Build It*, teaches Pentaho Reporting's PRPT bundle format, along with the details of Pentaho Reporting's Java API. This chapter focuses on the composition of the PRPT file representing the Pentaho report and how to build it using the Java API.

Chapter 12, *Developing Using Data Sources*, shows various methods of loading data into the Pentaho Reporting Engine, and digs deep into how the Pentaho Reporting Engine interacts with these data sources to render a report.

Chapter 13, *Internationalization, Subreports, and Cross Tabs Using Java*, covers the details of report parameterization. You also learn the various ways to dynamically render a report, including learning all the available functions and expressions but from a Java perspective.

Chapter 14, *Building Interactive Reports*, teaches you to enable interactive functionality within reports. You will also be able to modify report definitions to generate hyperlink events and many different HTML JavaScript events. You will learn how to render an HTML report on a server, along with including external script files within the HTML, rendered report.

Chapter 15, *Using Reports in Pentaho Business Analytics Platform*, shows the basics of the Pentaho Business Analytics Platform and the best practices on using Pentaho Reports stored in the repository or through dashboards.

Chapter 16, *Using Reports in Pentaho Data Integration*, covers how to use the developed Pentaho reports inside the Pentaho suite, particularly with Pentaho Data Integration (Kettle) to develop jobs/transformations managing Pentaho reports.

Chapter 17, *Pentaho Reporting Nightly Build and Support*, covers a potpourri of useful, short, and advanced Pentaho Reporting subjects.

What you need for this book

Pentaho Reporting tools are cross-platform applications and will run in Linux, Windows, macOS, and other Java supported environments. The Reporting Engine is backward-compatible with previous versions of JDK, but it is always recommended to use the latest one. In the case of Pentaho 8, JDK version 1.8 is suggested.

All the examples contained into this book are developed using an Ubuntu operating system v16.04 LTS with 4 GB of RAM and an Intel i7 processor. The development environment was composed by Java JVM 1.8.0_131, Apache Maven 3.3.9, Git version 2.7.4. This configuration is not mandatory for you to run the examples, but it is shared as a reference and suggestion to run the examples with success.

If you are an information technologist and don't want to cover the development tasks, Apache Maven and Git need not be installed into your laptop.

Who this book is for

This book is written for two types of professionals and students: information technologists with a basic knowledge of databases and Java developers with medium seniority. Developers will be interested to discover how to embed reports in a third-party Java application.

Conventions

In this book, you will find a number of text styles that distinguish between different kinds of information. Here are some examples of these styles and an explanation of their meaning. Code words in text, database table names, folder names, filenames, file extensions, pathnames, dummy URLs, user input, and Twitter handles are shown as follows: "You will also learn the details of the Pentaho Reporting Engine data API specification, allowing you to implement your own `DataFactory`, if necessary."

A block of code is set as follows:

```
// Defining the connection provider.
DriverConnectionProvider provider = new DriverConnectionProvider();
provider.setDriver("org.hsqldb.jdbcDriver");
provider.setProperty("user", "pentaho_user");
provider.setProperty("password", "password");
provider.setUrl("jdbc:hsqldb:./resources/sampledata/sampledata");
```

When we wish to draw your attention to a particular part of a code block, the relevant lines or items are set in bold:

```
// Defining the connection provider.
DriverConnectionProvider provider = new DriverConnectionProvider();
provider.setDriver("org.hsqldb.jdbcDriver");
provider.setProperty("user", "pentaho_user");
provider.setProperty("password", "password");
provider.setUrl("jdbc:hsqldb:./resources/sampledata/sampledata");
```

Any command-line input or output is written as follows:

```
mvn clean install
 mvn package
 java -jar target/dependency/jetty-runner.jar target/*.war
```

New terms and **important words** are shown in bold. Words that you see on the screen, for example, in menus or dialog boxes, appear in the text like this: "Clicking the **OK** button moves you to the next screen."

 Warnings or important notes appear like this.

 Tips and tricks appear like this.

Reader feedback

Feedback from our readers is always welcome. Let us know what you think about this book-what you liked or disliked. Reader feedback is important for us as it helps us develop titles that you will really get the most out of. To send us general feedback, simply email feedback@packtpub.com, and mention the book's title in the subject of your message. If there is a topic that you have expertise in and you are interested in either writing or contributing to a book, see our author guide at www.packtpub.com/authors.

Customer support

Now that you are the proud owner of a Packt book, we have a number of things to help you to get the most from your purchase.

Downloading the example code

You can download the example code files for this book from your account at http://www.packtpub.com. If you purchased this book elsewhere, you can visit http://www.packtpub.com/support and register to have the files emailed directly to you.

You can download the code files by following these steps:

1. Log in or register to our website using your email address and password.
2. Hover the mouse pointer on the **SUPPORT** tab at the top.
3. Click on **Code Downloads & Errata**.
4. Enter the name of the book in the **Search** box.
5. Select the book for which you're looking to download the code files.
6. Choose from the drop-down menu where you purchased this book from.
7. Click on **Code Download**.

Once the file is downloaded, please make sure that you unzip or extract the folder using the latest version of:

- WinRAR / 7-Zip for Windows
- Zipeg / iZip / UnRarX for Mac
- 7-Zip / PeaZip for Linux

The code bundle for the book is also hosted on GitHub at `https://github.com/PacktPublishing/Pentaho-8-Reporting-for-Java-Developers`. We also have other code bundles from our rich catalog of books and videos available at `https://github.com/PacktPublishing/`. Check them out!

Downloading the color images of this book

We also provide you with a PDF file that has color images of the screenshots/diagrams used in this book. The color images will help you better understand the changes in the output. You can download this file from `https://www.packtpub.com/sites/default/files/downloads/Pentaho8ReportingforJava Developers_ColorImages.pdf`.

Errata

Although we have taken every care to ensure the accuracy of our content, mistakes do happen. If you find a mistake in one of our books-maybe a mistake in the text or the code-we would be grateful if you could report this to us. By doing so, you can save other readers from frustration and help us improve subsequent versions of this book. If you find any errata, please report them by visiting http://www.packtpub.com/submit-errata, selecting your book, clicking on the **Errata Submission Form** link, and entering the details of your errata. Once your errata are verified, your submission will be accepted and the errata will be uploaded to our website or added to any list of existing errata under the Errata section of that title. To view the previously submitted errata, go to https://www.packtpub.com/books/content/support and enter the name of the book in the search field. The required information will appear under the **Errata** section.

Piracy

Piracy of copyrighted material on the internet is an ongoing problem across all media. At Packt, we take the protection of our copyright and licenses very seriously. If you come across any illegal copies of our works in any form on the internet, please provide us with the location address or website name immediately so that we can pursue a remedy. Please contact us at copyright@packtpub.com with a link to the suspected pirated material. We appreciate your help in protecting our authors and our ability to bring you valuable content.

Questions

If you have a problem with any aspect of this book, you can contact us at questions@packtpub.com, and we will do our best to address the problem.

1
Introduction to Pentaho Reporting

Pentaho Reporting is an easy-to-use, open source, lightweight suite of Java projects built for one purpose: report generation. In this book, you will discover how easy it is to embed Pentaho Reporting into your Java projects, or use it as a standalone reporting platform. Pentaho Reporting's open source license—the GNU **Lesser General Public License (LGPL)**—gives developers the freedom to embed Pentaho Reporting into their open source and proprietary applications at no cost. An active community participates in the development and use of Pentaho Reporting, answering forum questions, fixing bugs, and implementing new features. While many proprietary reporting options are available, none can offer the openness and flexibility that Pentaho Reporting provides its users with.

As with most successful open source projects, Pentaho Reporting has a proven track record, along with a long list of features. Most of this history has been documented in open forums and in email threads, which are still available for folks to browse through and glean ideas from. Starting as a side hobby and turning into an enterprise reporting suite over the course of many years, the Pentaho Reporting Engine and its suite of tools, such as the Report Designer, Reporting Engine, and Reporting SDK, are used as critical components in countless corporate, educational, governmental, and community-based information technology solutions.

In most business software applications, a reporting component is necessary, be it for summarizing data, generating large numbers of customized documents, or simply for making it easier to print information that would be useful in various output formats. With a complete set of features, including PDF, Microsoft Excel, HTML, Text, XML, CSV, and RTF report generation, along with advanced reporting capabilities such as subreports and cross tabs, Pentaho Reporting can crack the simplest of problems quickly, along with solving the more advanced challenges when designing, generating, and deploying reports.

Read on in this chapter to learn more about Pentaho Reporting, its typical uses, history, and origins, along with a more detailed overview of the reporting functionality that Pentaho Reporting provides.

In this chapter, you will cover the following topics:

- Introduction to Pentaho Reporting
- Typical uses of Pentaho Reporting
- Pentaho Reporting history
- Pentaho Reporting architecture

Introducing Pentaho Reporting

As introduced, Pentaho Reporting is an easy-to-use, open source, lightweight suite of Java projects, built to let the report developer be able to create pixel-perfect reports of his/her data in PDF, Microsoft Excel, HTML, Text, RTF, XML, and CSV formats. These computer generated reports easily refine data from various sources into a human readable form, and can be accessed via an integrated web viewer, saved as files and sent by email to a predefined list of recipients. It is also possible to generate reports as part of a Pentaho Data Integration transformation, to distribute the generated files according to more complex business rules (`http://community.pentaho.com/projects/reporting`).

 Pentaho Data Integration transformations are used to describe the data flows in a process, such as reading from a source, transforming data, and loading it into a target location. You will learn more in `Chapter 16`, *Using Reports in Pentaho Data Integration*.

As it renders such high performance, consuming, considerably low amount of memory, the report processing can tower from small footprint embedded scenarios to large-scale enterprise reporting scenarios. Pentaho Reporting integrates perfectly with the Business Analytics Platform and allows you to share reports with coworkers and peers.

Pentaho Reporting styling is flexible and it permits the report designer to choose the granularity at which they desire to manipulate the entire user interface, right down to the minute details like the font styling on individual characters. In addition to this, you can also add your own images and logos to these reports and select from the various layouts, charts, and tables the one that you wish to apply.

Introducing Pentaho Reporting tools

Pentaho Reporting can be defined as a suite of open source tools and can be described as being composed of the following:

- **Report Designer**: This is a desktop application providing a design, develop, and test environment to enable the knowledge worker to easily create simple as well as complex reports. The tool is designed to be used by experienced and power users, who are familiar with few technical concepts.
- **Reporting Engine**: This engine is born as an evolution of the JFreeReport project, a free Java class library for creating reports. The library can be used in both client-side (Report Designer, for example) and server-side applications (web applications, for example).
- **Reporting SDK**: This is a packaging of several resources (the engine, some documentation, and all the libraries required to embed the Pentaho Reporting Engine into your application), to be a valid support for all the developers, particularly, for all the Java developers.

In this book, we will look at the Report Designer and the Reporting SDK in detail, assuming they are the right tools for developers and report designers, to use the Reporting Engine in real life use cases.

Types of users and required knowledge

Pentaho Reporting is designed and developed to make life easier for report designers, with less limitations on flexibility and the ability to develop sophisticated and rich reports. For this reason, the Report Designer can be used by developers (not necessarily Java developers) but also by information technologists with a basic knowledge of databases and technical concepts.

For advanced development, especially using the Reporting SDK, technical skills on Java development are required, and you must be familiar with importing JARs into a project and be comfortable reading inline comments in code, to figure out advanced functionality on your own.

If you are an information technologist with a basic knowledge of databases and technical concepts, the chapters dedicated to the Report Designer and how to use reports in Pentaho Data Integration and Pentaho Business Analytics Platform, are the topics you might be interested in. If you are a Java developer, the chapters about the Reporting SDK could also be interesting to you.

Technological advantages

Pentaho Reporting offers the following unique functionalities, not found in competing embeddable solutions:

- **Requires a Java runtime environment, not necessarily a JDK.** Even if you need a JDK installed on your development environment, you do not need a JDK to run an application that embeds the Pentaho Reporting Engine. Only a Java runtime environment is required.

- **Potentially backwards compatible.** In theory, Pentaho Reporting can run use dated versions of the Java virtual machine. Pentaho highly suggests to use JRE 1.8.0, but it is possible to use the Reporting Engine in older JRE versions (few integrations would be required).

- **All Processing is done in memory.** All the processing, calculations, and algorithms are designed and developed to run in memory only, without the use of temporary files, tables, or any sort of memory mass usage.

- **Low memory requirement.** An application based on Pentaho Reporting can run with only 64 MB of memory, even though 128 MB would dramatically increase the report processing speed.

- **Dynamically library loading.** Pentaho Reporting Engine is able to detect JAR libraries at runtime. By adding new JARs or removing the existing ones, you can expand the engine's capabilities or remove unnecessary libraries to reduce your application's memory and disk space usage.

- **Parameterization at runtime.** All the report elements, and we can say the same for styling, functions, and queries, are completely customizable through parameters passed to the Reporting Engine at run time.

- **OpenFormula standard.** OpenFormula is an open standard that will be introduced in the next chapters. You will be able to create your own custom formulas or customize the existing ones using a known standard.

- **Easy resource management.** Thanks to the use of the **OpenDocument Format** (**ODF**), the Pentaho Reporting Engine can bundle all the requested resources, including the data source connection information, query, and even binary resources like images into a regular file, simplifying the resource management.

A business friendly open source license

One very attractive feature of Pentaho Reporting is its license. Pentaho Reporting is available for free under the GNU LGPL. This license, as shown in the following screenshot, allows other open source and proprietary projects to embed Pentaho Reporting without fear of large license fees or viral open source limitations. As an open source project, developers also have unprecedented access to the engine and to a large group of software developers within the Pentaho Reporting community. This community includes open discussion forums and **Internet Relay Chat (IRC)**, along with commercial support and licensing, if required.

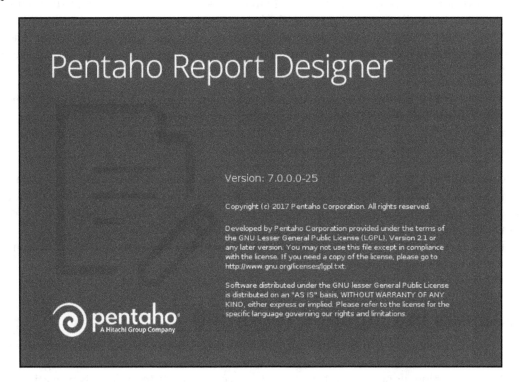

Typical uses of Pentaho Reporting

Business users need access to information in many different forms for many different reasons. Pentaho Reporting addresses the following typical uses of reporting, along with many other types that will be covered in this book.

Operational reporting

One of the most commonly used forms of reporting is operational reporting. When a developer or an IT organization decides to generate reports directly from their operational data sources for the purpose of detailed transaction level reporting, it is referred to as operational reporting. In this scenario, the database is designed to solve an operational problem, and usually contains live data supporting critical business functions. Users of Pentaho Reporting can point directly to this data source and start generating reports.

Some examples of operational reporting include building custom reports directly based on a third-party software vendor's database schema. These reports might include summaries of daily activity, or detailed views into a particular project or users in the system. Reports might also be generated from data originating from an in-house custom application. These reports are typically based on an SQL backend, but could be generated from flat log files or directly from in-memory Java objects.

Pentaho Reporting's parameterization capabilities provide a powerful mechanism to render up-to-the-minute customized operational reports. With features such as cross tabs and interactive reporting, business users can quickly view their operational data and drill back into operational systems that might require attention.

However, there are limitations when developing reports based on live operational data. Developers need to be careful to make sure that queries in the operational system do not impact the performance of regular operations. An extreme CPU-intensive query could delay a transaction from taking place. Also, certain historical questions, for example, state transitions or changes to particular informational fields such as address, aren't traditionally captured in an operational schema design.

Business intelligence reporting

When you've reached the limits of operational reporting, the next logical step is to move your data into a data warehouse. This move is often referred to as business intelligence reporting. Reporting alone does not provide the necessary tools to make this transition. You will need an **Extract, Transform, Load** (ETL) tool, such as Pentaho Data Integration, along with a sensible warehouse design, such as a snowflake schema.

 A **snowflake schema** is a logical arrangement of tables in a multidimensional database, such that the entity relationship diagram resembles a snowflake shape. A multidimensional database is defined as "a variation of the relational model that uses multidimensional structures to organize data and express the relationships between data".

This type of use allows business users to monitor changes over time. It also helps gain performance benefits by pre-calculating aggregations and defining schemas that are built in mind for summarized reporting. Until recently, data warehousing and business intelligence had been limited to large enterprises due to the cost of software and limited expertise. With open source tools becoming more widely available, a large number of small and medium size businesses are deploying data warehouses in order to get solutions for the critical questions in their business domain. Common examples of data warehouse reporting include combining sales and inventory data into a single location for reporting, or combining internal proprietary sales data with publicly available market trends and analysis.

Pentaho Reporting's flexible data source support makes it easy to incorporate reports in your business intelligence solutions. Also, with Pentaho Reporting's speed and scalability, you can deploy Pentaho Reporting with the confidence that reports will be executed efficiently.

As with all approaches, there are limitations to this approach. In traditional warehousing, data is usually batched nightly, weekly, or monthly. Therefore, business users rarely get to see up-to-the-minute reports on business operations. Also, when designing a warehouse, it is important to ask the correct business questions. Unfortunately, it is possible to build a data warehouse and still not address the business users' needs, if not investigated ahead of time.

Financial reporting

The financial reporting is a very specific, but very common, form of reporting, geared towards generating financial summaries for accountants, managers, and business investors. Standard reports that fall into this category include balance sheets, income statements, retained earning statements, and cash flow statements. Unlike business intelligence or operational reporting, many of these reports are required by law, with regulations around their content and presentation. Financial reports often include computations for assets, liabilities, revenues, and expenses.

Following is a screenshot showing one such report:

Steel Wheels		Steel Wheels, Inc. Income Statement From June 1 through June 30, 2005
Revenue		
Direct Sales	400,000	
Channel Sales	150,000	
Total Revenue		**$ 550,000**
Beginning inventory	40,000	
Net purchases	325,000	
Ending inventory	35,000	
Gross Margin		**$ 330,000**
Cost of goods sold		**$ 220,000**
Expenses		
Selling expenses		
Sales salaries	48,000	
Nonrecurring item	12,000	
Other	13,000	
Total Selling expenses		73,000
General and administrative expenses		
Office salaries	27,100	
Depreciation	5,500	
Amortization	3,200	
Bad debt	4,500	
Other	24,200	
Total General and administrative expenses		64,500
Total Expenses		**$ 137,500**
Other revenues		
Interest	5,200	
Dividends	7,200	
Gain on sale of equipment	8,600	
Total Other revenues		$ 21,000
Other expenses		
Interest	9,400	
Writeoff - goodwill	5,000	
Unusual item - loss on sale of long-term investment	5,100	
Total Other expenses		$ 19,500
Income tax expense	33,600	
Extraordinary item - gain on disposal of business segment	24,000	
Other Comprehensive Income	12,000	
Net Income		**$ 86,400**

Report Run: Sun Apr 02 12:50:19 CEST 2017

With features such as group summary aggregations, Pentaho Reporting makes it very easy for developers to implement custom financial reports that business managers and owners require.

Typically, this type of data exists in a controlled form, be it in a proprietary system such as QuickBooks or SAP, or in a secure database system such as Oracle or MySQL. Due to the sensitivity of this data, developers need to be conscious of who has access to the reports and may want to implement features such as audit logging.

Production reporting

Another typical use of Pentaho Reporting includes production reporting. This type of reporting includes reports such as customized form letter, invoice, or postcard for a large audience, as well as automated mail merging. Normally, batch processing is involved in this form of reporting. However, custom reports based on a standard template, generated for individuals, can also fall under this category.

The following is a screenshot that presents such a report:

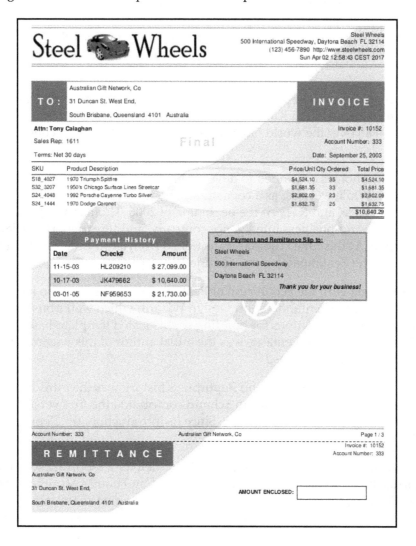

There are certain specific features in Pentaho Reporting, such as dynamically incorporating images from a data source, as well as pixel accurate formatting, which can be of real help when implementing production reporting.

Pentaho Reporting history

Pentaho Reporting began as JFreeReport, a Java-based Reporting Engine and Swing widget, back in 2002. David Gilbert, author of JFreeChart, implemented the initial version of JFreeReport to address report rendering needs. Soon after launching the project, Thomas Morgner became the primary developer. He added critical functionalities, such as report functions and XML report definitions, launching JFreeReport into a successful open source Java project.

Since the beginning, Pentaho Reporting has been an international project. David was located in Hertfordshire, United Kingdom, and Thomas was located in Frankfurt, Germany. Many others from all over the world have contributed translations and code to Pentaho Reporting.

From 2002 to 2006, Thomas continued to develop JFreeReport into an enterprise-worthy Reporting Engine. While working as a consultant, Thomas added support for a variety of outputs, including Excel and RTF. At the beginning of 2006, Thomas and JFreeReport joined Pentaho, an open source business intelligence company, and JFreeReport officially became Pentaho Reporting. At this time, Thomas transitioned from a full-time consultant to a full-time developer on the Pentaho Reporting Engine and suite of tools.

In January 2006, along with the acquisition of Pentaho Reporting, Pentaho announced the general availability of the Pentaho Report Design Wizard, which walks business users through a set of simple instructions for building sophisticated template-based reports. Mike D'Amour, a senior engineer at Pentaho, was the initial author of this wizard, which is now used in many Pentaho applications.

Another important milestone in Pentaho Reporting's history was the introduction of Pentaho Report Designer. In 2006, Martin Schmid contributed the first version of the Pentaho Report Designer to the community. Since its introduction, the Report Designer has evolved with the Reporting Engine.

In 2007, Pentaho teamed up with Sun's OpenOffice to deliver a reporting solution for OpenOffice's database tool set. This project was headed by Thomas Morgner, and is now known as the Pentaho Reporting Flow Engine. While this engine shares many of the concepts from the classic engine discussed in this book, it is a separate project with dramatically different features and functionalities than Pentaho's classic reporting project.

Beginning in Pentaho Business Intelligence Platform release 1.6, Pentaho Reporting also tightly integrates with Pentaho's Metadata Engine, allowing easy-to-use web-based ad hoc reporting by business users who may not have SQL expertise, data driven formatting in reports, as well as column and row level data security. The same functionality is available inside Pentaho Report Designer for query and report building, allowing business users to go from a quick template-based report to a full-fledged custom report.

Today, Pentaho Reporting is definitely a core part of the Pentaho platform, and it is maintained and enhanced as a official and powerful component of the entire business intelligence suite.

Feature overview

In this quick introduction to the various features available in Pentaho Reporting 8, you'll have an executive summary of how Pentaho Reporting works and what it can accomplish for your reporting needs. The topics that will follow are covered in more depth in later chapters of the book.

An advanced reporting algorithm

The reporting algorithm is at the heart of Pentaho Reporting. This algorithm manages the layout and rendering of the entire report, no matter which output format is being rendered. This algorithm combines a reporting template and a dataset on the fly, in order to generate the final report. There is no unnecessary compilation step. All other Pentaho Reporting features can be described in the context of the overall reporting algorithm.

This algorithm allows reports to render with a page header and footer, a report header and footer, group headers and footers, as well as a details band. The reporting algorithm traverses the dataset multiple times to render the report. In the first pass, the algorithm performs calculations and determines how to separate the data into groups, along with calculating the height and width of text and images. After the initial pass, the algorithm traverses the dataset a second time, in order to render the output.

A multitude of available data sources

Pentaho Reporting defines a standard Java API for accessing data. Many data source implementations are made available with Pentaho Reporting. The most commonly used implementations include JDBC and JNDI database connectivity, XML XPATH capability, and multidimensional OLAP data access using MDX and MongoDB NoSQL database support.

Java Naming and Directory Interface (JNDI) is a Java API for a directory service that allows Java software clients to discover and look up data and objects via a logical name, decoupling the implementation from the configuration and settings.

Online Analytical Processing (OLAP) is an approach to answering multidimensional analytical queries swiftly in computing. **Multidimensional Expressions (MDX)** is a query language for OLAP databases. Much like SQL it is a query language for relational databases.

Additional data sources that are available include a Pentaho Data Integration data source, a **Hibernate Query Language (HQL)** data source, a Pentaho Metadata data source, a scripting data source (in JavaScript, Python, TCL, Groovy, and BeanShell), a simple table defined as a static list of rows and columns, and other advanced data sources (OpenERP data access, community data access, and sequence generator).

Using Pentaho's Data Integration data source, it is easy to use Excel, logs, or other file formats as inputs to a report, without the need to write any code. All these data sources interact with the Reporting Engine through a standard API, which is easy to extend.

The following screenshot shows the available data sources in Pentaho Reporting:

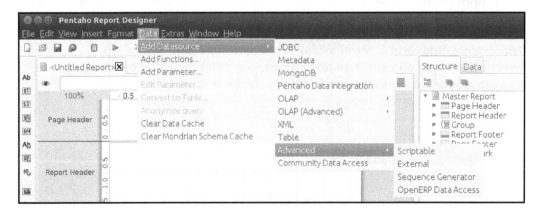

By combining Pentaho Reporting's data source functionality with Pentaho's Data Integration Engine, most known data formats and systems are available for input. This includes combining data sources into a single report. An example might include a Microsoft Excel file on a remote shared drive, with a plain text log file from an HTTP server.

A wide variety of output formats

Pentaho Reporting has the ability to render to the most widely used output formats, including Adobe's PDF standard using the iText library, Microsoft's Excel standard using the POI library, and HTML, all highlighted in the following screenshot. Other available formats include XML, plain text, RTF, and CSV. In addition to these output formats, a Pentaho report can be rendered in Swing and directly printed using PostScript formatting, allowing print previewing capabilities.

The following is a screenshot showing one such report obtained using Report Designer and rendered in PDF (top left), Microsoft Excel (top right), HTML (bottom left), and CSV (bottom right):

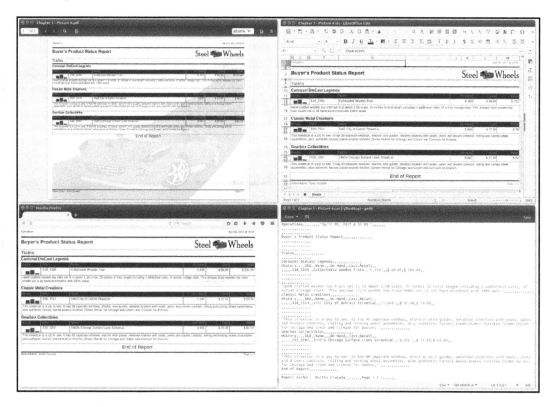

Pixel accurate rich formatting

Reports defined in Pentaho Reporting can specify at the pixel level where objects such as text or images should render. Using Pentaho Report Designer, it is easy to align fields and group items that need to stay aligned. While not always possible due to different format types, such as XML, CSV, and plain text, the three main graphical outputs, HTML, PDF, and Excel, strive to look as similar as possible.

Rich formatting includes the `TrueType` system font selection, the ability to render geometrical shapes and lines, along with the ability to include images and other objects in a report. This rich formatting is specified under the covers through styles similar to CSS, separating out the format from the report detail. This makes it easier to modify and maintain reports, and also to apply corporate styles through the report wizard, as shown in the following image:

Embedded charts

The Pentaho Reporting Engine and suite of tools make it easy to embed charts in reports, originally developed using the JFreeChart Engine. Many chart types are available, including bar, histogram, pie, and line charts, as shown in the following diagram:

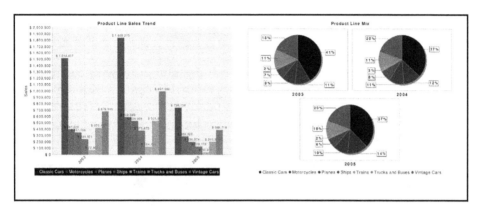

Report parameterization

Pentaho Reporting provides easy-to-use tools to parameterize a report, allowing users to specify ranges and other values to customize the output of a report. Parameter values can be selected from a list of hardcoded values or driven from a query. With parameterization, end users may control the amount of information that is displayed on a report. The following screenshot is an example of parameter input from within Pentaho's business intelligence server:

Formulas and style expressions

Report builders may define custom formulas and style expressions, using the OpenFormula standard, allowing for calculated values and dynamic formatting in their reports, such as aggregations, number formatting, as well as traffic lighting.

Subreports

Pentaho Reporting allows report developers to include subreports within a master report. This provides a powerful capability, which allows reports to contain different smaller reports, both side-by-side and within the various bands of a report. These subreports may be based on different data sources. The following screenshot is an example of a report that includes a separate chart subreport:

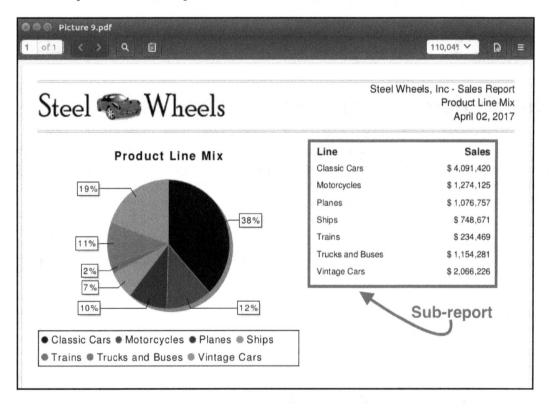

Cross tab reports

Cross tab reports present data in a spreadsheet-like format, making it easy to view summaries of data. Cross tab reports present both row and column headers, as well as cells of data, all of which can be customized through report elements. The following image shows how a cross tab report looks:

Product Line	Years	Quarters	Markets All Markets APAC	EMEA	Japan		NA
Classic Cars	2003		1,052	5,853	898	12,762	4,959
Classic Cars	2004		1,785	8,976	307	16,085	5,017
Classic Cars	2005		1,015	3,463	122	6,705	2,105
Motorcycles	2003		654	1,428	205	4,031	1,744
Motorcycles	2004		540	2,177	380	5,906	2,809
Motorcycles	2005		658	1,501	44	2,771	568
Planes	2003		456	1,723	677	3,833	977
Planes	2004		723	2,326	547	5,820	2,224
Planes	2004	QTR1	318		322	971	331
Planes	2004	QTR2		311		1,113	802
Planes	2004	QTR3		977		1,178	201
Planes	2004	QTR4	405	1,038	225	2,558	890
Planes	2005		151	1,464		2,207	592
Ships	2003			1,968	174	2,844	702
Ships	2004		396	2,144	127	4,309	1,642
Ships	2005		32	696	81	1,346	537
Trains	2003		33	384	174	1,000	409
Trains	2004		106	977		1,409	326
Trains	2005			183	49	409	177
Trucks and Buses	2003		91	2,261	415	4,056	1,289
Trucks and Buses	2004		801	1,558	102	5,024	2,563
Trucks and Buses	2005		488	836		1,921	597
Vintage Cars	2003		1,243	3,094	308	7,913	3,268
Vintage Cars	2004		1,587	5,472	229	10,864	3,576
Vintage Cars	2005		1,067	1,094	84	4,116	1,871

Interactive reporting

While most reports are static after being rendered, a subset of reporting includes functionalities such as drill through, pivoting, and other interactivity. Pentaho Reporting provides a straightforward Java and JavaScript API for manipulating a report after it has been rendered, allowing report builders to create very interactive reports. Pentaho Reporting's interactive functionality is available when rendering a report in HTML, Excel, or Swing. Links to external documents can also be added to PDF documents.

The following screenshot shows a report with links, that when clicked, collapses/expands the row in detail:

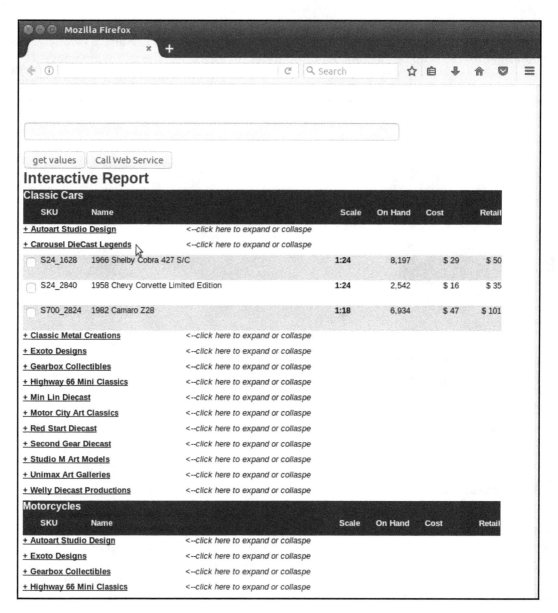

Rich authoring tools

While it is possible to build Pentaho reports using either XML or a Java API, most reports begin as templates built by the Pentaho Report Designer. Pentaho Report Designer is a **What You See Is What You Get** (**WYSIWYG**) report editor that exposes the rich set of features provided by the Pentaho Reporting Engine. In addition to building a report from scratch, the Report Design Wizard, included as a part of the Pentaho Report Designer, walks a report author through building a report, which will then be displayed in the Report Designer, as shown in the following screenshot, for further customization:

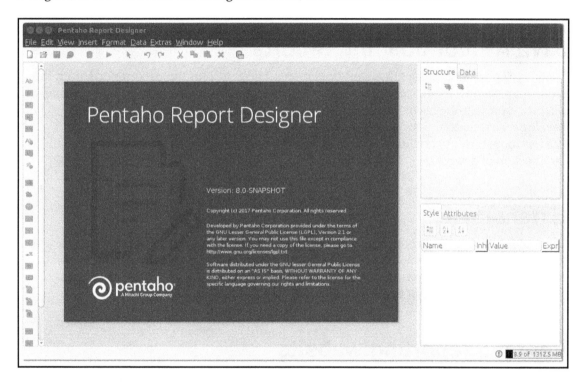

Reporting server

As part of the Pentaho suite, reports created by Pentaho Reporting may be published, executed, and scheduled on Pentaho's Analytics Platform. The Pentaho Analytics Platform offers authentication and authorization, as well as a central repository, to manage your business reports. The Pentaho Analytics Platform also hosts the web-based ad hoc reporting user interface for creating Pentaho Metadata-based reports. By combining the use of Pentaho Report Designer and Pentaho Analytics Platform, there is no need to write any code to get your business up and running with Pentaho Reporting.

Java API for building reports

Pentaho Reporting comes with a well-documented Java API for building reports from the ground up, so developers can stick with the Java programming language when customizing existing report templates or building reports from scratch. This Java API allows the developers to create and modify the various sections of a report, including the various header, footer, group, and detail bands, along with creating and modifying objects within each section of a report.

Extensibility

Pentaho Reporting is designed from the ground up in pure Java, exposing many interfaces for extension. From implementing basic formulas and functions that can be embedded in reports, to writing a custom data source or output format, Pentaho Reporting's source code and API interfaces are well documented and easy to work with.

Pentaho reporting website

In addition to these features, Pentaho Reporting is in active development. Visit `http://community.pentaho.com/projects/reporting/` to learn more about what additional features and functionalities are being considered for development, or to access early release versions of the product.

Pentaho Reporting architecture

Pentaho Reporting Engine is mainly a Java class library, broken up into other Java projects, which are then combined to render reports. The library is optimized for performance and a small memory footprint, and can run completely in memory without generating temporary files or requiring extra compilation steps. The source code is available, under the terms of the GNU LGPL Version 2.1, in the GitHub repository `https://github.com/pentaho/pentaho-reporting`.

The GitHub repository includes the Pentaho Report Designer, providing a graphical editor for report definitions and used as a standalone desktop reporting tool. In addition, there are also other related open source tools and projects in the Pentaho Reporting landscape, including the Report Engine Demo, Report Design Wizard, Report Designer, and the web-based ad hoc reporting user interface.

The following is an introduction of the Java project defining the Pentaho Reporting Engine, with a focus on the libraries, the Reporting Engine core, and the Reporting Engine extensions.

Reporting Engine's libraries

The Pentaho Reporting Engine uses the following libraries to render reports:

- **Flute**: This is a CSS 2 parser written in Java that implements SAC (`https://www.w3.org/Style/CSS/SAC/`). SAC is a standard event-based API for CSS parsers, closely modeled on the SAX API for XML parsers.
- **LibBase**: This is the root library for all other Pentaho Reporting libraries. This library contains common capabilities, such as debug and error logging utilities, library configuration, along with library initialization APIs, for consistent startup and shutdown management of the Reporting Engine.
- **LibDocBundle**: This abstracts the management of Pentaho Reporting file bundles, which are by default stored as ZIP files, and implements the ODF. This makes it simpler for other parts of the Reporting Engine to work with and manipulate Pentaho Reporting's file formats.
- **LibFonts**: This allows Pentaho Reporting to work with TrueType system fonts, extracting the necessary metadata from font types and populating an abstract interface to allow appropriate rendering in various contexts, including PDF and Excel views.

- **LibFormat**: This is a string formatting library, which can render dates and numbers appropriately, based on format strings. This library is focused on memory and CPU efficiency for high performance report rendering.

- **LibFormula**: This is a formula parsing and execution library based on the OpenFormula standard. You can learn more about OpenFormula by visiting `http://wiki.oasis-open.org/office/About_OpenFormula`. This library is similar in function to Excel-based formula definitions. LibFormula is a very general library and is used outside Pentaho Reporting in other projects that require OpenFormula style parsing and execution. LibFormula-UI is a formula editor for OpenFormula expressions based on LibFormula.

- **LibLoader**: This manages the loading and caching of all necessary resources required for generating reports in a generic way, providing a simple API for other parts of the Reporting Engine that control static and dynamic content, including data sources and images.

- **LibPensol**: This is an access layer for accessing a remote Pentaho solution repository via an Apache VFS filesystem. It handles all HTTP calls, the parsing of the XML file, and all client-side state managements.

- **LibPixie**: This is a WMF-file reading library, originally written by David R. Harris as converter for the Pixie-image viewer. Pixie was long time dead and has now been resurrected as WMF-reader and image producer for Java 1.2.2 or higher. Pixie lacks the support for most bitmap-formats, but everything else works fine.

- **LibRepository**: This abstracts the input and output of hierarchical storage systems, such as file systems, that Pentaho Reporting interacts with. This makes it possible for a custom storage system, such as FTP, to be implemented and to be mapped to the API, giving Pentaho Reporting access to the system.

- **LibSerializer**: This provides helper methods for serializing non-serializable objects. This is necessary so that the Reporting Engine can serialize standard Java classes that don't implement Java's serializable interface.

- **LibSparkline**: This is a library developed to render sparkline graphs. Sparklines are small-scale bar or line charts that are inserted into text to provide visualized information along with the textual description.

- **LibSwing**: This is a common helper class storage for design-time elements, so that they don't have to move into the engine project, where they potentially bloat up the project due to third-party dependencies or a large amount of code.

- **LibXml**: This provides utility classes for **Simple API for XML (SAX)** parsing and XML writing, based on Java's **Java API for XML Parsing (JAXP)** API. This library assures the speedy loading and validation of Pentaho Reporting XML template files.

Reporting Engine core

The Reporting Engine core project contains the main reporting algorithm for rendering reports, along with the necessary functionality to support styling. This project also contains the algorithms for rendering specific outputs, including PDF, Excel, CSV, XML, and more. The engine relies on the already mentioned libraries for managing the loading, parsing, formatting, rendering, and archiving of generated reports.

Reporting Engine extensions

The Reporting Engine extensions project contains third-party extensions to the Reporting Engine, which are very useful, but increase dependencies. Extensions in this project include JavaScript expression support using the Rhino project, a hibernate data source factory, bar code support using Barbecue, sparkline support using the LibSparkline, along with additional JDK 1.4 support for configuration and printing. Additional extension projects exist that include charting and many of the data sources discussed in this book.

 The following are some links to the quoted projects for further details:
Rhino: `https://developer.mozilla.org/en-US/docs/Mozilla/Projects/Rhino`
Hibernate: `http://hibernate.org`
Barbeque: `http://barbecue.sourceforge.net`

Summary

In this chapter, we introduced Pentaho Reporting and highlighted some typical uses, providing you with baseline ideas for implementing your own solutions. Typical uses for embedded reporting include operational, business intelligence, financial, and production reporting.

We briefly described the unique history of Pentaho Reporting, from its JFreeReport roots, and also learned a great deal about the rich features included in the release 8.0. Core features include a wide variety of data source integration, along with PDF, HTML, and Excel rendering. On the other hand, more advanced features include subreports and cross tab reports. Additionally, developer-oriented features, such as open Java APIs, along with the available source code and a business-friendly LGPL open source license, gives Pentaho Reporting a leg up on all other Java reporting toolkits.

The architecture of Pentaho Reporting is also covered in this chapter, providing developers with a twenty thousand foot view of where they might be able to modify or contribute to the Pentaho Reporting Engine, along with giving them the ultimate flexibility of access to source code.

You'll soon be able to apply the rich feature set of Pentaho Reporting to your use case.

In the following chapter, we'll introduce you to Pentaho Reporting's easy to use Report Designer and Java API, making it fun and easy to embed reporting into your Java application.

2
Getting Started with Report Designer

After the introduction of Pentaho Reporting and an overview from twenty thousand feet, in this chapter, you will start with a practical hands-on session, learning how to run Pentaho Report Designer for the very first time. In addition, you will take your first steps in creating a report with your preferred layout, using some initial data as an example.

You will begin by setting up an environment for building reports. From there, you will walk through some initial details of the user interface, like menus, toolbars, report element palettes, report canvas tab panels, report explorer, element properties, and messages. After learning more about the user interface, you will walk through the creation of a report from scratch. At this stage, you will be using the easy wizard available in Pentaho Report Designer, to make the session more practical, you will see how to save your report in the filesystem. This will be useful to store it safely for the following sessions, according to your needs and use cases. Along the way, you will receive the first details on building a report and getting data into it, along with generating a preview and iterating between design and preview, for the best result.

This chapter is written as a tutorial for developers and information technologists. The best way to learn is to follow the instructions on your laptop while reading. At the end of this chapter, you will feel comfortable with the basics of building a Pentaho report. Later chapters will assume that your environment is configured appropriately and that you have retained the knowledge that you gained in this chapter, so read carefully and pay attention.

Prerequisites of your environment

As described in `Chapter 1`, *Introduction to Pentaho Reporting*, Pentaho Reporting is a suite of open source tools, including Report Designer, Reporting Engine, and Reporting SDK. All the preceding tools are written in pure Java, allowing any operating system that supports the Java runtime environment to run the application. The latest version of Pentaho Reporting, the 8th, requires the use of JDK 8 or more recent version.

Pentaho Reporting tools are cross-platform applications and will run in Linux, Windows, macOS, and other Java supported environments. The Reporting Engine is backward compatible with previous versions of JDK, but it is always recommended to use the latest one.

As stated in the introduction, in this chapter we are going to focus our attention on Pentaho Report Designer. The discussion on Pentaho Reporting SDK will be covered in the next chapter. About Reporting Engine, it is used as core component in the designer and the SDK, so it will be treated during the description of the other two tools.

Talking about the Pentaho Report Designer, the only prerequisite your environment should have onboard is obviously Sun's JDK. To get started, visit `http://java.sun.com` and download the latest patch release of the Java SE development kit 8. Once downloaded, you can easily install it in your environment, mainly unzipping and setting few variables accordingly to your operating system. We won't show more details here, because it is assumed it will be straightforward for you to find the most recent tutorial about this task by googling a little bit. To verify your installation, run `java -version` on the command line and, if correctly installed, you will see something similar to what is shown in the following screenshot:

```
pentaho@pentaho: ~
pentaho@pentaho:~$ java -version
java version "1.8.0_121"
Java(TM) SE Runtime Environment (build 1.8.0_121-b13)
Java HotSpot(TM) 64-Bit Server VM (build 25.121-b13, mixed mode)
pentaho@pentaho:~$
```

Now that everything is ready in your environment, let's move a step forward and install Pentaho Report Designer.

Setting up the Pentaho Report Designer

As you can expect, the first task for our goal is to download Pentaho Report Designer from the correct website. The distribution packages are available in a couple of places: on the SourceForge website (`https://sourceforge.net/projects/pentaho`) and directly on the official Pentaho website (`http://community.pentaho.com/projects/reporting`). In every case, the distribution packages are free for downloading and no fee or costs should be asked.

If you choose to download Pentaho Report Designer from the official Pentaho website, an automatic redirect will send you to the SourceForge website. To find the right distribution in the SourceForge website, follow the `Report Designer` folder in the `Files` repository. There you will find one subfolder for each version. Choose the latest available, in our case version 8.0.

In the distribution folder, you can find three packages available (let's ignore the `.sum` files containing checksum strings only). The first two packages, `prd-ce-mac-*.zip` and `prd-ce-*.zip`, contain the binary distribution for macOS and Windows/Linux operating systems. The third package, `pre-classic-sdk-*.zip`, contains the Reporting SDK.

Once you have downloaded the binary distribution of the Pentaho Report Designer, create a directory in your machine and, inside that, unzip the content of the package. Once the content is unzipped, you will find a script named `report-designer` in the main directory.

 Of course, if you are working with a Windows-based operating system, run the `report-designer.bat` script. If you are working with a Linux-based operating system, run the `report-designer.sh` script. If you are on macOS, find the Pentaho Report Designer in your finder and double-click directly on the application.

After running the script, the user interface should appear and a welcome screen, similar to the following one, will be shown on your desktop:

At this point, you may want to create a shortcut to your desktop or something that will make the run easier. In any case, congratulations, you have successfully installed Pentaho Report Designer!

Pentaho Report Designer, by default, comes packaged with the core Pentaho Reporting Engine libraries, so you now have the necessary reporting components to complete the examples described in this book.

If you have experienced difficulties installing Pentaho Report Designer, there are some common troubleshooting issues that you will want to verify. The most common issue is related to the Java virtual machine and SDK that you have installed. The `report-designer` script uses the first Java command found on the system path. Therefore, you will want to verify that your path is configured correctly. You can do this by executing the command `java -version` in a command window, in order to see which version of Java you are using.

The SamplaData schema

Together with the distribution package, the installation of Pentaho Report Designer comes with a database schema called `SampleData`. The `SampleData` schema contains a complete set of tables and data, to be used in your tests and training in general. In this book, you are going to use this database in all of the exercises. You will see for yourself that `SampleData` is a great starting point for every common need around reporting.
Nothing has to be done to setup and use the `SampleData` schema. Pentaho Report Designer comes with the HyperSQL RDBMS onboard and it is a natural choice considering that HyperSQL is an engine completely written in Java and does not require any installation or complex task to make it work.

 If you want more information about HyperSQL RDBMS, you can check the huge quantity of documentation and tutorials available on the web or directly in the official website (`http://hsqldb.org`).

As you probably know, a HyperSQL database is contained in a bunch of files, all stored in a unique folder of the filesystem. In case of `SampleData`, you can find it on the `<report-designer>/resources/sampledata` path.

Database apart, Pentaho Report Designer contains bundled a data source connected to the `SampleData` schema. We will see in detail what a data source is and how a data source is used in your reports, but for now, it's enough for you to know that you can easily have access to it from inside the Pentaho Report Designer, immediately and automatically after a correct installation.

To complete the introduction of the SampleData schema, let's take a look at the list of tables included in it. This is relevant because you will use these tables in queries several times in this book and, hopefully, you will use them in all your initial tests and experiments, as follows:

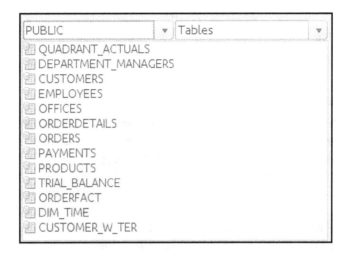

We won't see more than this the SampleData schema, but this introduction has been relevant for you, because now you can easily understand all the queries we are going to develop. As you will see soon in the following sections, queries are the first step in developing all the reports using Pentaho Reporting.

Introduction to the user interface

Now that you have Pentaho Report Designer installed in your environment and you know how to launch it, let's move another step forward, introducing the user interface. After launching the Pentaho Report Designer, you will notice the following six main graphical components. All together, the components work with the unique goal to create the report. From the top left to the bottom right of the window, you can recognize:

- The menu and toolbar, where you can request the execution of all the possible actions on reports
- The report element palette, where you can select report elements for your report
- The report canvas tab panel, which displays your report
- The report explorer panel, with the **Structure** and **Data** tabs, displaying the entire report in object tree form

- The element properties panel, displaying all the styles and attributes associated with the currently selected report element
- The messages panel, displaying warnings and errors related to the currently opened report

The following is a screenshot highlighting the listed components and their place in the Pentaho Report Designer user interface:

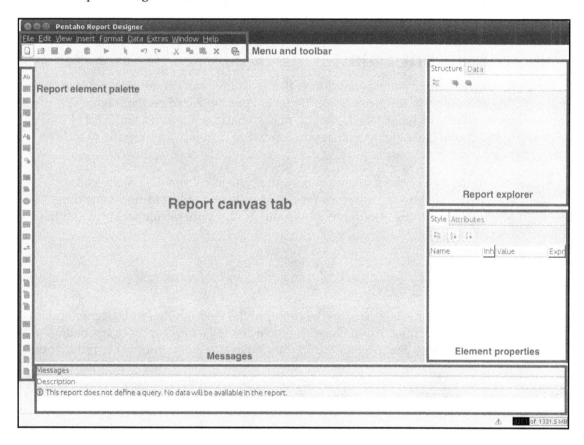

Considering that the components should be managed with high confidence to have great results, following are their brief descriptions, to ensure you understand their uses and their purposes in the report's development from the very beginning.

Menu and toolbar

The menu and toolbar contain useful functionalities to make building a report easier. Along with basic functionalities like saving, opening, and publishing, you have access to a lot of advanced features. Many of the options in the menu and toolbar are available as shortcut keys. The purpose of the Pentaho Report Designer's menu and toolbar is not different from a standard menu and toolbar. They contain all the available features, collected in a sequence of descriptions and icons, all clickable to complete a specific task.

Report element palette

The report element palette panel is located on the left side of the Pentaho Report Designer and contains an icon list of the types of elements that can be placed on the report. The report element palette includes labels, shapes, fields, charts, subreports, and a lot of interesting and useful basic elements that you can use to develop your reports exactly as you (or your customers) want.

 To add an element to your report, drag the icon from the palette and drop it directly into the report canvas. Probably, you will start understanding that everything is extremely easy and not for pure developers only (at this stage).

Report canvas tab

The report canvas tab panel is located in the center of the Pentaho Report Designer and it is sort of a preview of your final result. Once you have created a new report or opened an existing one, this is where you drag and drop the elements to build your preferred layout.

In design mode, the canvas displays some so-called report bands (we will see in detail in the next chapters what report bands are and what they do). The canvas offers many visual features that allow you to manage the alignment and sizing of your report elements. This is the place where the magic happens and you will be able to move, adjust, and tune the report to be exactly what you (or your customers) want. In addition to the design canvas, you can also preview the current report directly in this panel.

 You can quickly toggle between live data and the report template in this fashion. This will make the development of your report easier and immediately tested from a user perspective.

Report explorer

The report explorer, located on the right side of the Pentaho Report Designer, includes the **Structure** tab panel and the **Data** tab panel. The **Structure** tab panel contains the tree structure of the report, including all the report bands. The **Data** tab panel contains all the data sources, functions, and parameters of your report. On right-clicking various portions of the structure and data trees, the interface shows a lot of possible options, such as adding new data sources and subgroups. The report explorer may be hidden through the window application menu. Together with the canvas tab and the element properties, it is one of the most powerful components of the Pentaho Report Designer.

 It is highly recommended to start understanding as soon as possible how the report explorer works, as it can help you a lot, especially during the fine tuning of the precise placement of the elements in the report.

Element properties

The element properties panel is located following the report explorer panel, on the right side of the Pentaho Report Designer, and displays the details of the currently selected item in the report explorer or canvas. All styles and attributes, which are editable, appear in this panel. Many editable properties provide additional dialogs for advanced editing capabilities. The report explorer may be hidden through the window application menu. Together with the canvas tab and the report explorer, it is one of the most powerful components of the Pentaho Report Designer.

 It is highly suggested to start understanding as soon as possible how the element properties works, as it can help you a lot, especially during the fine tuning of the precise placement of the elements in the report.

Messages

The **Messages** panel is located at the bottom of the Pentaho Report Designer and displays any active warning or error that is present in the report. Selecting a message, the Report Designer will automatically select the element and property in question, making it easy to track down issues in your report. The **Messages** panel is hidden by default and can be made viewable through the window application menu. It is highly suggested to check the **Messages** panel quite often, because it contains the details of the potential issues your report could have when it is deployed into a production environment and, worst, submitted to a final user.

You can easily check for warnings or errors by looking at the small icon at the very bottom right of the user interface. You can see an example of the icon as a yellow triangle in the next screenshot. If you see an icon there, it is recommended to check the message box, as there is something you should solve in your report.

The following screenshot shows the **Messages** panel displaying an active warning:

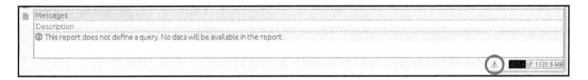

Creating your first report using the wizard

Now that you have successfully installed Pentaho Report Designer and you are more confident with the user interface, in this section, you will walk through building a first complete report. The report you are going to develop will list all the products in the catalog defined in the SampleData schema and more precisely, stored in the PRODUCTS table. Before you begin, create a directory called my_reports on your laptop, to manage the files you will develop in this book.

In the GitHub repository available at https://github.com/fcorti/pentaho-8-reporting-for-java-developers, you can find the source code described in all the examples of this book. In the Chapter 02 - Getting started with Report Designer/my_reports folder, you can find the example described here, in the file named my_first_report.prpt.

Introducing the Report Design Wizard

There are a two possible ways to create a report with Pentaho Report Designer: starting from a blank report or using the wizard. Neither of the two ways is better than the other. Each way has advantages and disadvantages and you should mature your own idea, after some experiences and some successes (or difficulties) in following one path instead of the other.

The development starting from a *blank* report is suggested if you want to have full control over the details and behavior. The development using the wizard is suggested if your goal is to develop a standard report, quite simple in terms of structure, and also simple in terms of layout and customization. One of the most attractive advantages of the wizard is that you can choose the layout from a set of available templates, most of them nice enough to guarantee to be appealing to your users.

As you can expect, in this book you will cover both the possible ways, but you are going to start by using the wizard because it is faster and simpler. After this first example, you will leave the wizard approach, preferring to start from a blank report.

Before starting to develop the report using the wizard, let's underline again one best practice: some developers prefer to start modifying a report built with the wizard, instead of starting from scratch. In principle, this is not bad, but what can be experienced is that you could have less control on some details, especially in fine tuning of the layout or some unexpected behaviors in particular cases.

To start the Pentaho Report Design Wizard, check the upper menu and click on the **File** item, and then on **Report Design Wizard**. Note that you can also use shortcuts (*Ctrl + Shift + N* in this case) as alternative to selecting the items from the menu. The following screenshot shows what the upper menu looks like:

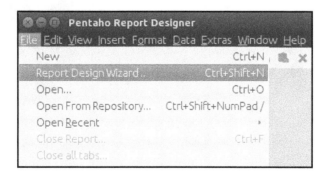

Once you start the Pentaho Report Design Wizard, a model window appears, describing four steps:

1. **Look and Feel**, where you choose your preferred layout from a list of possible templates
2. **Data Source and Query**, where you define the dataset to use in your report
3. **Layout Step**, where you define grouping and fields to show in the report
4. **Format Step**, where you define the look and feel of each single item shown in the report

A small description for each step, describing further details of the user interface you are going to see in your laptop, is presented as follows.

Defining the look and feel

The modal window, shown as first task in the Report Design Wizard, defines the look and feel step. In this step, you can choose the layout of your report from a collection of possible templates. The following screenshot shows what the window looks like:

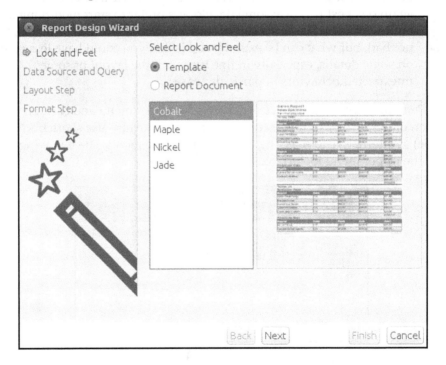

As you can see from the screenshot, the templates are previewed in a small image, giving the opportunity to see in advance what your report will look like. With **Report Document**, you can also use an existing report as a template. Be careful to use this feature or, at least, try to use it before any final decision (sometimes the result is not exactly as nice as you imagined). Once you have chosen the best template for your report, click on **Next** to move forward. In our exercise, you will use the **Cobalt** template as an example.

Defining the data source and query

The second step of the Report Design Wizard is selecting the set of data. The set of data is usually identified as a query on a database, but can be defined on several other types of sources (called data sources). In our example, we are going to use the `SampleData` tables. In particular, we are going to inquire the table named `PRODUCTS`.

Starting from the wizard window, on the top right corner, you should see a plus icon ( ). Clicking on the plus icon ( ), a window appears, asking you to select the type of data source you want to define. In the later chapters, we will see in detail all the available types of data sources, but at this stage, select `JDBC` to setup a standard query on a database schema. Immediately after the selection, a new window for the **JDBC Data Source** definition is shown as follows:

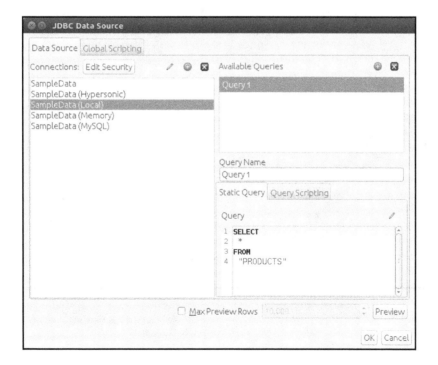

In the preceding screenshot, you can see the final result where all the data is correctly filled. In your environment, the parts related to the queries (**Available Queries** and **Static Query**) should be empty. Starting from your environment, select the **SampleData (Local)** connection to instruct the wizard to use this as a source. Then press the green plus icon 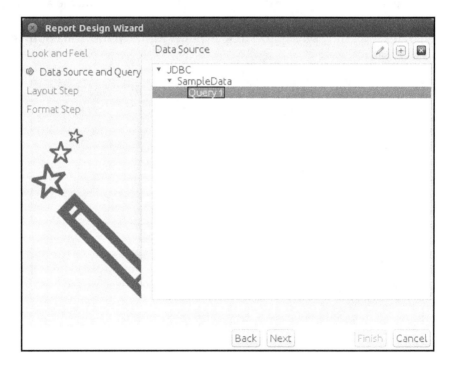 () on the right of **Available Queries**; this action will add a new query to the list of the available ones (**Available Queries**). The new query is defined with the name Query 1. You can decide to change the name of the query by typing into the **Query Name** field. We choose to keep the default name as an example in our first report. Now that the query is added, type the SQL command in the **Query** text field or press the pencil icon (✐) to open a visual query composer.

To test the data source, press the **Preview** button to execute the query and see the resulting dataset. If the preview shows the dataset, it means that everything is well defined. If not, check the connection to the SampleData schema and the syntax of the SQL command. To save the data source and use it in the report, click the **OK** button and you will return to **Report Design Wizard**. Once the data source is created, the wizard will show you a window, as follows:

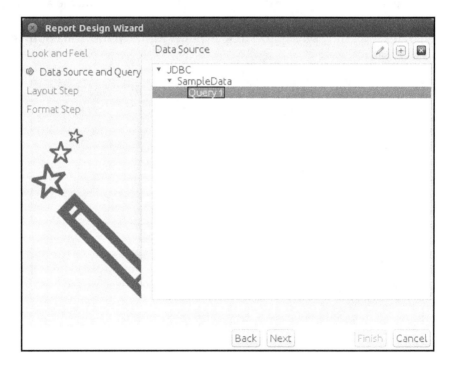

Select the new query (in our case Query 1) and move forward to the layout setup by pressing the **Next** button.

Defining the layout

Now that you have completed the data source definition, it's time to set up the layout of your report. In this step, you are going to select a subset of fields of the data source, defining the list of visible fields in the report. To create complex reports, the fields selected in this step are classified in two subsets: the group items and the detail items. In the group items, the wizard includes all the fields used to group the details (showing each value in a header of the resulting report). In the detail items, the wizard includes all the fields shown in the report as maximum level of detail.

In our example, let's act on the wizard's window, selecting the fields of the data source from **Available Items** and pressing the yellow arrows, depending on the classification you want to give to the field: press the upper yellow arrow to include the field in **Group Items** or press the lower yellow arrow to include the field in **Selected Items** (the detail items). The following screenshot shows how the window looks after the correct grouping of the fields:

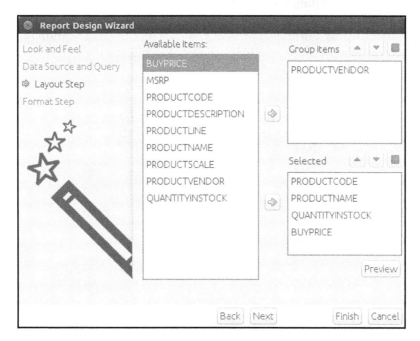

As you can see, not all the available fields of the data source are included in the group items or in the detail items. This feature helps a lot if you want to reuse the data sources in different reports. As an example, we can imagine using this data source to develop two similar (but different) reports: one showing the products per quantity and one showing the products per buy price.

Looking at our example, we set up the product vendor as a group item, and product code, product name, quantity in stock, and buy price as details of the report. With this configuration, the resulting report will show a list of product vendors and for each vendor, a list of details of the product, showing the code, the name, the quantity in stock, and the buy price.

Once the layout step is completed, click on the **Next** button to move forward to the last step of formatting the fields.

Formatting the fields

As a last step, the wizard requests to define the format of each field. Formatting definition is required for all the types of fields: the ones grouped in the group items and the ones grouped in the detail items. Formatting really depends on the classification of the field; for the fields in the group items, only a label is requested, while for the fields in the detail items, more details can be customized.

We won't cover further details about the possible settings, because it's straightforward to understand how to setup the formatting using the wizard. To show the differences between the two, in the following screenshot is shown the settings defined for the field of the group items (in our example, only the PRODUCTVENDOR field):

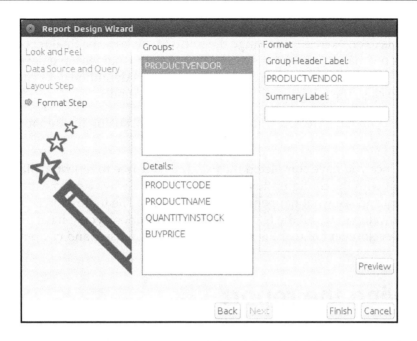

The following screenshot shows the settings defined for the fields in the detail items (in our example, we see PRODUCTCODE only):

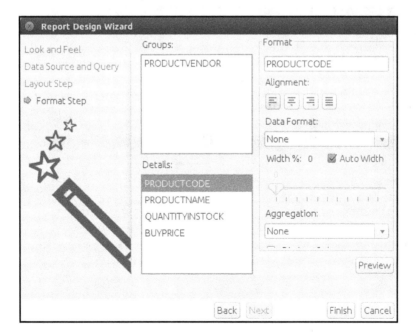

Back to our example, it is not required to modify any default settings. You can decide to modify the labels as an exercise, or change the setup to see how the final report changes, but in our case, it is not mandatory and we can be happy with what we have developed using the default setup. Now that we are happy with the report's definition, let's click on the **Finish** button to close the wizard and access the resulting report.

Congratulations, you have created your first Pentaho report using the Report Design Wizard.

Once you have completed the example, feel free to repeat it, playing a little bit with the configuration and settings. It is always a good experience to try and see what happens to the final result. The more exercises you develop to try all the features, the more solutions you'll have during the development of real-life reports for your final users and customers.

Previewing the report

Now that the Report Design Wizard has completed its job, you have a fully featured report in your Pentaho Report Designer. The following screenshot shows what the user interface looks like:

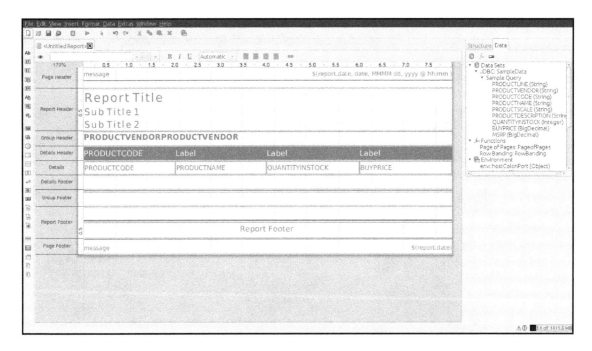

If you don't understand the details of the structure and the meaning of each label, don't worry. In the later chapters, we will cover all the details about the Pentaho Report Designer and you will practice a lot to became a real expert of the entire tool.

Before any other task, let's update the title and subtitles to make them more meaningful. To modify the title, double-click on the Report Title text and replace the content with My first report. After this, double-click on SubTitle 1 and SubTitle 2 and remove the text in both. At the end of the changes, the titles should look like the following screenshot:

Now that the title has been modified, everything seems to be ready to preview the report in its final version for the users. To cover this need, Pentaho Report Designer has a great feature, which is really useful during the development. If you look at the top left corner of the report canvas, immediately below **<Untitled Report>**, there is an eye icon (👁). The eye icon is definitely a friend of the developers and represents the preview of the report. Clicking on the eye icon, you can see your first report running. The following screenshot shows how the preview looks like for the developed report:

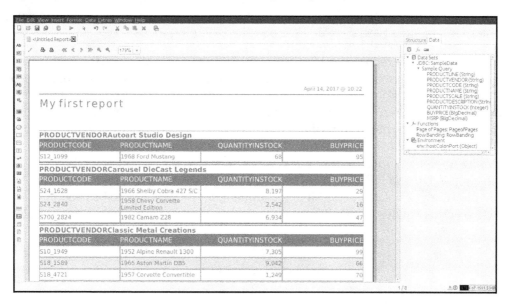

As you can see from the preview, something more can be done to make it perfect. For example, the distance between the title and the table can be reduced, the label for the product vendor can be changed, and probably a lot of minor issues can be fixed. OK, it's true, but don't be too demanding. You have reached a great result in a very short time and we have several chapters to read to reach perfection.

Now that you can see the preview of your report, you probably want to toggle back to the design mode to do some changes. To switch again to the design mode, check at the top left corner of the report canvas, immediately below **<Untitled Report>**. Where earlier there was an eye icon, there is now a pencil icon (✎) representing the switch to the design mode. Clicking on the pencil icon (✎), you are back to the initial view, ready to modify the report and then preview it again. Sounds easy, isn't it?

Iterating between design mode and preview mode, all the times you will need until you will like your report, it's the right approach to the development. You should always remember this if you are going to develop reports using the wizard or starting from an empty one.

Saving and opening the report

After the definition of the first Pentaho report, you will probably want to understand more about saving it somewhere for future use. Before seeing it in action in our exercise, let's introduce all the possible ways. Pentaho Reporting has two different places where you can ask to store reports: the filesystem and the so called Pentaho repository.

Saving (and loading) a report into (and from) the filesystem is not very different from saving (and loading) a regular file. A different solution is the Pentaho repository. The Pentaho repository is managed by the Pentaho Analytics platform directly and is mainly a collaborative space where developers and users can read, write, update, and delete content, in a manner similar to content repository. The Pentaho Analytics platform implements its repository using Apache Jackrabbit (`http://jackrabbit.apache.org`), a fully conforming implementation of the content repository for Java technology API (JCR, specified in JSR 170 and JSR 283). The Pentaho repository can be accessed using the API of the Pentaho Analytics platform and it is recommended, by Pentaho, to be used in production environments. You will cover all of this in `Chapter 15`, *Using Reports in Pentaho Business Analytics Platform*.

Even if the Pentaho repository should be preferred, in our practical example, we start using the filesystem as a repository. To save the first report into the filesystem, Pentaho Report Designer has a clear feature: the **Save** and **Save As...** items in the upper menu (under the **File** group). Clicking on the **Save** item (**Save As...** has the same user experience), a window similar to the following one will appear. As you can easily check by yourself, a disk icon (▣) is visible in the toolbar as shortcut for the saving feature. As described, this feature is not different to saving a regular file, as shown here:

What to do with the **Save** window is definitely understandable: identify a folder on the filesystem, specify a name for the report, and press the **OK** button. In our case, we call the report my_first_report and save it into the my_reports folder. As you should remember, at the very beginning of this chapter, we created the my_reports folder to store all the reports created during the exercises of this book.

Once safely stored in the filesystem, you can check what the report looks like by accessing the my_reports folder. As shown in the following screenshot, the report looks like a single file with the extension .prpt. We will cover in Chapter 11, *The PRPT Format and the Java API to Build It,* what a .prpt file is. At this stage, it is nothing more and nothing less than a single file containing a Pentaho report in one place. A Pentaho report in the .prpt format can be copied, moved, deleted, and renamed as a regular file and nothing really changes in terms of user experience.

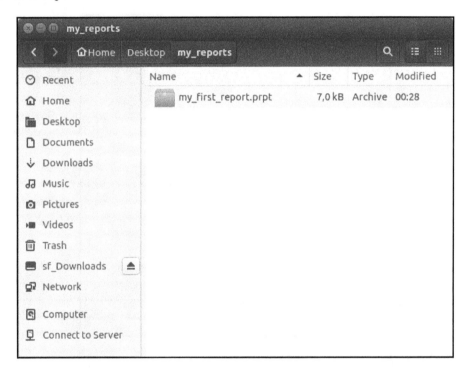

To complete the life cycle of our report, as the last topic in this chapter, let's briefly discuss how to open a report from the filesystem. The task is not difficult to do and to understand. In addition to that, like the save task, opening a Pentaho report is not different from opening a regular file. To open a Pentaho report from the Report Designer, click on the **File** item in the menu and then select **Open....** Select the .prpt file from the filesystem and click **OK**. That's all.

The report will be imported again into the Pentaho Report Designer and be ready to be modified and previewed again, as we discussed in the previous sections. As we saw for **Save** and **Save As...**, a folder icon (🗁) is visible in the toolbar as a shortcut for the **Open...** feature of the upper menu.

 Feel free to check into the GitHub repository available at `https://github.com/fcorti/pentaho-8-reporting-for-java-developers`, where you can find the `my_first_report.prpt` file stored in the `Chapter 02 - Getting started with Report Designer/my_reports` folder.

Summary

In this chapter, you have walked all the way through a complete reporting example, with step-by-step instructions on how to create a Pentaho report with your preferred layout. You started off learning how to install Pentaho Report Designer together with the `SampleData` schema on a HyperSQL database, used to train and experiment Pentaho Reporting's features. Hopefully, you installed Pentaho Report Designer into your laptop, because it will be used along with all the exercises of this book.

After the installation, you moved the first step with the user interface and you walked through the creation of a report using the easy wizard available in Report Designer. After completing the task, you learned how to preview it and how to toggle between design and preview mode, as best practice in report development. To complete the report's life cycle, you saw how to save it into the file system for future use and safe storing. Last but not the least, you saw how to open the report again, to start using it or to iterate again developing enhancements.

Now that you have read this chapter, you should feel comfortable with what Pentaho Report Designer is and how to use the Pentaho wizard to create a report. In the next chapter, you will be introduced to Pentaho Reporting SDK to create a project using Maven and Java.

3

Getting Started with Reporting SDK

After the introduction of Pentaho Reporting and the development of a first report using the Report Design Wizard, in this chapter, you are going to leave the world of what-you-see-is-what-you-get report building and enter the Java land of Pentaho Reporting SDK. At the end of this initial discovery, you will learn how to create a web application in Java using Pentaho Reporting, with the goal to preview the Pentaho report you developed in previous chapter.

You will begin by downloading and setting up the Pentaho Reporting SDK. From there, you will understand more about the anatomy of the SDK package, through some initial details of the directory structure and the various libraries and samples included with it. To make the discovery more practical, you will see how to include the samples in an Eclipse project.

After the introduction of the Pentaho Reporting SDK, the hands-on session will be dedicated to a different topic: creating a web application in Java, including Pentaho Reporting, and developing it using Apache Maven as a software project management and comprehension tool. To make the discussion more practical, you will see how to start from scratch: creating a standard Java web application, then including the Pentaho Report Engine, and only as a last step, previewing an existing Pentaho report. To create a connection with what you have learnt till now, the Pentaho report developed in the last chapter, using the Report Designer Wizard, will be used as an example.

This chapter is highly technical and written as a tutorial for pure Java developers. If you are an information technologist with not much knowledge in development, feel free to skip this read, even if it's a relevant part of the Pentaho Reporting tools. The best way to learn is to follow the instructions on your laptop while reading. At the end of this chapter, you will feel comfortable with the basics of embedding a Pentaho report into an existing Java web application. Later chapters will assume that you will be able to manage and set up a web application in Java using Pentaho Reporting Engine, so read carefully and be sure you are confident with all the concepts explained.

Obtaining the Pentaho Reporting SDK

In `Chapter 2`, *Getting Started with Report Designer*, you saw where to find all the Pentaho Reporting tools: at the SourceForge website (`https://sourceforge.net/projects/pentaho`), particularly in the `Report Designer` folder of the `Files` repository. In the `Report Designer` folder, you find a ZIP file called `pre-classic-sdk-*.zip`, containing the whole Pentaho Reporting SDK. As you can imagine, download the ZIP file into your laptop and that's all. As introduced for Report Designer, the distribution packages are always free for downloading and no fee or costs should be required.

Once you have downloaded the distribution package of Pentaho Reporting SDK, create a directory on your machine and unzip the contents inside. This is all you have to do to get Pentaho Reporting SDK available in your environment. Before moving forward, note the PDF file called `embedding_pentaho_reporting_engine` in the `documentation` folder. This file is extremely useful and we highly recommend you read it, to understand more about Pentaho Reporting SDK and its use.

 Considering the existence of this PDF guide, in this book you will find only an introduction of the main concepts about the examples and what is included in the package. Instead of repeating what is just covered in the PDF, we prefer to focus the content on practical exercises, creating a web application in Java, including Pentaho Reporting and developing using Apache Maven as software project management and comprehension tool.

Anatomy of the Pentaho Reporting SDK

Before any further steps, let's introduce the directory structure of Pentaho Reporting SDK and a brief description of its content. A description of how the `PentahoReportingEngineSDK` folder looks is shown as follows:

```
PentahoReportingEngineSDK
  |- documentation
  |- licenses
  |- samples
  |- build-res
  |- lib
  |- source
  |- sql
  |- WebContent
   |- META-INF
   |- WEB-INF
```

Following are brief descriptions of the contents of each folder:

Folder	Description
`PentahoReportingEngineSDK`	Root of Pentaho Reporting SDK.
`documentation`	Location where the `embedding_pentaho_reporting_engine` PDF file is located.
`licenses`	Contains text files with licensing information.
`samples`	The project directory for Eclipse, containing some samples described in the PDF guide.
`build-res`	Includes folder for the Apache Ant scripts (`http://ant.apache.org`).
`lib`	The directory of libraries which makes up the Pentaho Reporting Engine.
`source`	The source files used to make up the reporting samples.
`sql`	The file-based HyperSQL database instance used with the samples. This is the exact `SampleData` schema introduced in the previous chapters.
`WebContent`	Web content information used by one of the examples (mainly `WEB-INF/web.xml`).

Before going ahead with other concepts, take a look at the content of each folder to be familiar with the SDK structure and content. In the PDF guide mentioned earlier, you will find further information about the anatomy of the Pentaho Reporting SDK. Feel free to read the guide before continuing to read the following paragraphs.

Using the included Eclipse project

As described in the PDF guide, if you use Eclipse or IntelliJ IDEA IDEs, you can use the Eclipse project included with the Pentaho Reporting SDK to work directly with the examples. In practice, select the unpacked Pentaho Reporting SDK directory as your workspace and everything should work. You can also launch the `Sample1.java` and `Sample2.java` example applications directly from the file browser in Eclipse.

We won't provide more than these details about the Eclipse project, as it is well covered in the guide. From another point of view, we prefer to spend our next sections on the most modern approach, using Apache Maven (`https://maven.apache.org/`) as software project management and comprehension tool.

Introducing the included examples

There are five interesting examples included in the Pentaho Reporting SDK. The examples are described in the PDF guide, together with an overview introducing the interaction with the Reporting Engine. All the source code described in the PDF guide is available in the `sample` folder, and the names of the files are strictly connected with the examples. Following are brief descriptions of each example for reference:

- `Sample0`: The base class. The `AbstractReportGenerator` class is extended by `Sample1` and `Sample2`. It contains the basic logic that creates a report, leaving the details of input and output to the classes that extend it.
- `Sample1`: Static report definition, JDBC input, PDF output. The simplest embedding scenario produces a static report (no user input regarding data source or query), with JDBC input from the Pentaho-supplied `SampleData` HyperSQL schema, and produces a PDF on the local filesystem.
- `Sample2`: Static report definition, JDBC input, HTML output. This example produces a static report (no user input regarding data source or query), with JDBC input from the Pentaho-supplied `SampleData` HyperSQL schema, and produces an HTML file on the local filesystem.

- `Sample3`: Dynamically generated, JDBC input, Swing output. `Sample3.java` generates the same report as created in `Sample1.java`, but it uses a Swing helper class defined in the Reporting Engine to render the report in a Swing preview window.
- `Sample4`: Dynamically generated, JDBC input, Java servlet output. `Sample4.java` is `HttpServlet` which generates an HTML report similar to `Sample2`. This example assumes you have a Java application server, such as Tomcat or JBoss, installed, configured, running, and accessible to you.

Feel free to read the content of the PDF guide and the description of the five examples in detail, before continuing to read the content of the following paragraphs. It would be great if you could test the examples in your environment. As mentioned in the previous section, we will continue introducing a different approach using Apache Maven.

Creating a web application using Pentaho Reporting and Maven

In this section, you'll learn how to create a web application from scratch, using the Pentaho Reporting Engine. This example is useful if you also want to understand how to embed the Pentaho Reporting Engine into an existing web application. In this example, in particular, you will see how to create a Java web application showing the Pentaho report you developed in `Chapter 2`, *Getting Started with Report Designer*. As you probably remember, we saw how to create a Pentaho report using the Report Design Wizard and we named it `my_first_report`.

Differently from the examples introduced in the Pentaho Reporting SDK, in this book we are going to use Apache Maven, the most used software project management and comprehension tool for Java.

To better describe the tasks and give you the opportunity to test the correct results, we are going to split the project into a few subtasks: one paragraph for each task, with source code and screenshots to be sure you can reproduce the example with success in your environment.

 In the GitHub repository available at `https://github.com/fcorti/pentaho-8-reporting-for-java-developers`, you can find the source code described in the examples of this book. In the `Chapter 03 - Getting started with Reporting SDK/pentaho-reporting-web-app` folder, you can find the source code of these examples in particular.

Prerequisites of your environment

In Chapter 2, *Getting Started with Report Designer*, we introduced the only prerequisite your environment should have: Sun's JDK Version 8. Considering that we are going to use Apache Maven, be sure that you have it installed in your development environment. The suggested version is 3 or more recent. To verify your installation, run the following command from the command line:

```
mvn --version
```

If correctly installed, you will see something similar to what is shown in the following screenshot:

```
pentaho@pentaho: ~
pentaho@pentaho:~$ mvn --version
Apache Maven 3.3.9
Maven home: /usr/share/maven
Java version: 1.8.0_121, vendor: Oracle Corporation
Java home: /usr/lib/jvm/java-8-oracle/jre
Default locale: en_US, platform encoding: UTF-8
OS name: "linux", version: "4.4.0-72-generic", arch: "amd64", family: "unix"
pentaho@pentaho:~$
```

If you don't have it already, the installation of Apache Maven is a simple process of extracting the archive and adding the bin folder with the mvn command to PATH. For further details on how to install Apache Maven in your environment, check the official web page at https://maven.apache.org/install.html.

 Another obvious requirement is the availability of an internet connection from your machine/environment. Apache Maven is based on the idea of public repositories where the commands get libraries, source code, and everything that is needed to compile and run your application. Be sure your laptop is connected to the internet during the execution of the following tasks.

Creating a web application in Java

Now that your development environment is correctly set up, the next step is creating a new Java web application. This particular task may not interest you if you already have an existing web application and want to include the Pentaho Engine with it. However, we prefer to cover the entire life cycle of the development for completeness, assuming you will try the example in your environment for better comprehension.

Let's start from the very beginning by creating a Java web application from scratch, and then add an initial page before the compilation and the first run.

Creating a Java web application using Apache Maven

Creating a Java web application from scratch using Apache Maven is straightforward, thanks to the Maven Archetypes. In short, an Archetype is a Maven project template toolkit defined as an original pattern or model from which all other things of the same kind are made. For our needs, we are going to use `maven-archetype-webapp` to start a simple web application.

 In this book, we won't detail the Maven Archetypes and we assume you are confident with the basics around their use and behavior. If not, don't worry, because we will describe a step-by-step approach. If you want to understand more, read the Apache Maven documentation at `https://maven.apache.org/guides/introduction/introduction-to-archetypes.html`.

Back to our task, identify a folder in your machine to put in your new Java application (we will use `Desktop`). Open a Terminal, move into the working folder (in our case, `Desktop`), and execute the following command:

```
mvn archetype:generate
  -DarchetypeArtifactId=maven-archetype-webapp
  -DinteractiveMode=false
  -DgroupId=com.example
  -DartifactId=pentaho-reporting-web-app
```

Looking at the command, the `archetypeArtifactId` parameter specifies the Maven Archetype, the `interactiveMode` parameter tells Maven to ask (or not to use) questions of the user instead of defaults, the `groupId` parameter defines the root package of your Java source code, and the `artifactId` parameter defines the name of your web application.

 Note that a brand new folder named `pentaho-reporting-web-app` is created. The new folder is going to contain the whole project, including configuration files, libraries, source code, and resources. This folder is the natural candidate to be stored in a version control repository (GitHub, SVN, and others).

You will see that the execution of the command is quite verbose and a lot of log messages will be shown on the Terminal. The log messages describe that you are downloading all the libraries and configuration files, and everything is needed to create, compile, and run your new Java web application. After some time, you should see a message similar to the following screenshot:

```
○ ○ ○   pentaho@pentaho: ~/Desktop
[INFO] ------------------------------------------------------------------------
[INFO] Parameter: basedir, Value: /home/pentaho/Desktop
[INFO] Parameter: package, Value: com.example
[INFO] Parameter: groupId, Value: com.example
[INFO] Parameter: artifactId, Value: pentaho-reporting-web-app
[INFO] Parameter: packageName, Value: com.example
[INFO] Parameter: version, Value: 1.0-SNAPSHOT
[INFO] project created from Old (1.x) Archetype in dir: /home/pentaho/Desktop/pentaho-reporting-web-app
[INFO] ------------------------------------------------------------------------
[INFO] BUILD SUCCESS
[INFO] ------------------------------------------------------------------------
[INFO] Total time: 11.946 s
[INFO] Finished at: 2017-04-30T11:05:01+02:00
[INFO] Final Memory: 19M/258M
[INFO] ------------------------------------------------------------------------
pentaho@pentaho:~/Desktop$ 
```

Checking into the filesystem, a brand new folder called `pentaho-reporting-web-app` is created, containing the whole project corresponding to your Java web application. Take your time to dive into its structure to understand the composition (as you will see, it is very straightforward).

We won't detail the anatomy of a Java project created with Apache Maven here (you can find a lot of resources describing the details by just googling it), but all the magic happens through the `pom.xml` file, used to declare that everything is requested to compile, test, and run the project with success.

Before considering the task completed, let's add Eclipse Jetty to the project. Eclipse Jetty (`http://www.eclipse.org/jetty`) is a Java HTTP (web) server and Java servlet container, released as open source and available for commercial use and distribution. To include Eclipse Jetty in the project, add the following XML code to the `pom.xml` file located in the `pentaho-reporting-web-app` folder:

```xml
<project ...>
  ...
  <dependencies>
    ...
  </dependencies>
  <build>
    <finalName>pentaho-reporting-web-app</finalName>

    <!-- Add This here. -->
```

```
    <plugins>
      <plugin>
        <groupId>org.apache.maven.plugins</groupId>
        <artifactId>maven-dependency-plugin</artifactId>
        <executions>
          <execution>
            <phase>package</phase>
            <goals><goal>copy</goal></goals>
            <configuration>
              <artifactItems>
                <artifactItem>
                  <groupId>org.eclipse.jetty</groupId>
                  <artifactId>jetty-runner</artifactId>
                  <version>9.4.4.v20170414</version>
                  <destFileName>jetty-runner.jar</destFileName>
                </artifactItem>
              </artifactItems>
            </configuration>
          </execution>
        </executions>
      </plugin>
    </plugins>

  </build>
</project>
```

After the `pom.xml` file has been saved, the project is ready for being compiled in its initial version. To compile the Java web application, open a Terminal, move into the `pentaho-reporting-web-app` folder, and run `mvn package`. At the end of the execution, a `BUILD SUCCESS` message, similar to the previous screenshot, will appear, and you will find a new folder called `target` in `pentaho-reporting-web-app`.

To deploy the WAR package in the Eclipse Jetty server and run it, simply execute the following command:

```
java -jar target/dependency/jetty-runner.jar target/*.war
```

After a few seconds and some lines of log messages, the web application is up and running on port 8080. The following screenshot shows what your browser should look like, opening the page `http://localhost:8080`:

To stop the Eclipse Jetty server, break the execution of the previous command by pressing *Ctrl + C* or a similar combination of buttons, depending on your operating system.

Creating the first page of the Java web application

Now that the new project is created in the `pentaho-reporting-web-app` folder, let's add a first page as endpoint for the Java web application. The creation of a page in a Java web application is straightforward, thanks to the Java servlet.

In this book, we won't detail the Java servlet and we assume you are confident with the basis around their use and behavior. If not, don't worry, because we will describe a step-by-step approach to drive you through the creation of your Java web application. To understand more, use Google to find the best tutorial for you: Java servlet is a well known solution to develop pages (and endpoints) in a Java web application.

To add the Java servlet API to the project, add the following XML code to the `pom.xml` file located in the `pentaho-reporting-web-app` folder:

```
<project ...>
  ...
  <dependencies>
    ...

    <!-- Add This here. -->
    <dependency>
      <groupId>javax.servlet</groupId>
      <artifactId>javax.servlet-api</artifactId>
```

```
      <version>3.1.0</version>
    </dependency>

  </dependencies>
  <build>
    ...
  </build>
</project>
```

After the `pom.xml` file has been saved, create the following folder structure `pentaho-reporting-web-app/src/main/java/com/example`, together with a new file named `PentahoServlet.java`. In `PentahoServlet.java`, write the following content:

```java
package com.example;

import javax.servlet.ServletException;
import javax.servlet.http.HttpServlet;
import javax.servlet.http.HttpServletRequest;
import javax.servlet.http.HttpServletResponse;
import java.io.IOException;
import java.io.PrintWriter;

public class PentahoServlet extends HttpServlet {

  @Override
  public void doGet(
    HttpServletRequest request,
    HttpServletResponse response)
    throws ServletException, IOException {

    doPost(request, response);

  }

  @Override
  public void doPost(
    HttpServletRequest request,
    HttpServletResponse response)
    throws ServletException, IOException {

    PrintWriter out = response.getWriter();
    out.println("PentahoServlet Executed");
    out.flush();
    out.close();

  }
}
```

This Java code creates a response of the servlet, in case of the GET method call and the POST method call. In both cases, a simple the **PentahoServlet Executed** message is shown as result.

After the PentahoServlet.java file has been saved, it's time to update the web.xml file stored in the pentaho-reporting-web-app/src/main/webapp/WEB-INF folder with the following configuration:

```
...
<web-app>
  <display-name>Archetype Created Web Application</display-name>

  <!-- Add This here. -->
  <servlet>
    <servlet-name>reporting</servlet-name>
    <servlet-class>com.example.PentahoServlet</servlet-class>
  </servlet>
  <servlet-mapping>
    <servlet-name>reporting</servlet-name>
    <url-pattern>/reporting</url-pattern>
  </servlet-mapping>

</web-app>
```

These settings create a link between the endpoint /reporting and the PentahoServlet class. After the web.xml file has been saved, the project is ready for being compiled and run again. To compile the Java web application, open a Terminal, move into the pentaho-reporting-web-app folder, and run the following commands:

```
mvn clean
mvn package
```

At the end of the execution of each command, a BUILD SUCCESS message should appear. At the end of the package command, the target folder is going to contain the WAR package named pentaho-reporting-web-app.war. To deploy the WAR package in the Eclipse Jetty server and run it, execute the following command:

```
java -jar target/dependency/jetty-runner.jar target/*.war
```

After a few seconds and some lines of log messages, the web application is up and running on port `8080`. The following screenshot shows what your browser should look like, opening the page `http://localhost:8080/reporting`:

To stop the Eclipse Jetty server, break the execution of the previous command by pressing *Ctrl + C* or a similar combination of buttons, depending on your operating system.

Including Pentaho Reporting Engine in a web application

Once the Java web application is created using Apache Maven, the next task is to include the Pentaho Report Engine. Thanks to Pentaho's openness, all the requested artifacts are available in a public Nexus repository at `http://repository.pentaho.org`.

 Being open source does not necessarily mean being free of charge. However, all the artifacts related to community editions are free of charge, so no fee or cost should be asked during their download and use.

The requested artifacts are mainly composed of all the JAR libraries defining the Pentaho Report Engine (see `Chapter 1`, *Introduction to Pentaho Reporting*, for the complete list). To include the Pentaho Report Engine in your Java web application, follow the tasks described in the next section.

Adding the Pentaho repository

The very first task is about including the Pentaho Nexus repository as source for your web application. To add the Pentaho Nexus repository in the Java project, add the following XML code to the `pom.xml` file located in the `pentaho-reporting-web-app` folder:

```
<project ...>
  ...

<!-- Add This here. -->
<repositories>
  <repository>
    <id>pentaho-releases</id>
    <url>http://repository.pentaho.org/artifactory/repo/</url>
  </repository>
</repositories>

<dependencies>
  ...
</dependencies>
<build>
  ...
</build>
</project>
```

This `repositories` section defines the URL of the Pentaho repository where all the dependencies related to Pentaho will be downloaded. Save the `pom.xml` file to complete the task.

Adding the Pentaho dependencies

Once the Pentaho Nexus repository is included in your web application, it's time to declare the dependencies of all the components defining the Pentaho Report Engine. To add the Pentaho dependencies in the Java project, add the following XML code to the `pom.xml` file located in the `pentaho-reporting-web-app` folder:

```
<project ...>
  ...
  <repositories>
    ...
  </repositories>
  <dependencies>
    ...

    <!-- Add This here. -->
```

```
<dependency>
  <groupId>pentaho-reporting-engine</groupId>
  <artifactId>pentaho-reporting-engine-classic-core</artifactId>
  <version>8.0-SNAPSHOT</version>
</dependency>
<dependency>
  <groupId>pentaho-reporting-engine</groupId>
  <artifactId>pentaho-reporting-engine-classic-extensions</artifactId>
  <version>8.0-SNAPSHOT</version>
</dependency>
<dependency>
  <groupId>pentaho-reporting-engine</groupId>
  <artifactId>pentaho-reporting-engine-wizard-core</artifactId>
  <version>8.0-SNAPSHOT</version>
</dependency>
<dependency>
  <groupId>pentaho-library</groupId>
  <artifactId>libbase</artifactId>
  <version>8.0-SNAPSHOT</version>
</dependency>
<dependency>
  <groupId>pentaho-library</groupId>
  <artifactId>libdocbundle</artifactId>
  <version>8.0-SNAPSHOT</version>
</dependency>
<dependency>
  <groupId>pentaho-library</groupId>
  <artifactId>libfonts</artifactId>
  <version>8.0-SNAPSHOT</version>
</dependency>
<dependency>
  <groupId>pentaho-library</groupId>
  <artifactId>libformat</artifactId>
  <version>8.0-SNAPSHOT</version>
</dependency>
<dependency>
  <groupId>pentaho-library</groupId>
  <artifactId>libformula</artifactId>
  <version>8.0-SNAPSHOT</version>
</dependency>
<dependency>
  <groupId>pentaho-library</groupId>
  <artifactId>libloader</artifactId>
  <version>8.0-SNAPSHOT</version>
</dependency>
<dependency>
  <groupId>pentaho-library</groupId>
  <artifactId>librepository</artifactId>
```

```
        <version>8.0-SNAPSHOT</version>
      </dependency>
      <dependency>
        <groupId>pentaho-library</groupId>
        <artifactId>libserializer</artifactId>
        <version>8.0-SNAPSHOT</version>
      </dependency>
      <dependency>
        <groupId>pentaho-library</groupId>
        <artifactId>libxml</artifactId>
        <version>8.0-SNAPSHOT</version>
      </dependency>
      <dependency>
        <groupId>com.lowagie</groupId>
        <artifactId>itext</artifactId>
        <version>2.1.7</version>
      </dependency>
      <dependency>
        <groupId>com.lowagie</groupId>
        <artifactId>itext-rtf</artifactId>
        <version>2.1.7</version>
      </dependency>
      <dependency>
        <groupId>commons-logging</groupId>
        <artifactId>commons-logging</artifactId>
        <version>1.2</version>
      </dependency>

    </dependencies>
    <build>
      ...
    </build>
  </project>
```

If you want to use charts in your report, you should add the following dependencies too:

```
<dependency>
  <groupId>pentaho-reporting-engine</groupId>
  <artifactId>pentaho-reporting-engine-legacy-charts</artifactId>
  <version>8.0-SNAPSHOT</version>
</dependency>
<dependency>
  <groupId>org.jfree</groupId>
  <artifactId>jfreechart</artifactId>
  <version>1.0.19</version>
</dependency>
<dependency>
  <groupId>bsf</groupId>
```

```
    <artifactId>bsf</artifactId>
    <version>2.4.0</version>
</dependency>
```

At the time of the development of this book, the latest available version of the Pentaho Reporting SDK was 8.0. Of course, this will change in the future, so you should replace the content of the version tags accordingly. At the time of the development of this book, the latest available version of the Pentaho Reporting SDK was 8.0. Of course, this will change in the future, so you should replace the content of the version tags accordingly. The suggestion is to check the Pentaho Nexus server at `https://public.nexus.pentaho.org` and search the latest version available, using the search term `pentaho-reporting-engine-classic-core`.

Showing an existing Pentaho report in a web application

Now that the Java web application is ready to manage the Pentaho content, in this last task, you will finally learn how to modify the Java web application to show a Pentaho report developed using the Report Design Wizard. In particular, the goal is to show `my_first_report`, previously developed as an example.

In the following chapters, you will see that the management of Pentaho reports not developed using the Report Design Wizard is approximately the same. For this reason, this content is valuable for you to learn how to manage an existing Pentaho report from a Java application.

As usual, we are going to split the task into smaller subtasks, because it will be easier to describe, check, and control.

Including an existing Pentaho report

The very first task is to include `my_first_report` in the Java web application. Remembering that the `my_first_report.prpt` file contains everything that is requested to render the Pentaho report, create the path `pentaho-reporting-web-app/src/main/resources/reports` and copy the `my_first_report.prpt` file into it.

Believe it or not, but this is all you need to do to make the report available to the Java web application.

Including the SampleData schema

As described in Chapter 2, *Getting Started with Report Designer*, the my_first_report report uses the SampleData schema as data source. For this reason, you need to include it in the Java web application. Including the SampleData schema in the Java web application is possible with two simple tasks: making the SampleData HyperSQL database available in the project and adding the HyperSQL client as dependency.

To make the SampleData HyperSQL database available in the Java web application, create the path pentaho-reporting-web-app/resources and copy the sampledata folder from <report-designer>/resources into it.

To add the HyperSQL client as dependency of the Java web application, change the pom.xml file located in the pentaho-reporting-web-app folder, according to what is described as follows:

```
<project ...>
  ...
  <repositories>
    ...
  </repositories>
  <dependencies>
    ...

    <!-- Add This here. -->
    <dependency>
      <groupId>org.hsqldb</groupId>
      <artifactId>hsqldb</artifactId>
      <version>2.3.2</version>
    </dependency>

  </dependencies>
  <build>
    ...
  </build>
</project>
```

This is all you need to do to include the SampleData schema in your Java web application.

Updating the PentahoServlet

As a last task, before previewing the Pentaho report, you need to change the Java servlet to use and render `my_first_report`. To complete the task, replace the content of the `PentahoServlet.java` file stored in the `pentaho-reporting-web-app/src/main/java/com/example` folder. The following is the new version of the content to replace in `PentahoServlet.java`:

```java
package com.example;

import java.io.IOException;
import java.net.URL;

import javax.servlet.ServletConfig;
import javax.servlet.ServletException;
import javax.servlet.http.HttpServlet;
import javax.servlet.http.HttpServletRequest;
import javax.servlet.http.HttpServletResponse;

import org.pentaho.reporting.engine.classic.core.ClassicEngineBoot;
import org.pentaho.reporting.engine.classic.core.MasterReport;
import
org.pentaho.reporting.engine.classic.core.modules.output.pageable.pdf.PdfRe
portUtil;
import org.pentaho.reporting.libraries.resourceloader.Resource;
import org.pentaho.reporting.libraries.resourceloader.ResourceManager;

public class PentahoServlet extends HttpServlet {

  @Override
  public void init(
    ServletConfig config)
    throws ServletException {

    super.init(config);
    ClassicEngineBoot.getInstance().start();

  }

  @Override
  public void doGet(
    HttpServletRequest request,
    HttpServletResponse response)
    throws ServletException, IOException {

    doPost(request, response);
```

```
    }

    @Override
    public void doPost(
      HttpServletRequest request,
      HttpServletResponse response)
      throws ServletException, IOException {

      // Prpt file.
      String reportPath = "file:" +
this.getServletContext().getRealPath("WEB-
INF/classes/reports/my_first_report.prpt");

      try {

        // Resource manager.
        ResourceManager manager = new ResourceManager();
        manager.registerDefaults();

        // Get report.
        Resource res = manager.createDirectly(new URL(reportPath),
MasterReport.class);
        MasterReport report = (MasterReport) res.getResource();

        // Generate report in PDF into the response.
        response.setContentType("application/pdf");
        PdfReportUtil.createPDF(report, response.getOutputStream());

      } catch (Exception e) {
        e.printStackTrace();
      }

    }
  }
```

Before moving forward to the previewing of the Pentaho report, we suggest you double-check the source code to understand how the prpt file is managed and how the objects are used to render the PDF file in the response. It is not a big deal, as you can see there are few lines of code between the try and catch commands.

Previewing the Pentaho report

Now that the web application has been updated, the last task is about compiling and running the project, as we already saw earlier in the chapter. To compile the Java web application, open a Terminal, move into the `pentaho-reporting-web-app` folder, and run `mvn clean package`. At the end of the execution of each command, a `BUILD SUCCESS` message should appear. At the end of the `package` command, the `target` folder will contain the WAR package named `pentaho-reporting-web-app.war`. To deploy the WAR package in the Eclipse Jetty server and run it, execute the following command:

```
java -jar target/dependency/jetty-runner.jar target/*.war
```

After a few seconds and some lines of log messages, the web application will be up and running on port `8080`. The following screenshot shows what your browser should look like, opening the page `http://localhost:8080/reporting`:

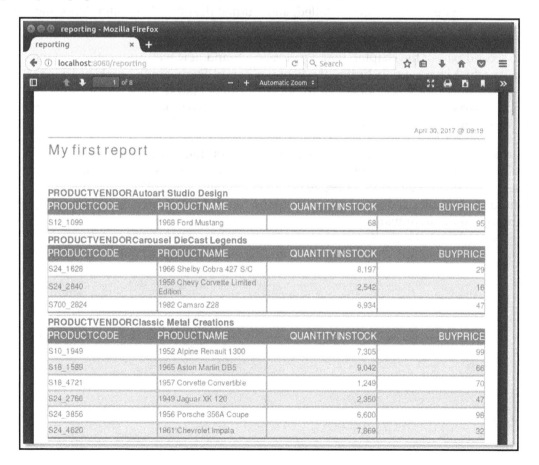

As you can see, the Java servlet is previewing the `my_first_report.prpt` file in PDF format, using the Pentaho Report Engine integrated into the Java web application.

 Feel free to check the GitHub repository available at `https://github.com/ fcorti/pentaho-8-reporting-for-java-developers`, in particular, in the `Chapter 03 - Getting started with Reporting SDK/pentaho- reporting-web-app` folder, where you can find the source code of this example.

Summary

In this chapter, you have walked through a complete example with step-by-step instructions on how to embed Pentaho Reporting in a Java J2EE Application. In the first part of the chapter, you downloaded, installed, and studied the official Pentaho Reporting SDK, discovering its structure, the samples, and the provided guide.

In the second part of the chapter, you developed a brand new web application in Java, using Apache Maven and including the Pentaho Report Engine in the project. To make the example more practical, you saw how to manage the Pentaho report developed in the previous chapter from the Java code. The goal has been to preview the Pentaho report in PDF format, using your browser.

Now that you have read this chapter, you should be confident with the basics about Pentaho Reporting SDK and how to build a Java application consuming Pentaho reports. In the next chapter, you will start a deep learning of Pentaho Report Designer, understanding the funding principles and developing a Pentaho report from scratch, instead of using the wizard as you did in previous chapter.

4
Creating a Report with Report Designer

In the previous two chapters, you learned the basis of Report Designer and Reporting **Software Developers Kit** (**SDK**). Reporting Engine has been treated as part of the other two tools. In this chapter, you are going to use Pentaho Report Designer again, with the goal to better understand it and start becoming a real expert. With this chapter, starts a collection of six chapters entirely dedicated to the desktop reporting tool. Starting from here, you will see all the advanced features, with the goal of being able to develop the best reports for your manager and customers.

To get started, you will first learn how to develop a Pentaho report from scratch, not using the Report Design Wizard as you did in `Chapter 2`, *Getting started with Report Designer*. The manual creation of a Pentaho report will give you the opportunity to see in action, all the features (basic and advanced) of the Pentaho Report Designer. As usual, the description will be driven by a practical example and a step-by-step approach to the tasks. To make the example more practical, you are going to develop a Pentaho report based on the inventory of products stored in the `SampleData` database.

To complete the initial description of the Report Designer's features, you will see how to customize the resulting report with a nice header, footer, and grouping of details. In the last (but not the least) topic, you will be introduced to the charts, before being shown how to preview reports in all the possible formats.

This chapter is again written as a tutorial for developers and information technologists. The best way to learn is to follow the instructions on your laptop while reading. At the end of this chapter, you will feel comfortable with the manual development of easy and complex Pentaho reports developed using Pentaho Report Designer. Later chapters will assume that you are able to manually develop a Pentaho report, so read it carefully and pay attention.

Creating a Pentaho report

As we discussed in `Chapter 2`, *Getting Started with Report Designer*, the creation of a Pentaho report starting from a blank report is an alternative to using the Report Design Wizard. Neither of the two ways is better than the other. Each way has advantages and disadvantages, and you should mature your own idea after some practice.

The development starting from a blank report is suggested if you want to have full control over the details and behaviors. The development using the wizard is suggested if your goal is to develop a standard report, quite simple in terms of structure, and also simple in terms of layout and customizations.

 Let's underline again one best practice: some developers prefer to start modifying a report built with the wizard, instead of starting from scratch. In principle this is not bad, but what can be experienced is that you have less control over some details, especially in fine tuning of the layout or some unexpected behaviors in particular cases.

In this section, you are going to learn how to develop a Pentaho report starting from a blank report. The goal is to develop a very simple example and then add elements to elements till you get a nice result in terms of layout and complexity.

To make the example more practical, you are going to develop a Pentaho report based on actuals, stored in the `SampleData` schema. The report will include information about the actuals and the budget for each role of a company, along with a summary pie chart to give an idea of the distribution in the various departments. This example will also include a static image and a title in the report header, and a page count and the username in the page footer of the report.

Creating a new Pentaho report

Creating a Pentaho report starting from a blank report is really straightforward. From Pentaho Report Designer, use the upper menu (click on the **File** item and then on **New**) or the toolbar, as shown in the following image:

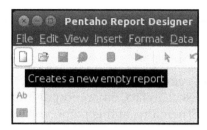

Once the blank report is created, an empty report is shown, similar to the following screenshot:

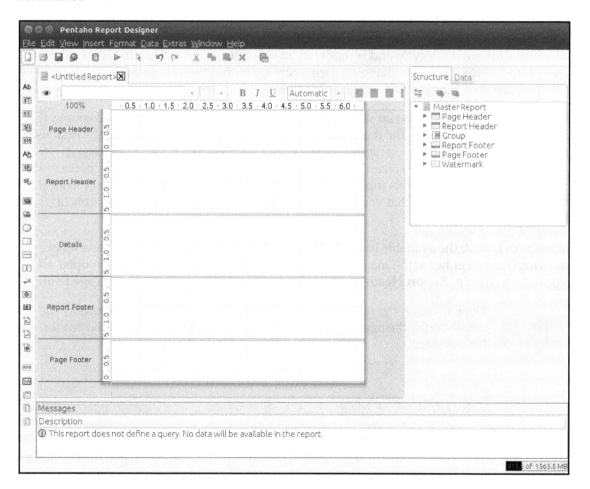

Before moving ahead with another task, let's give some colors to the report canvas. The report canvas, shown in the center of the screenshot, is where you define the look of your report.

Note that, at this point, you haven't decided if the report will be rendered as PDF, RTF, or Excel. In fact, any report definition can be rendered in all of these formats. Therefore, at this point, you do not have to worry about that.

The report canvas contains a set of **bands** that together make up a report. Bands include **Report Header** and **Report Footer** bands, individual **Group Header** and **Group Footer** bands (hidden by default), as well as a **Details** band that is rendered for each row of data. Reports may also contain **Page Header** and **Page Footer** (visible by default). Each band has a different life cycle and is rendered based on its context. You can hide any of the panels around the canvas by changing their visibility within the **Window** menu. This can help manage your screen while designing reports.

In real life scenarios, reports can vary a lot in terms of structure and content. Of course, the content is mostly driven by the data sources, but the layout really depends on the final user and the type of report that you have to develop. Not all the layouts are same, even if Pentaho Reporting is able to face all the possible requests (maybe). In this section, we would like to draw some light on this topic, pointing your attention to the fact that you can easily face all the future requests that your colleague or customer may ask of you in terms of report layout.

In terms of layout, the available bands in Pentaho Report Designer can help you a lot in showing the data either at the maximum level of details (**Details Body**) or as grouped and aggregated (**Group**, **Report Header** and **Report Footer**, and **Page Header** and **Page Footer**).

Depending on the report that you have to develop, feel free to use only the details, only the aggregations, or both, to define your preferred layout for the best result.

Creating a datasource in Pentaho reports

Before starting to develop the appearance of the report, you need to define a **data source**. The data source is the basis of every report, as it defines the list of fields requested for the viewing of results, for the making of charts, for the calculating of formulas, and so on. Starting from the empty report, by selecting the **Data** tab on the top right and right-clicking on **Data Sets**, as shown in the following picture, it is possible to define a new dataset and choose its type from a wide list of options. The following is an image showing what the selection looks like:

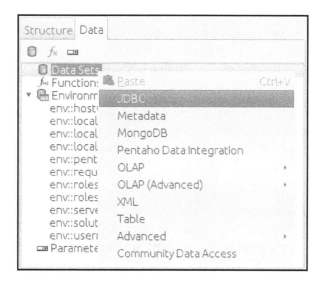

In the following chapters, we will discuss all the available types of data sets , but in our example, we are going to use the most common one, the JDBC.

  Java Database Connectivity (JDBC) is an **application programming interface** (**API**) for the Java language, which defines how a client may access a database. It provides methods to query and update data in a database and is oriented towards relational databases. See `https://en.wikipedia.org/wiki/Java_Database_Connectivity` for further details.

By clicking on **JDBC**, you will get a panel similar to the next image, which has a connection canvas on the left, the available queries in the top right, and query details on the bottom line. In the connection canvas, you will find five different types of associations to the SampleData schema. Take your time to examine each connection and their differences.

By selecting one connection and clicking on the pencil icon (✐), you will have access to the connection parameters and settings. Even if all the connections point to the SampleData schema, the type of access is different, and the different parameters and settings. We won't detail the differences between the types of connections, but will wait for the chapter dedicated to the data sources to discover further details.

 It's important to note that the default installation of Pentaho Report Designer does not provide all the JDBC drivers to the sources, even if they are listed in this panel. To install a JDBC driver, simply copy the JAR file implementing the driver into the `<report-designer>/lib/jdbc` folder and restart.

Even if you are going to use an existing connection, it is very simple to create a new one by using the green plus icon (⊕). As an exercise, try to click the green plus icon (⊕) to see what the window looks like.

After having introduced the connection canvas, select SampleData (local) and continue defining a query over the connection. To define a query, press the green plus icon (⊕) on the right of the Available Queries panel. Once clicked, a new named Query 1 will be defined. To change its name to be meaningful, select it and change the value in the Query Name field. In our case, we are going to call it Actuals.

Now that the query is available but should be defined, let's focus on the bottom panel containing the query definition. At the bottom right of the canvas, digit the query or compose it using **SQLeonardo Query Builder**. The simple query builder is accessible through the pencil icon (✐) on the right. In both cases, you can select a single table or define a more complex query over multiple tables. Once finished, click on **Preview** to see the resulting data set.

In our example, let's define the query as described in the following screenshot:

Note that in this way, you can define a collection of available queries for your report. Even if you decide to develop a report with multiple queries, always remember that you have to elect one as *main*. The main query will be used in the report and all the others will be used in sub-reports (see the following chapters for a detailed description) or for parameters (see the following chapters for a detailed description).

Click on **Preview** to see the resulting data set and check if the data source is correctly defined. If the preview of data appears without any error, click the **OK** button and the Actuals query will appear in the **Data** tab of the Report Designer.

Adding details to Pentaho reports

Now that the first data source is defined, let's go ahead with the layout, building a very simple report with the available fields in the Actuals query. In order to develop the report using the Actuals query, you need to focus your attention on two different parts of the report: the **Data** tab in Report Explorer and the **Details** band in the report canvas.

By dragging the query field from the Report explorer on the right and dropping it into the **Details** band in the report canvas, you can define the content of the report. As you can see trying into your development environment, in this way you can decide the precise position where to visualize the data, their order in the layout, and the length and height of each field. As you can expect, you can easily control a lot of settings, like for example, font and dimension, format and masks, coloring, alignment, and a lot of other useful things. All the customizations and configurations are possible using the Element properties panel in both the **Style** tab and the **Attributes** tab. Don't worry if you feel that you don't have the full knowledge and control of the capabilities; you will learn more about the fine tuning in the following chapters of the book.

Considering that often, experience is the best teacher, it would be great if you could play a little bit with the report, trying and testing what the report looks like if you change one of the settings instead of the other. Don't worry about trying to change values, settings, and properties. You cannot break things, so feel free to try as much as you can.

Now that you know how to compose the details of your report starting from the query fields, let's define the layout for this specific use case. You can see the screenshot of the **Details** band containing the POSITIONTITLE field, the ACTUAL field, and the BUDGET field as follows. Try to reproduce it in your development environment, as described previously, paying attention to the details of the position and length of each query field.

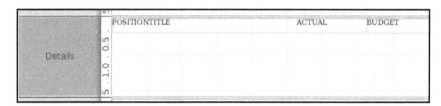

During the composition of the **Details** band, you have probably experienced the behavior described in the following screenshot. In case you overlap two fields, even partially, you will see one of the fields highlighted in red. In addition to this, a warning message will appear in the **Message** window with the description: Element ... overlaps with Element ... and will not be printed in table-exports. The following screenshot shows what the red highlight looks like:

What the warning message means and the implication of the overlap is quite easy to understand: overlapping the fields could cause problems in the final rendering of the report, hiding portions of the content. If this happens, don't worry and adjust the position and dimension of the elements until the red highlight disappears. This behavior is perfectly regular during the development of a report and Pentaho Report Designer gives you a lot of help for the best result.

Previewing and saving a Pentaho report

Now that a report is developed with few and basic elements, you probably want to preview it to check the final result. As you learnt in Chapter 2, *Getting Started with Report Designer*, click on the eye icon ( ) in the top left corner of the report canvas, and a preview similar to the following screenshot will be shown:

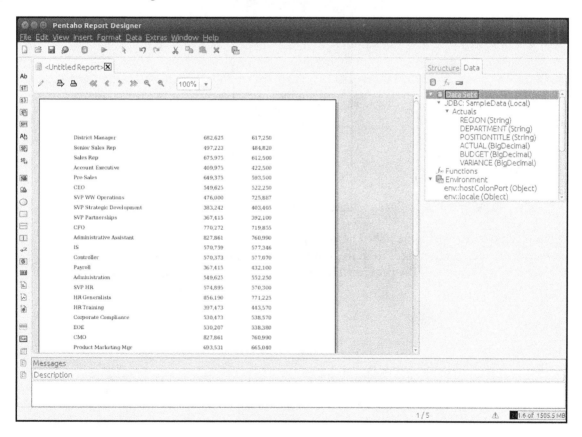

As you can see, the report is extremely basic in terms of layout and elements. In the following paragraphs, we will see how to make it more appealing. However, what we would like to bring to your attention now is that a report like this could be useful in case you want to define some kind of data exports in machine readable formats, like CSV, Microsoft Excel (XLSX), or text.

To learn something new about previewing a report, let's see how to preview the report in Microsoft Excel format (XLSX) instead of the PDF format (the default preview format by clicking on the eye icon (👁)). Previewing a report in one of the available formats is, again, really straightforward. As you can see in the toolbar, there is a green arrow icon (▶) in the middle. By clicking on the green arrow (▶) icon, a menu similar to the following screenshot is shown:

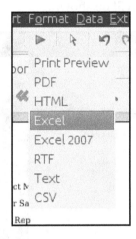

As you can easily expect, the list of items represents the possible formats of the preview. As an example, click on the **Excel** item to generate your report in Microsoft Excel (XLSX) format. Once completed, the preview should look like the following screenshot:

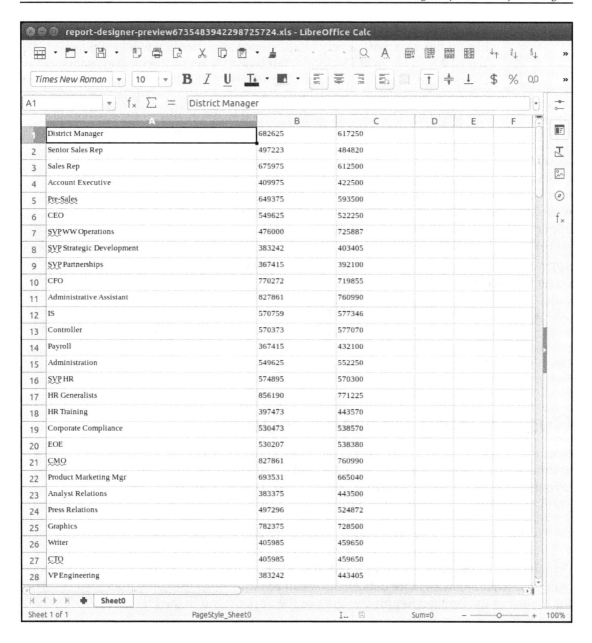

You can play with the other preview formats to see what your report looks like. In this case, with a very simple report, the preview will be always acceptable in terms of rendering, but when the report is complex, some issues could arise due to automatic rendering. This is to say, find the best compromise between complexity of the layout and formatting, otherwise you could experience some issues related to the quality of the final result and the satisfaction of your customers (or colleagues).

Now that the preview confirms that the report is what you need, let's save it with the report_01.prpt name in the my_reports folder. Saving the report has been introduced in Chapter 1, *Introduction to Pentaho Reporting* with more details, but it can be easily done using the disk icon (🖫) in the toolbar of the Pentaho Report Designer or the upper menu in the File group (using the **Save** or **Save as** items). Once done, close the report using the **X** icon, close to the report_01.prpt title of the tab in report canvas, the upper menu in the **File** group (a Close report item is listed), or use *Ctrl + F* if you'd prefer to learn and use shortcuts.

You can find report_01.prpt in the https://github.com/fcorti/ pentaho-8-reporting-for-java-developers repository, more precisely in the Chapter 04 - Creating a report with Report Designer/my_reports path.

Customizing Pentaho reports

Now that a first version of the report is developed (and tested using the preview), it's time to think about a second iteration, with the goal of enriching it by adding complexity to the layout with new elements. Before starting this new task, let's duplicate the previous report with a different name.

Duplicating an existing report is really straightforward: copy the report_01.prpt file as report_02.prpt in the my_reports folder. Once copied, open the report using the Pentaho Report Designer. Opening a report has been introduced in Chapter 1, *Introduction to Pentaho Reporting* with more details, but it can be easily done using the folder icon (📂) in the toolbar of the Pentaho Report Designer or the upper menu in the **File** group (using the **Open** item).

Customizing the font

We can do a lot for our report to make it more appealing for the users, and sometimes a few basic changes can improve the quality of the final result. As an example of customization, we are going to change the default font.

To change the font, click on the **Master Report** item of the **Structure** tab in the **Report Explorer**. You will see the **Element** properties appear. Click on the **Style** tab and search for the **family** item in the **font** group. Change the value to **SansSerif**, as shown in the following screenshot:

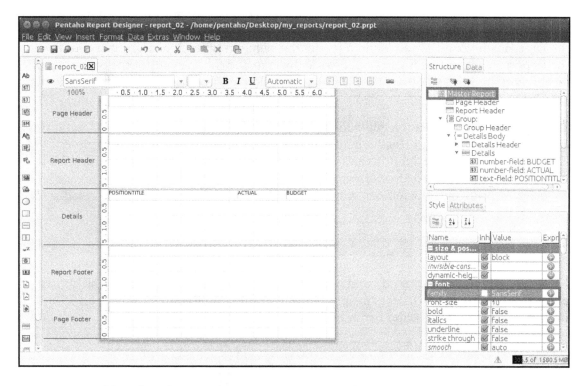

Note that this simple customization introduces you to one of the most powerful approaches to fine tuning of the elements of a report: the properties in the **Style** and **Attributes** tabs. Always remember that everything that can be customized and changed in an element, can be controlled acting on those tabs. The best way to learn how to do it, is to practice and play in samples, so try and try and try again until you find the best layout for your report.

Previewing the report (by clicking on the eye icon (👁) in the top left corner of the Report canvas), you will see the new font used in the whole content. Before continuing with the customizations, toggle again to the design mode by clicking on the pencil icon (✏).

Customizing the report header

Now that the font is refined and closer to the idea of a professional report, let's add a logo identifying the company and a title to be more meaningful in its printed version.

The very first decision to take on each customization of your report is how to develop the layout. In this case, the decision is where to put the logo and the title. You could decide for the **Page Header** band, if you want to render the elements on each page, or you could use the **Report Header** band, if you prefer to see the logo and the title only at the beginning of your report. In this task, let's choose the second option: putting the elements in the **Report Header** band.

To prepare the header, we are going to change the background color and the default text color, selecting the **Report Header** item from the **Structure** tab in the **Report Explorer**. Changing the color is straightforward using the Style tab of the **Element** properties. More particularly, identify the text-color and **bg-color** properties and set them to white and #77b3d4 respectively. The following image shows what the two fields should look like:

Now that the colors are correctly updated, let's add the logo identifying the company. To add a picture to the report, drag the image icon (🖼) from the **Report Element** palette and drop it into the **Report Header** band, as shown in the following screenshot:

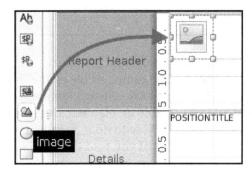

Double-click on the picture in the **Report Header** band to access its configuration. Once clicked, the configuration panel will ask you the path to the image to include or the URL, if you'd prefer to use an image from the internet. In both cases, you could decide to link the image as external source or embed the image in the report.

Most of the time, it's a good idea to embed the image in the report to avoid problems in case the internet connection is not available or the link is broken.

In our case, let's point to the image named `world.64x64.png` stored in the `Chapter 04 - Creating a report with Report Designer/resource` path of the `https://github.com/fcorti/pentaho-8-reporting-for-java-developers` repository. To point to the image from Pentaho Report Designer, clone the project locally or download the image directly into your laptop.

Now that the logo is correctly positioned in your report, let's add the title. The task is very similar to the previous one: drag the label icon (**Ab**) from the **Report Element** palette and drop it into the **Report Header** band, as shown in the following screenshot. Note that the label is positioned in the middle of the image and its length has been extended till the end of the page.

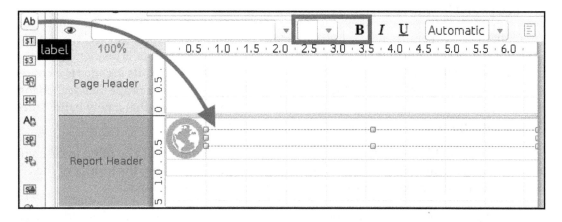

Click on the label element in the Report Header band and change the format, acting on the toolbar highlighted in the image. Select bold option by clicking on the **B** button and change the font dimension to `20` in the drop-down menu. Now that the format is updated, double-click on the `label` element to have access to the content. Change the text to `Actuals per position title` and press *Enter* to confirm the new content of the label.

Now that the header is correctly updated, let's preview it by clicking on the eye icon (👁). The following screenshot shows how the preview should look:

Actuals per position title		
District Manager	682,625	617,250
Senior Sales Rep	497,223	484,820
Sales Rep	675,975	612,500
Account Executive	409,975	422,500

Before continuing with the customizations, toggle again to the design mode by clicking on the pencil icon (✏).

Adding the details header and customizing the details

Now that the title is correctly developed in the report, we should work on the details again to improve the appeal of the final result. To reach that goal, let's see how to add the header to the details and how to add alternate row coloring.

By default, the report comes with a hidden details header band (as you can see, the details header band is not visible in the **Report Canvas** tab). To show the details header, select the **Details Header** item in the **Structure** tab of the Report explorer (**Details Header** is a child of **Details Body**). After this, toggle to the **Attributes** tab in the **Element** properties and change the `hide-on-canvas` property to `false`. Immediately, you will see that a new band called details header appears in the Report canvas.

As you can expect, this band can be used as a regular band and should be filled in case you want to show something in your final version of the report, regarding the header of the details. In our example, we want to show one label as title for each field.

Before adding the labels, click again on the **Style** tab of the Element properties and change the value of the `text-color` property to `#77b3d4`. This will give the labels a different coloring for a better result.

To add the labels, drag the label icon (**Ab**) from the **Report Element** palette and drop it into the **Details Header** band. You should repeat this easy operation three times (one for each field of the details) and place the label in correspondence with the detail field in the **Details** band.

For each label, set the font format to bold (clicking the **B** button in the font toolbar) and double-click the element to change the content to `Position title` (for the first), `Actuals` (for the second), and `Budget` (for the third). For the `Actuals` label and the `Budget` label, click on the right alignment icon (⊟) in the font toolbar.

 To make the final version of the report more appealing, try to leave a small space (from 10 to 15 pixels) from the top of the band to the labels. This will give your report a cleaner layout, adding a small distance between the title bar and the details header.

To complete the task, select the `Actuals` field and the `Budget` field from the **Details** band and click on the right alignment icon (⊟) in the font toolbar. At the end of the task, the Report canvas should look like the following image:

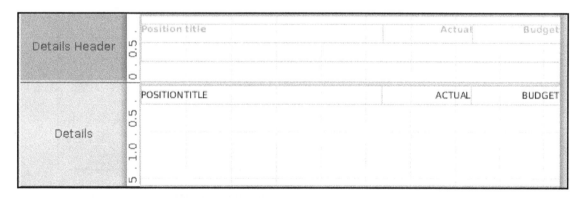

 With the default setup, the details header will be shown in the first page only. To repeat the header on each page, select the `Details Header` item from the `Structure` tab in the Report explorer. In the `Style` tab of the Element properties, you will find the `repeat-header` property in the `page-behaviour` group. Change the value to `true` and preview the result using the eye icon (👁). Scroll the pages using the navigation bar and you will see the header appear on each one. Before continuing with the customizations, toggle again to the design mode by clicking the pencil icon (✏).

Now that the details header is developed, let's continue customizing the details fields. In particular, we are going to add alternate row coloring. To complete the task, select the Details item from the Structure tab in the Report explorer and search for the bg-color property in the text group of the Style tab. In this case, we are going to evaluate the property with a dynamic expression. To set up the **expression**, click on the green plus icon (⬤), close to the property. At this stage, a configuration window will appear. In the Formula text field, in the bottom right of the window, digit the following formula:

```
=IF(ISEVEN(ROWCOUNT()); "white"; "#d2e8f4")
```

As final tuning, change the v-align property to the MIDDLE value. Now that the customizations are complete, let's see what the report looks like by previewing the report using the eye icon (👁):

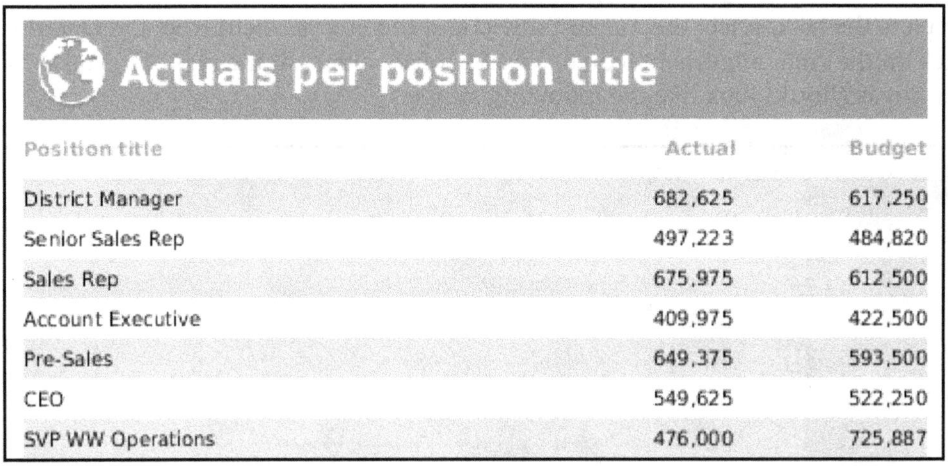

Actuals per position title

Position title	Actual	Budget
District Manager	682,625	617,250
Senior Sales Rep	497,223	484,820
Sales Rep	675,975	612,500
Account Executive	409,975	422,500
Pre-Sales	649,375	593,500
CEO	549,625	522,250
SVP WW Operations	476,000	725,887

Before continuing with the customizations, toggle again to the design mode by clicking the pencil icon (✏).

Customizing the page footer

Customizing the page header and page footer is nothing different from what we saw for the report header. The bands in the Report canvas are definitely helpful and they are going to enable you to develop everything as requested for this task. Our goal now is to add the user executing the report and the page number in the page footer.

To prepare the page footer, we are going to change the default text color by selecting the **Page Footer** item from the **Structure** tab in the **Report Explorer**. Changing the color is straightforward using the **Style** tab of the **Element** properties. In particular, identify the text-color property and set it to #77b3d4.

To add the user to the report, let's use a bundled **parameter** called env:username. To use the parameter in your report, select the Data tab in the Report explorer and scroll down until you find the **Environment** group. As usual, drag the env:username parameter and drop it into the **Page footer** band, on the left:

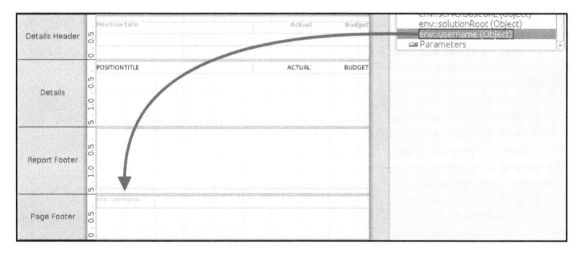

To add the page number, you need to create a new **function** using a formula. To create the function, right-click on the `functions` group of the **Data** tab in **Report Explorer**. Once clicked, a simple menu will show you the **Add function ..** item. Click on it to access the window:

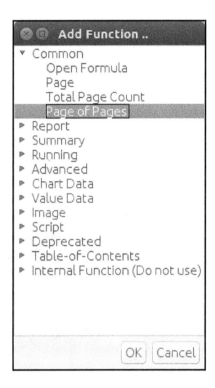

Expand **Common** and select **Page of Pages**, and then click on the **OK** button to add the new formula to the **functions** group. Now that the **Page of Pages** function is available, drag it from the **functions** group and drop it close to the right of the **Page footer** band. To complete the task, click on the right alignment icon (⬚) in the font toolbar:

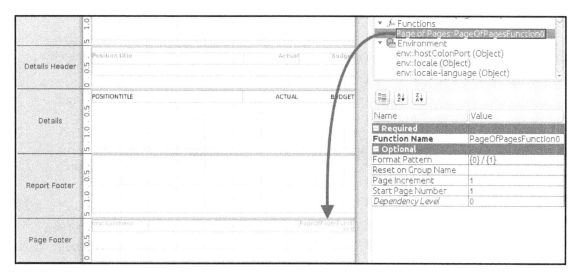

Now that the customizations are complete, let's see how the report looks by previewing it using the eye icon (👁):

EOE	530,207	538,380
CMO	827,861	760,990
Product Marketing Mgr	693,531	665,040
Analyst Relations	383,375	443,500
Press Relations	497,296	524,872
Graphics	782,375	728,500
Writer	405,985	459,650
CTO	405,985	459,650
Designer		1 / 6

As you will see, the page footer is repeated for each page and the page numbering will change accordingly. Before continuing with the customizations, toggle again to the design mode by clicking the pencil icon (✎).

Grouping the details

At this stage, the Pentaho report seems to be more appealing for the final user, but we are not happy yet and what we would like to discuss now is about grouping the details. Grouping the details in a report is a common request and we would like to show an example using the DEPARTMENT field in our Actuals.

To prepare the task, we need to modify the data source, to be sure that all the details are ordered by the DEPARTMENT field.

 If you will use grouping in reports, be sure you are correctly ordering the rows by the grouping fields. If you forget this tip, you will experience some unexpected results, without any exception or error message. The reason for this behavior is quite easy to understand; Pentaho Reporting Engine changes the group comparing the current value of the grouping fields with the previous one, so if they are not ordered, the report could show a wrong result.

To change the data source, select the **Data** tab in the Report explorer and right-click on the Actuals query. Select the Edit query item and replace the query with the one described next:

```
SELECT *
FROM "QUADRANT_ACTUALS"
ORDER BY "DEPARTMENT" ASC
```

As you can see, the only difference is the ORDER BY keyword. Press **Preview** and the **OK** button later on, if the preview shows the data set.

Once the data source is prepared, the next task is defining the layout. Looking at the **Structure** tab of the **Report Explorer**, you can find the Group element. Click on it and select the **Attributes** tab from the **Element** properties. In the list of properties, you can find the group property in the common group. Change the value to DEPARTMENT using the **...** button. Once done, nothing really changes to the layout but the grouping is correctly set in your report.

To change the layout, click on **Group Header** in the Report explorer and change the hide-on-canvas property to FALSE, as we did for **Details Header**. As we saw for the Details Header band, the Group Header band immediately appears in the Report canvas and we can add elements to it.

To add an element to `Group Header`, drag the `DEPARTMENT` field from the `Actuals` query in the `Data` tab of the Report explorer, dropping it into the `Group Header` band. To complete the task, extend the length of the field to cover the whole width of the page and set the font format by setting the dimension to `14` and the style to bold (clicking the **B** button in the font toolbar).

> To make the final version of the report more appealing, try to leave a small
> space (from 10 to 15 pixels) from the top of the band to the field. This will
> give your report a cleaner layout, adding a small distance between the
> grouping field and the details header.

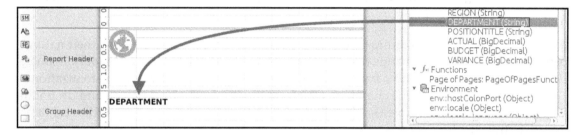

Now that the report grouping is correctly defined, let's preview it by using the eye icon 👁:

🌐 **Actuals per position title**		
Executive Management		
Position title	Actual	Budget
CEO	500,000	478,750
SVP Partnerships	531,780	519,179
SVP Strategic Development	226,000	226,395
SVP WW Operations	249,800	249,184
CEO	500,000	488,750

Before continuing with the customizations, toggle again to the design mode by clicking on the pencil icon (✏).

Using the same approach as described previously, you will be able to create multi-level grouped reports. Using Pentaho Report Designer, you can add hierarchical groups of fields, together with group header and footer bands on each group.

Adding charts

For the last (but not the least) customization to the report, let's see how easy it is to add a chart. The ability to easily create charts in various formats is a great feature in Pentaho Reporting, and in our example, we are going to see how to add a chart summarizing the actual values per department.

As you can expect, charts require a dataset to show data, and most of the time, their natural place is in the aggregation bands (usually **Report Header**, but also **Group Header**). In our example, we are going to add a bar chart in **Report Header** with some easy customizations. To add the bar chart, drag the chart icon (⬚) from the Report element palette and drop it in the **Report Header** band. Note that the chart is placed immediately under the title and its length is stretched to cover the width of the page:

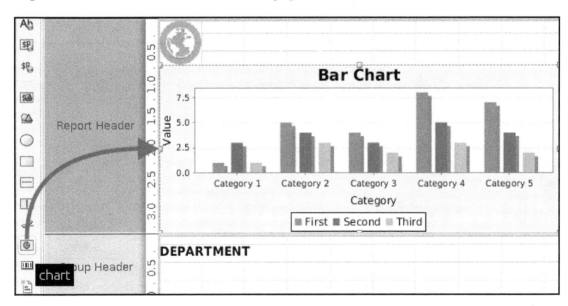

Once the chart is positioned in the `Report Header` band, double click on the chart element to access the editing panel. In the following image, you can see highlighted all the changes to do. As you can see, the changes are related only to three properties: the `category-column` property pointed to the `DEPARTMENT` query field, the **value-column** property pointed to the `ACTUAL` query field, and the **show-legend** property set to **False**.

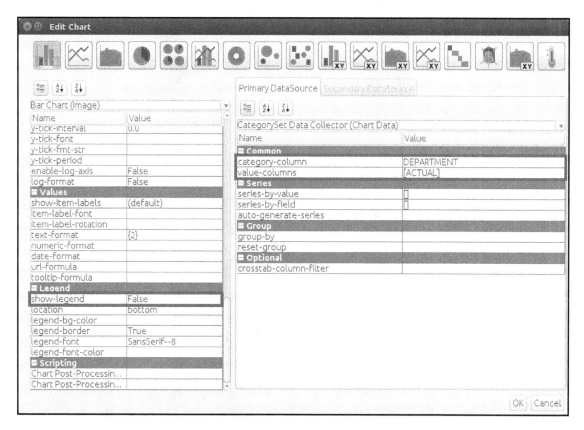

Once done, click the OK button and that's all. Congratulations, your report is completed and customized, and you can preview it using the eye icon (👁):

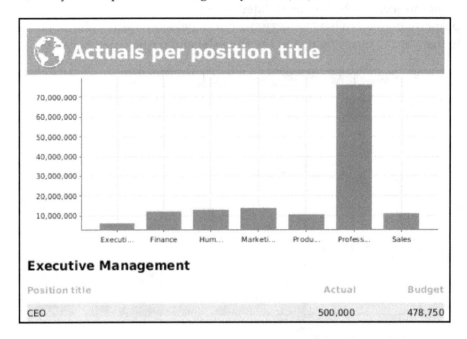

Before continuing with new things to learn, let's save the report with `report_02.prpt` in the `my_reports` folder. Saving the report has been introduced in Chapter 1, *Introduction to Pentaho Reporting* with more details, but it can be easily done using either the disk icon 💾 () in the toolbar of the Pentaho Report Designer or the upper menu in the **File** group (using the **Save** or **Save as** items).

> You can find `report_02.prpt` in the https://github.com/fcorti/ pentaho-8-reporting-for-java-developers repository, more precisely, in the Chapter 04 - Creating a report with Report Designer/my_reports path.

Previewing Pentaho reports in different formats

Now that you have two brand new reports (`report_01.prpt` and `report_02.prpt`) developed starting from a blank page, let's see how to preview `report_02.prpt` in different formats. As you learnt in the introduction, Pentaho Reporting Engine is able to generate reports in several formats, independently from the development.

To preview a report choosing the format, click on the green arrow icon (▶) visible in the toolbar. Once clicked, you will see a short menu appear with a list of possible formats. The following screenshot shows what the menu looks:

Choosing the **Print Preview** item is like choosing the default format; the default format is generated and downloaded locally. If you select the PDF format, you will see that the report is entirely generated and downloaded locally. If your client environment has a reader (or software) associated with the format, you will see that it will be opened and previewed. On other hand, if the format of your report is not associated to any reader or software, it will be asked to be saved as a regular file.

The following are some screenshots showing `report_02.prpt` rendered in PDF format (top left), HTML format (top right), Microsoft Excel format (bottom left), and RTF (bottom right):

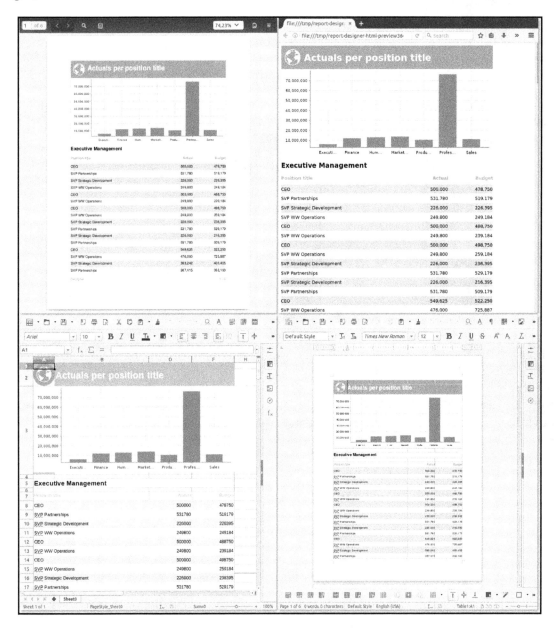

Before leaving this feature, let's share some practical considerations on the relation between the developed report and the final format (or formats). As you can see in the previous example with `report_02.prpt`, Pentaho Reporting Engine is really powerful and is able to generate the best version of the report in all the available formats. As you can imagine, this has some obvious limitations. If you take a look at the Microsoft Excel version, the rendering is not perfect and is probably not suitable for a release in production. Right or wrong, this is a regular behavior on complex layouts and this is something you should always consider in your future developments.

If you have to develop a report that will be released in formats with limited capabilities, like Microsoft Excel, CSV, or Text, always remember to *keep it simple*. The more complex the layout, the more difficult it is for Pentaho Reporting Engine to render the report in its final version. On other hand, if you are going to render a report in PDF format, the Pentaho Reporting Engine is almost magic and will be able to render very complex layouts. From this point of view, report development and final formats are strictly related.

Train yourself to learn faster

We have already mentioned that experience is the best teacher for a report developer. In this section, we shared some exercises you could develop by yourself, so you can try creating and customizing a Pentaho Report using Pentaho Report Designer.

If don't have Pentaho Report Designer already installed on your laptop, check Chapter 2, *Getting Started with Report Designer*, for a step-by-step description of how to install it. If one or more exercises appear too difficult, don't worry. In the next chapters, you will cover all the details of the development and you will become a real expert.

In the meantime, remember that the solutions to all the suggested exercises can be found in the https://github.com/fcorti/pentaho-8-reporting-for-java-developers repository, more precisely in the Chapter 04 - Creating a report with Report Designer/my_reports path.

- **Exercise 1**: Starting from `report_02.prpt`, change the color of the orange bars to #77b3d4. As a suggestion, check the `series-color` property in the chart editor. For the solution, check the `report_03.prpt` file.

- **Exercise 2**: Starting from `report_02.prpt`, change the grouping to `REGION` instead of `DEPARTMENT`. As a suggestion:
  - Check the `group` property in the `Attributes` tab of the `Group` element.
  - Check the `field` property in the `Attributes` tab of the `text-field` element under `Group Header`.
  - Check the `category-column` in the chart editor.

For the solution, check the `report_04.prpt` file.

- **Exercise 3**: Starting from `report_01.prpt`, set the color of the text to white and the background of the even rows to `#273B09` and the odd rows to `#002400`. As a suggestion, check the `text-color` property of the `Details` element and set the expression for the `bg-color`, as you saw in the example described in this chapter. For the solution, check the `report_05.prpt` file.

Summary

In this chapter, you have walked through an advanced use of Pentaho Report Designer, starting from a blank report and learning how to develop a Pentaho report from scratch, not using the Report Design Wizard. The manual creation of a Pentaho report gave you the opportunity to see in action all the features (basic and advanced) of the Pentaho Report Designer.

As experienced in the previous chapters, the description has been driven by practical examples and a step-by-step approach to the tasks. At the end of the chapter, you saw how to develop a very simple report with an easy layout (`report_01.prpt`), and a complex report with a nice header, footer, grouping of details, and also a chart (`report_02.prpt`). In the last (but not the least) topic, you were introduced to a preview of the reports in all the available formats, with some highlights on the relation between the development and the final format.

This chapter is again written as a tutorial for developers and information technologists. We hope you enjoyed following the development on your laptop while reading, and hopefully, you feel comfortable with the manual development of easy and complex Pentaho reports, developed using Pentaho Report Designer.

In the next chapter, we will dive deep into the details of the various elements available to designers, how they are used, and what they might be used for.

5
Design and Layout in Report Designer

In the previous chapters, you were introduced to Pentaho Report Designer and you started to use it, developing simple and complex reports either by using the wizard or starting from scratch. In this chapter, you will dive deep into the concepts and functionality of Pentaho Report Designer related to the design and layout of a report.

You will first refresh the basics around Report Designer's user interface and you will then learn more about the core layout bands presented in the Report Designer, including detail and group bands. From there, you will explore in detail the various elements available to designers, how they are used, and what they might be used for.

You will also learn the ins and outs of visual layout within the reporting canvas, including advanced concepts such as grids and guides. You will close the chapter with more details about working with the various output formats supported by Pentaho Reporting.

This chapter is written as a reference manual for developers and information technologists. The goal is to share all the relevant and advanced features of Pentaho Report Designer. At the end of this chapter, you will feel comfortable with its user interface and you should be able to use it to the best of its capabilities.

Report Designer user interface components

In Chapter 2, *Getting Started with Report Designer*, you discovered the composition of the user interface, and in Chapter 4, *Creating a Report with Pentaho Designer*, you used Report Designer to develop both very simple and complex reports, discovering most of the relevant features regarding designing and layout. Before completing the discovery of the whole features, as a reminder, let's recap in the following list the components you can recognize in Report Designer user interface, as shown in the screenshot that follows. This will be useful in the following sections, to discuss the details and the advanced features connected to design and layout.

- The menu and toolbar on the upper part of the window
- The report element palette, on the left, where you can select report elements for your report
- The report canvas tab panel, which displays your reports
- The report explorer panel with the structure tab (and the **Data** tab) which displays the entire report in object tree form
- The element properties panel, which displays all the styles and attributes associated with the currently selected report element
- The messages panel, which displays warnings and errors related to the currently opened report

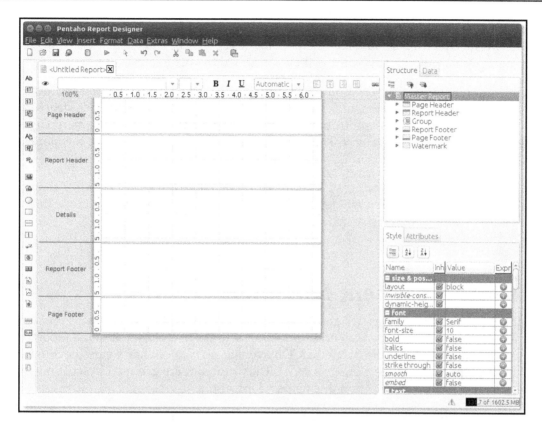

In the following sections, you are going to dive deep into the most useful features about design and layout in Report Designer user interface.

The Structure tab in report explorer

As described in the previous section, the report explorer panel has a tab called **Structure**, which displays the entire report in object tree form. This tab, or rather the tree structure represented in it, is one of the key tools in the hands of the developers. Using this tool, the developers can control the fine tuning of the report.

In the tree structure is represented a hierarchy of objects, each one identifying one (and only one) element of the report. Everything in the report is an element and every element has a parent with zero or more children. One element must have one parent only and it cannot have multiple or zero parents. A unique exception is the root, who has any parent.

About the root: on top of the hierarchy there is always a unique element called **Master Report**. **Master Report** is an invisible element in the report, but it is where everything starts defining design, layout and everything that is included in your report.

Moving (or deleting) an element from the report will also move (or delete) the entire subtree of elements. Try to add an element to the report canvas and check how the tree structure changes. Try to move an element from its parent to a different element in the hierarchy and see how the report canvas changes. The more you use the tree structure now, the more confident you will be with report development in your future projects.

Take your time to play with the structure tab in the report explorer. Being confident with it will let you have full control of your report and the fine tuning of all the structure, properties, and so on.

The report element properties

Another key concept in report designing is the element's property. An element's property is the atomic value or description or configuration or settings of an element in the report. Each element can have zero or more properties. On average, an element has a variable number of properties (depending on the element's type). The properties are grouped in sets for better understanding and better selection during development.

The main place to find the list of properties is the element property panel. The element property panel is defined by two tabs: the **Style** tab containing all the properties related to the layout and rendering, and the **Attributes** tab containing all the properties related to all the generic settings and configurations.

Each tab is defined by a list of properties related to an element, each one showing a couple of objects: the property name and the property value (or values). The property value can be defined by a value (depending on the type of property) or a dynamic formula. The majority of the properties in the element property panel have a green plus icon ( ) on the right. Clicking the green plus icon ( ) gives you access to the formula editor (we will introduce the formula editor in the following chapters). The following is an example of a property as presented in the user interface. In this case, font-size is the property with a value of 10.

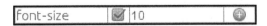

Selecting an element in the report and then selecting one of the children, you can easily notice that the values of the common properties are inherited from one element to the other. This give us the opportunity to talk about the inheritance of the properties of one report: each element defined in a report inherits the value of the common properties from the parent, and the parent from its parent, and so on.

 If you want to change a global property for a report (font, size, colors, borders, and so on), it may be enough for you to change the value of the corresponding property in `Master Report`. The value of the property will be propagated to all the descendants (that is, to the whole report) until one of them explicitly rewrites the value.

You can easily recognize that a property value is inherited from the parent if the flag ☑ is checked in the corresponding item in the element property panel. As you can imagine, you can break the inheritance, changing the value of the property. Doing this, the flag is automatically set to *unchecked*. From that point onwards, all the descendant elements will inherit the new property value, until another explicit change is set up. Clicking again on the flag (☑) icon, you can instruct Report Designer to again inherit the property value from the parent element, as it was by default.

The properties in each tab are grouped in sub-sets, for better selection and search during the development. The sub-sets are named using a meaningful description, like: `size & position`, `font`, `text`, `text-spacing`, `object`, `link`, `excel`, `padding`, `border`, `query`, `common`, `query-metadata`, `parameter`, `wizard`, `html`, `html-event`, `pdf-event`, `swing-event`, `advanced`, `pentaho`, and a few more.

Selecting an element in the report (using the report canvas, using the report explorer, or any other possible way using the Report Designer), the element property panel will show all its available properties. Each change of the property value is immediately reflected in the report preview in the report canvas.

Master report and report bands properties

Now that the concepts of element and property have been introduced, let's start talking about the root of a report (the `Master Report` element) and the first level in the tree structure, the bands. Specifically, we are going to describe the properties related to each type of element, starting from the common ones and then describing the specific ones, element per element.

Every Pentaho report you create has a `Master Report` element as the root of the tree hierarchy. The `Master Report` element is not explicitly visible in the preview or the report canvas, but it contains a set of general properties. In the following section, dedicated to the `Master Report` element, you will learn more about the specific properties of this root element.

When first creating a report, in your canvas and report explorer structure tree, you will see: `Page Header`, `Report Header`, `Details`, `Report Footer`, and `Page Footer` band. These bands, along with other bands, including `Group`, `Watermark`, and `No Data`, make up the entire visual report. All bands may contain elements from the palette and act as containers for rendering these elements. Each band has a different life cycle and is rendered based on its context.

To better explain the importance of the properties and their role in a report's development, you will find quoted some examples of Pentaho reports in the `https://github.com/fcorti/pentaho-8-reporting-for-java-developers` repository; more precisely, in the `Chapter 05 - Design and layout in Report Designer/my_reports` path. Each report shows the use of a relevant property (or a set of properties) as an example and can be a guide for your understanding and learning.

Common properties

As introduced in the section *The report element properties*, the inheritance of property values between nested elements is a relevant feature of Pentaho Reporting. Of course, the inheritance works if the same property is used in both the parent element and the child element. This concept introduces the principle that a bunch of common properties are shared (and inherited) between the various elements. In this section, you will dive deep into the common properties between the `Master Report` element and the various types of bands.

Size and position properties

This set of properties defines the size and position for the band. These properties may be edited together by selecting the band in the structure tree and then clicking on the **Format | Size & Border...** menu item, or individually within the report element **Style** tab:

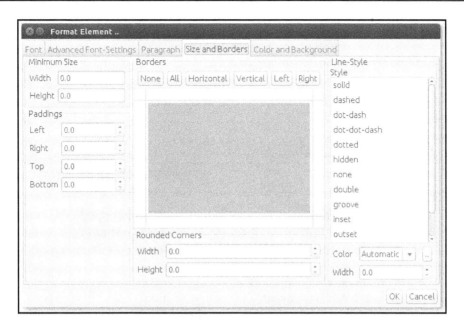

The following table lists the size and position properties you can find visible in the **Size & Border...** group of the **Style** tab in the report element explorer:

Name	Type	Description
layout	Selection	This is for bands only and defines how elements within the band are rendered. • The default layout is canvas, which allows you to specify exactly where each report element in the band should render. • The block layout stacks all the items in a band from top to bottom. • The inline layout stacks all the items left to right, with wrapping. • The row layout displays all the report elements in a single row. • The auto layout displays automatically the report elements to avoid overlaps. • The table related layout (including the specific table-body, table-header, table-footer, table-row, table-cell, table-col, and table-col-group) stacks all the items in a HTML table structure, once you export the report to HTML.
x	Integer	The x location of this element within its parent container.
width	Decimal	The width of this element. A number between -100 and 0 represents a percentage of the parent container's width.
y	Integer	The y location of this element within its parent container.
height	Decimal	The height of this element. A number between -100 and 0 represents a percentage of the parent container's height.
invisible-consumes-space	Boolean	If set to true, children of this band that are invisible will still consume space in the report.
visible	Boolean	If set to false, the element is not rendered.
dynamic-height	Boolean	If set to true, it informs the reporting engine that this element has a dynamic height.
preferred-width	Decimal	The preferred width of this element.
preferred-height	Decimal	The preferred height of this element.
min-width	Decimal	The minimum width of this element.

min-height	Decimal	The minimum height of this element.
max-width	Decimal	The maximum width of this element.
max-height	Decimal	The maximum height of this element.
x-overflow	Boolean	If set to true, text may overflow horizontally outside of the element.
y-overflow	Boolean	If set to true, text may overflow vertically outside of this element.
fixed-position	Integer	If specified, sets the fixed vertical position of this band within a report.
box-sizing	Selection	This is either set to content-box or border-box. If set to content-box, the sizing styles do not include the border, and if set to border-box, the sizing styles include the border box. The default value of this style is content-box.
table-layout	Selection	Advanced feature to instruct Pentaho reporting Engine to render tables with fixed or automatic size and position.

As you can see in your environment, clicking on the report element explorer and checking in the element properties tabs, only a small subset of these properties is available in the Master Report element, but most of them are available in all types of bands.

As an exercise, start from report_02.prpt as developed in Chapter 4, *Creating a Report with Report Designer,* and modify the chart to cover 50% of the page's width and extend the row height to 40 pixels. To see the final result, you can check the report_06.prpt file stored in the Chapter 05 – Design and layout in Report Designer/my_reports folder of the GitHub repository.

Font, text, and text-spacing properties

Font, text, and text-spacing are three basic sets of properties, entirely dedicated to text layout in your report. Differently from the previous set of properties, the majority of the properties are shared (and inherited) from Master Report and all types of bands. Let us take a look at each property in detail in the following sections.

Font properties

Pentaho Reporting uses Java's built-in font support for most of its font operations. Some additional functionality exists in `libfonts`, providing the report engine with additional information that is not available through Java's standard `Font` and `FontMetrics` API.

In Pentaho Report Designer, fonts may be modified in multiple ways. First, all text-based elements contain font properties. These properties allow the selection of font family, font size, and font style. When editing these properties through the menu **Format | Font...**, the following screen is presented:

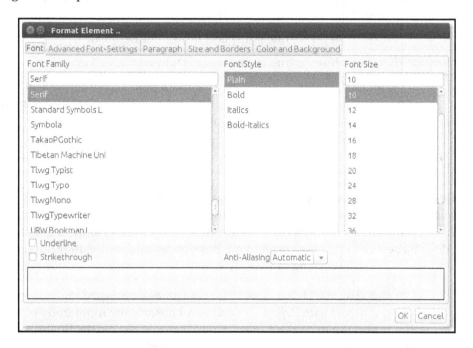

In addition to modifying the property, Pentaho Report Designer also provides a toolbar (shown in the following screenshot), where you can quickly modify the font name, size, style, and alignment:

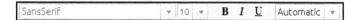

Another way to configure fonts is by using the element property that has the following properties available:

Name	Type	Description
family	Selection	A string that represents the font type, for instance SanSerif.
font-size	Integer	A number that represents the point size of the font.
bold	Boolean	If set to true, it displays the font in bold. For example, if the formula is set to true, the font will appear as bold.
italics	Boolean	If set to true, it displays the font in italic.
underline	Boolean	If set to true, it displays the font underlined.
strike through	Boolean	If set to true, it displays the font with a strikethrough.
smooth	Selection	If set to auto, the fonts above 8 points have anti-aliasing enabled. If set to always, all fonts have anti-aliasing enabled. Finally, if set to never, no fonts have anti-aliasing enabled.
embed	Boolean	If this style equals true, embeds the fonts included in the report, while rendering PDF.

Additional font-related issues may arise if a report is designed in one operating system environment and published in another. For instance, Windows operating systems come with a different standard set of fonts than Solaris, Mac, and Linux systems. Pentaho Reporting does its best to match the correct font, but you should verify after publishing that font sizes and styles are still working as expected.

 As an exercise, start from report_02.prpt as developed in Chapter 4, *Creating a Report with Report Designer*, and modify the font family of the entire report (so in Master Report) to Purisa. To see the final result, you can check the report_07.prpt file stored in the Chapter 05 – Design and layout in Report Designer/my_reports folder of the GitHub repository.

Text properties

Text properties are common (and inherited) to Master Report and bands, except for h-align and v-align. The following properties impact the appearance of text within report elements:

Name	Type	Description
h-align	Selection	The horizontal alignment of the text within the element. This property is also editable in the main toolbar.
v-align	Selection	The vertical alignment of the text within the element. This property is also editable in the main toolbar.
v-align-in-band	Selection	Specifies the vertical alignment of text in the band.
text-wrap	Selection	Specifies if the text should wrap. Appropriate values include none and wrap.
word-break	Boolean	Flag indicating to break text within words. If not defined, this defaults to true (breaks only at word-boundaries).
direction	Selection	The direction of text (for arabic text, as an example) indicating if it is left-to-right (ltr) or right-to-left (rtl).
text-color	String	The foreground font color. This property is also editable in the main toolbar.
bg-color	String	The background color of the text element.
line-height	Decimal	The value of the font's line height within the text element.
overflow-text	String	A text quote that is printed if the given text does not fully fit into the element bound.
trim	Boolean	A flag indicating whether leading and trailing white spaces will be removed.
trim-whitespace	Selection	Controls how the renderer treats white spaces.
encoding	String	Specifies the target text-encoding for the given field, in case the output supports per-field encodings.

About the `text-color` and `bg-color` properties, you should know that Report Designer has a helpful tool to for picking the color from a visual editor. The following image shows what the visual editor looks like.

As an exercise, start from `report_02.prpt` as developed in Chapter 4, *Creating a Report with Report Designer*, and modify the line height of the entire report (so in Master Report) to 30 pixels. To see the final result, you can check the `report_08.prpt` file stored in the Chapter 05 - Design and layout in Report Designer/my_reports folder of the GitHub repository.

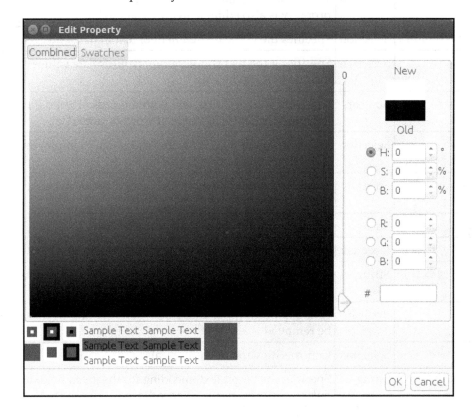

Text-spacing properties

`Text-spacing` properties let you control the space between letters and words in textual elements.

Name	Type	Description
`character`	Integer	Specifies the minimum character spacing between two letters
`word`	Integer	Specifies additional padding between words when rendering
`preferred-character`	Integer	Specifies the preferred character spacing between two letters
`max-character`	Integer	Specifies the maximum space between two letters

As an exercise, starting from the usual `report_02.prpt`, modify the character distance to 5.0 pixels. To see the final result, you can check the `report_09.prpt` file stored in the `Chapter 05 - Design and layout in Report Designer/my_reports` folder of the GitHub repository.

Object properties

`Object` properties control the general appearance of elements as described in the following table:

Name	Type	Description
`anti-alias`	Boolean	Flag indicating if anti-aliasing is enabled or not during the drawing of the element.
`keep-aspect-ratio`	Boolean	Flag indicating if the scaling should preserve the aspect ratio.
`fill`	Boolean	Flag indicating if the element should be filled.
`fill-color`	Selection	Defines the fill-color. If undefined, the foreground color is used.
`draw-outline`	Boolean	Defines whether the element outline should be drawn.
`stroke`	Selection	Defines the pen type and width that should be used to render the element.
`scale`	Boolean	Flag indicating if the content printed in the element should be scaled to fit the element's boundaries.

Links properties

`Links` properties manage the HTML links created from the report elements:

Name	Type	Description
pdf-bookmark	String	Adds a bookmark to the PDF output
html-anchor	String	The name of an anchor (link-target) embedded in the HTML output
url	String	The destination URL of the link
url-tooltip	String	The title of the link, displayed as a tooltip
url-window-target	String	The target window where the link should be opened

Excel properties

This is a set of properties related to Microsoft Excel:

Name	Type	Description
sheet-name	String	The name of the sheet to render the band.
format-override	String	The Excel cell data format string.
formula-override	String	The Excel cell data formula string.
wrap-text-override	Boolean	If true, wraps a text-based report element text within an Excel Cell. This value is inherited by text-based report elements within the band.
indention-text	Integer	Number of characters for indention.

Page-behaviour properties

`Page-behaviour` properties impact how bands are rendered relative to individual pages (available for bands only):

Name	Type	Description
display-on-firstpage	Boolean	Flag indicating if the element should be shown in the first page. Provided for page header/footer bands only.
display-on-lastpage	Boolean	Flag indicating if the element should be shown in the last page. Provided for page header/footer bands only.

Name	Type	Description
sticky	Boolean	Flag indicating if the page-header/footer and the repeated group-header/footer from Master Report should be repeated in the sub reports.
avoid-page-break	Boolean	Forces the band to skip to the next page instead of split rendering.
pagebreak-before	Boolean	Places a page break before rendering the band.
pagebreak-after	Boolean	Places a page break after rendering the band.
orphans	Integer	The number of contiguous bands to group before a page break occurs.
widows	Integer	The number of contiguous bands to group after a page break occurs.
widow-orphan-opt-out	Boolean	Flag indicating whether to include or not to include the bands from the widow's count.
repeat-header	Boolean	Flag indicating if the header/footer should be repeated in every printed page (header and footer elements only).

 As an exercise, starting from the report_02.prpt developed in Chapter 4, *Creating a Report with Report Designer*, set the repeat-header property of the Group Header to true. To see the final result, you can check the report_10.prpt file stored in the Chapter 05 - Design and layout in Report Designer/my_reports folder of the GitHub repository.

Padding properties

These properties define the padding and border definition for the band. Border information includes thickness, line type, and color. These properties may be edited together by selecting the band and then clicking on the **Format** | **Size & Border...** menu item, or individually within the report element **Styles** tab. You can refer to the image in the section *Size and position properties* for an example of how the window looks:

Name	Type	Description
top	Decimal	The height of the padding on the top of an element
bottom	Decimal	The height of the padding at the bottom of an element

Name	Type	Description
left	Decimal	The width of the padding on the left of an element
right	Decimal	The width of the padding on the right of an element

 As an exercise, starting from the report_02.prpt developed in Chapter 4, *Creating a Report with Report Designer,* set the left padding of the POSITIONTITLE text field to 20. To see the final result, you can check the report_11.prpt file stored in the Chapter 05 – Design and layout in Report Designer/my_reports folder of the GitHub repository.

Border properties

This set of properties controls the color, texture, and size of the border around the element, as described in the following table:

Name	Type	Description
top-style	Selection	The style of the top border. Style values include solid, dashed, dot-dash, dot-dot-dash, dotted, double, hidden, none, groove, ridge, inset, and outset.
top-size	Decimal	The width of the top border.
top-color	String	The color of the top border.
left-style	Selection	The style of the left border. Style values include solid, dashed, dot-dash, dot-dot-dash, dotted, double, hidden, none, groove, ridge, inset, and outset.
left-size	Decimal	The width of the left border.
left-color	String	The color of the left border.
right-style	Selection	The style of the right border. Style values include solid, dashed, dot-dash, dot-dot-dash, dotted, double, hidden, none, groove, ridge, inset, and outset.
right-size	Decimal	The width of the right border.
right-color	String	The color of the right border.

Name	Type	Description
bottom-style	Selection	The style of the bottom border. Style values include solid, dashed, dot-dash, dot-dot-dash, dotted, double, hidden, none, groove, ridge, inset, and outset.
bottom-size	Decimal	The width of the bottom border.
bottom-color	String	The color of the bottom border.
break-style	Selection	If the element is split, this is the style of the border where the break occurred. Style values include solid, dashed, dot-dash, dot-dot-dash, dotted, double, hidden, none, groove, ridge, inset, and outset.
break-size	Decimal	If the element is split, this is the width of the border where the break occurred.
break-color	String	If the element is split, this is the color of the border where the break occurred.
top-left-width	Decimal	The width of the top left corner's radius.
top-left-height	Decimal	The height of the top left corner's radius.
top-right-width	Decimal	The width of the top right corner's radius.
top-right-height	Decimal	The height of the top right corner's radius.
bottom-left-radius-width	Decimal	The width of the bottom left corner's radius.
bottom-left-radius-height	Decimal	The height of the bottom left corner's radius.
bottom-right-radius-width	Decimal	The width of the bottom right corner's radius.
bottom-right-radius-height	Decimal	The height of the bottom right corner's radius.

As an exercise, starting from the report_01.prpt developed in Chapter 4, *Creating a Report with Report Designer*, add the top border only, in dashed style and 1.0 pixels. To see the final result, you can check the report_12.prpt file stored in the Chapter 05 - Design and layout in Report Designer/my_reports folder of the GitHub repository.

Common properties in attributes

Starting from here, the sets of properties are related to the `attributes` tab and not to the `Style` tab. This set of properties contains the common ones as attributes.

Name	Type	Description
hide-on-canvas	Boolean	Flag indicating if the element should be hidden or used in the report. The default value is different according to the band type.
type	String	Not modifiable. Represents the type of element.
group	String	Defines the field to group by.
name	String	The name you want to assign to this element.
if-null	String	If the defined field or value returns null, shows the value defined here.
style-class	String	Style class assigned to the element.
id	String	Unique identifier of the element.

Query-metadata properties

This set of properties controls the metadata of queries:

Name	Type	Description
data-format	Boolean	Flag indicating if the number or date element should be formatted using the Report Wizard.
style-format	Boolean	Flag indicating if requested to use the style formatting from the Report Design Wizard or the data source.
enable-style-bold enable-style-italics enable-style-underline enable-style-strikethrough enable-style-font enable-style-fontsize enable-style-color enable-style-background-color enable-style-valignment enable-style-alignment	Boolean	Flag indicating if the specific style is enabled or not.

Wizard properties

This set of properties is related to the Design Wizard:

Name	Type	Description
`generated-content-marker`	Boolean	If enabled, clears out all bands affected by the `generated-content-marker` attribute and starts from scratch.
`label-detail-header`	Selection	Defines the detail band header.
`show-changes`	Boolean	Flag indicating if the changes are shown.
`grid-style`	Selection	Style of the grid. Style values include `solid`, `dashed`, `dot-dash`, `dot-dot-dash`, `dotted`, `double`, `hidden`, `none`, `groove`, `ridge`, `inset`, and `outset`.
`grid-width`	Decimal	Width to be used for the grid.
`grid-color`	String	Color to be used for the grid.
`padding-top` `padding-left` `padding-bottom` `padding-right`	Decimal	Padding values.

HTML properties

This set of properties is used to define and control the HTML rendering:

Name	Type	Description
`class` `name` `title` `xml-id`	String	Properties representing HTML class, `name`, `title`, and `xml-id` attributes
`append-header`	String	Inserts the text entered in this property into the `<header>` tag of the HTML output
`append-body`	String	Inserts the text entered in this property into the `<body>` tag of the HTML output
`append-body-footer`	String	Inserts the text entered in this property into the `<footer>` tag of the HTML output

Name	Type	Description
suppress-content	Boolean	Flag indicating if it is requested to suppress generated content for cells that have raw-content in HTML output

Excel properties in attributes

This set of properties is used to define and control the Microsoft Excel rendering:

Name	Type	Description
formula	String	String used as formula in the Excel format
page-header-text	String	Appends the string to the Excel page header
page-footer-text	String	Appends the string to the Excel page footer

HTML-events, PDF-events, and Swing-events properties

The group of properties included in this section will be better described later in this book, but here they are introduced to complete the documentation around the element properties related to bands and Master Report.

HTML-events properties

This set of properties is related to HTML-events raised when the report is generated in HTML format:

Name	Type	Description
on-click on-double-click on-mouse-down on-mouse-up on-mouse-move on-mouse-over on-mouse-enter on-mouse-out on-key-down on-key-pressed on-key-up	String	String used as formula in the HTML format

Pdf-events properties

This set of properties is related to `pdf-events` raised when the report is generated in PDF format:

Name	Type	Description
script	String	Name of the script in the PDF

Swing-events properties

This set of properties is related to `swing-events` raised when the report is used within a **Swing (Java) Framework**. Swing is a GUI widget toolkit for Java. It is part of Oracle's **Java Foundation Classes (JFC)**--an API for providing a **graphical user interface (GUI)** for Java programs.

Name	Type	Description
action	String	Java method
tooltip	String	Content of the tooltip

Master Report properties

As introduced in the beginning of this chapter, `Master Report` is the root element of the tree object structure, representing the report in report explorer. Even if `Master Report` is not visible in the report canvas, it is a key element for report development, as it enables you to change one element only and propagate all the changes to the whole report (thanks to the inheritance of common properties).

In this section, you will learn the specific properties of the `Master Report` element, in addition to the ones described in the previous sections.

Size and position properties

`Master Report` includes only few a properties of this group. All the properties related to position (`x`, `y`, `width`, `height`, and so on) are not provided because they are not useful for the root element.

Text properties

All the properties are provided except for `h-align` and `v-align` ones.

Page-behaviour properties

This group of properties is not provided for the `Master Report` element.

Query properties

This group of properties is provided for `Master Report` only and contains the properties for query management:

Name	Type	Description
query	String	Assigns a name to the selected query. If you are using a JDBC Custom data source, use the name field.
limit	Integer	Limit for the query execution and rows retrieve. The value -1 means no limit.
timeout	Integer	Timeout limit for the query.
design-timeout	Integer	Timeout limit when running from Report Designer.
auto-sort	Boolean	Flag indicating if the auto sort is requested.
shared-connection	Boolean	Flag indicating if the connection is shared to sub-reports.
data-cache	Boolean	Determines whether parameter result sets are cached, which would reduce the amount of reload time when switching parameters in a rendered report. This option can be further configured through the `org.pentaho.reporting.engine.classic.core.cache.InMemoryCache.CachableRowLimit` and `org.pentaho.reporting.engine.classic.core.cache.InMemoryCache.MaxEntries` engine settings. By default, the value is `true`.

Common properties in the attributes tab

In this group of properties, the `Master Report` element does not provide the `hide-on-canvas` property and has some additional specific properties:

Name	Type	Description
`output-format`	Selection	Sets preferred output type for the report. The selection is enabled from a long list of possible available formats.
`lock-output-format`	Booelan	Locks the output type specified in the `output-format` attribute so that no other output type can be chosen. By default, the value is `false`.
`compatibility-level`	Selection	Level of compatibility with previous version of the Report Engines.
`style-sheet-reference`	String	References the stylesheet to include in the report.

Wizard properties

In this group of properties, the `Master Report` element does not provide the `generated-content-marker` property and has one additional specific property:

Name	Type	Description
`wizard-enabled`	Boolean	If enabled, clears out all bands affected by the `generated-content-marker` attribute and starts from scratch

Excel properties

In this group of properties, the `Master Report` element does not provide the `page-header-*` properties and has a couple of additional specific properties:

Name	Type	Description
`freezing-left-position` `freezing-right-position`	String	The goal of this property is to provide to Pentaho Reporting Developers the ability to choose which panes, in Excel, they want to freeze

Advanced properties

This set of properties is provided for `Master Report` only:

Name	Type	Description
pre-processor	String	A report **pre-processor** is a customization component that can be added to a master or sub-report. This component provides a method to automatically modify an existing report definition on each report run. Pre-processors are registered during the reporting engine's boot process. You cannot use pre-processor implementations that are not registered in the reporting engine's metadata system.

Pentaho properties

This set of properties is provided for `Master Report` only:

Name	Type	Description
visible	Boolean	Flag to setup if the report is visible or not
staging-mode	Selection	Selection indicating how to stage reports before sending them back to the client
report-cache dynamic-report-cache	Boolean	Flags to control the report caching

Page Header and Page Footer properties

The `Page Header` and `Page Footer` bands appear at the beginning and end of each page, determined by the specific output format.

These bands differ slightly from the common properties defined earlier. The `pagebreak-before` and `pagebreak-after` properties do not apply to these bands. Also, the following properties are available in addition to the defaults: `display-on-firstpage`, `display-on-lastpage`, and `sticky`.

In addition to the common properties, the `table` set is provided with the following properties:

Name	Type	Description
col-span	Integer	Column span in case of HTML rendering
row-span	Integer	Row span in case of HTML rendering

In the `excel` set, `page-header-left`, `page-header-center`, and `page-header-right` are provided with decimal values.

Report Header and Report Footer properties

`Report Header` and `Report Footer` appear at the beginning and end of a report, and are often used to display the title and summary information, like charts, tables of contents, and so on. `Report Header` and `Report Footer` have the `table` set as additional properties beyond the common set.

Group Header and Group Footer properties

The `Group Header` and `Group Footer` bands may appear for each defined group configured as part of the report. A grouping defined in a report is a set of identical values in one or more selected data columns. A new group is triggered when the values change in the defined group column(s).

It's critical that columns defined as groupings are sorted appropriately before being passed into Pentaho Reporting, otherwise duplicate groups may appear in the rendered report.

`Group Header` and `Footer` differ slightly from the common properties defined earlier, because the following properties are available in addition to the defaults: `repeat-header`, `sticky`, `page-header-left`, `page-header-center`, and `page-header-right`. `Group Header` and `Footer` have the `table` set as additional properties beyond the common set.

Details body properties

Details Body consists of four distinct bands. The Details Header and Details Footer bands are rendered before and after a grouping of detail rows. A Details band is rendered for every row of data, and a No Data band is rendered when no data is available for the report. The Details Header, Details Footer, and No Data bands are hidden in the Report Designer by default.

The Detail Header and Detail Footer bands share the same additional properties, sticky, repeat-header, page-header-left, page-header-center, and page-header-right as the group bands. In addition, the table set are provided as additional properties beyond the common set. The table set of properties is also provided to the No Data band. The rest of the detail bands define no additional properties beyond the common set of properties.

Watermark properties

The Watermark band appears behind all the other bands, and is used for background images and styling of the report. The Watermark band has the table set as additional properties beyond the common set.

Report elements

All available **report elements** appear in the palette and may be dragged and dropped into the report canvas. Report elements make up the content of your report. They range from the label and text elements to the graphic, chart, and sub-report elements.

Like bands, the other report elements are also shown in the structure tab of report explorer and the list of properties is available in the report element properties. Like the elements described in the previous section, the report elements also inherit the existing properties from their parent and they propagate the common properties to the children elements.

In this section, you will learn the properties related to each type of element in the palette. As we saw in the previous section about bands, you will start from the common ones and then you will see a detailed description for each element.

Also valid in this case is the suggestion shared earlier in the book: play as much as you can with elements and Report Designer to have a direct experience. If you try adding elements to a sample report, you can check the properties in the panel and try to change the values, remembering the behavior. Again, direct experience is the best teacher.

Common properties

Like bands and `Master Report`, the report elements also have common properties organized in groups for better understanding. Luckily, most of the common properties of the report elements are the same common properties you saw for bands.

Thinking about this, it probably makes a lot of sense because report elements leave properties nested into bands, so it's natural to find some (or all) of the generic properties of the bands, inherited into the children's elements.

Considering that the report elements are very specific for one purpose (labels, charts, fields from data sources, shapes, and so on), it will happen that some properties of the bands will be inherited in some report elements and not in others. In any case, you will find detailed the specific differences in sections dedicated to each type of report element.

Back to common properties; the following are detailed descriptions of the sets of properties.

Size and position properties

This set of properties is the same as you saw for bands and `Master Report`, where it has sense. `Layout` is used in all the report elements that can be stretched or modified in width/length according to the report.

Font properties

This set of properties is the same as you saw for bands and `Master Report`, where it has sense. For some report elements, like shapes and lines, the font properties are not available because text is not used.

Text and text-spacing properties

Both these sets of properties are the same that you saw for bands and `Master Report`, where they have sense. For some report elements, like shapes, `simple-barcodes`, `survey-scale`, and lines, the `text` and `text-spacing` properties are limited to the following properties: `h-align`, `v-align`, `text-color`, and `bg-color`.

Rotation properties

This set is introduced here for the first time and it is valid only for text based elements, like labels and few others:

Name	Type	Description
`rotation`	Selection	Rotation with value 90 or -90

Object properties

This set of properties is the same as you saw for bands and `Master Report`. For some report elements, like shapes, `simple-barcodes`, `survey-scale`, images, and lines, the `object` properties are extended with all the available properties for this set.

Links properties

This set of properties is the same as you saw for bands and `Master Report`. For some report elements, like shapes, `simple-barcodes`, `survey-scale`, images, and lines, the `pdf-bookmark` property is not provided.

Excel properties

This set of properties is the same as you saw for bands and `Master Report`, where it has sense. For some report elements, like shapes, `survey-scale`, `simple-barcodes`, and lines, the `excel` properties are not available because they are not required. In some cases, like, for example, images, the `sheet-name` and `format-override` properties are not provided.

Page-behavior properties

This set of properties is composed of a subset of the ones you saw for bands and Master Report, in particular, avoid-page-break, orphan, widows, and widow-orphan-opt-out. In some cases, like, for example, on the band and sub-report elements, the pagebreak-before and pagebreak-after properties are also provided.

Padding and border properties

These sets of properties are exactly the same as you saw for bands and Master Report.

Common properties in attributes

This set of properties is the same as you saw for bands and Master Report. The number of available properties depends on the type of element.

Query-metadata properties

This sets of properties is exactly the same as you saw for bands and Master Report.

Wizard properties

This set of properties is composed of a subset of the ones you saw for bands and Master Report, in particular, label-detail-header and show-changes. For some report elements, other properties are also provided.

HTML properties

This sets of properties is exactly the same as you saw for bands and Master Report.

Excel properties in attributes

This set of properties is composed of a subset of the ones that you saw for bands and Master Report; in particular, formula.

HTML-event, pdf-events, Swing-events properties

These sets of properties are exactly the same as you saw for bands and `Master Report`.

Label and message

The `label` element and the `message` element contain exactly the same set of common properties as introduced earlier in the chapter, except for some differences, described as follows:

- The `object` set of properties is not defined for these elements.
- The `excel` set of properties contains only `format override` and `wrap-text-over`.
- `Common` properties in attributes have `message-null-value` for the `message` element only. The property contains the string used when the content of the element is null.
- The `HTML` set of properties doesn't provide the `append-header` property.
- The `Excel` set of properties only provides the `formula` property.

Fields and resources

This section is about `date-field`, `b`, `text-field`, `resource-message-field`, `resource-field`, and `resource-label`. These elements contain exactly the same set of common properties as introduced earlier in the chapter, except for some differences, described as follows:

- The `object` set of properties is not defined for these elements.
- The `excel` set of properties contains only `format override` and `wrap-text-over`.
- `Common` properties in attributes have the `resource_identifier` property for the `resource-*` elements and the `field` property for all the `*-field` elements. The `resource_identifier` property is a unique string for the element in report and the `field` property points on the field of the data source.
- `HTML` set of properties doesn't provide the `append-header` property.
- `Excel` set of properties only provides the `formula` property.

Image and image-field

This section is about the `image` and `image-field` elements. These elements contain exactly the same set of common properties as introduced earlier in the chapter, except for some differences, described as follows:

- The `excel` set of properties contains only `format override` and `wrap-text-over`.
- `Common` properties in attributes has the `field` property for the `image-field` element. The `field` property points to the field of the data source.
- `Encoding` set is introduced here with the following properties:

Name	Type	Description
`encoding-type`	String	Description of the encoding type (`image/png` as an example)
`encoding-quality`	Integer	Level of quality

- `HTML` set of properties doesn't provide the `append-header` property.
- `Excel` set of properties only provides the `formula` property.

Vertical-line, horizontal-line, rectangle, and eclipse

This section is about the `vertical-line`, `horizontal-line`, `rectangle`, and `eclipse` elements. These elements contain exactly the same set of common properties as introduced earlier in the chapter, except for some differences, described as follows:

- The `font` set of properties is not defined for these elements
- The `text` set of properties contains only `h-align`, `v-align`, `text-color`, and `bg-color`
- The `text-spacing` set of properties is not defined for these elements
- The `links` set of properties does not provide the `pdf-bookmark` property
- `Common` properties in attributes has very few properties, and `rectangle` has `arc-width` and `arc-height` to define the optional arcs on corners
- `HTML` set of properties doesn't provide the `append-header` property
- `Excel` set of properties only provides the `formula` property

Survey-scale

This section is about the `survey-scale` element. This element contains exactly the same set of common properties as introduced earlier in the chapter, except for some differences, described as follows:

- The `font` set of properties is not defined for these elements
- The `text` set of properties contains only `h-align`, `v-align`, `text-color`, and `bg-color`
- The `text-spacing` set of properties is not defined for these elements
- The `links` set of properties does not provide the `pdf-bookmark` property
- The `excel` set of properties is not defined for these elements
- The `Encoding` set is provided with the same properties as introduced for the `image` and `image-field` elements
- The `Survey-scale` set is introduced here with the following properties:

Name	Type	Description
highest	Integer	Scale max value (default is 5).
lowest	Integer	Scale min value (default is 1).
upper-bound	Integer	Bar plot max value.
lower-bound	Integer	Bar plot min value.
tick-mark-paint	String	Color of the tick mark.
upper-margin	Integer	Optional upper margin.
lower-margin	Integer	Optional lower margin.
default-shape	Selection	Shape to be used. Possible selections are various, from down triangle to diamond, circle, and so on.
outline-stroke	String	Color of the outline.

- The `HTML` set of properties doesn't provide the `append-header` property

Chart

This section is about the `chart` element. This element contains exactly the same set of common properties as introduced earlier in the chapter, except for some differences, described as follows:

- The `font` set of properties is not defined for these elements
- The `text` set of properties contains only `h-align`, `v-align`, `text-color`, and `bg-color`
- The `text-spacing` set of properties is not defined for these elements
- The `links` set of properties does not provide the `pdf-bookmark` property
- The `excel` set of properties is not defined for these elements
- The `Encoding` set is provided with the same properties as introduced for the `image` and `image-field` elements
- The `Chart` set is introduced here with the following properties:

Name	Type	Description
`primary-dataset-expression`	String	Formula in OpenFormula format (will be described in the following chapters)
`secondary-dataset-expression`	String	Formula in OpenFormula format (will be described in the following chapters)

- The `HTML` set of properties doesn't provide the `append-header` property
- The `Excel` set of properties only provides the `formula` property

Simple-barcodes

This section is about the `simple-barcodes` element. This element contains exactly the same set of common properties as introduced earlier in the chapter, except for some differences, described as follows:

- The `font` set of properties contains only `family`, `font-size`, `bold`, and `italics`
- The `text` set of properties contains only `h-align`, `v-align`, `text-color`, and `bg-color`
- The `text-spacing` set of properties is not defined for these elements
- The `links` set of properties does not provide the `pdf-bookmark` property

- The `excel` set of properties is not defined for these elements
- The Encoding set is provided with the same properties as introduced for the `image` and `image-field` elements
- The `Bar-code-settings` set is introduced here with the following properties:

Name	Type	Description
type	Selection	Select the type of barcode. Several types of barcodes are supported.
bar-height	Decimal	Height of bar image.
bar-width	Decimal	Width of bar image.
show-text	Boolean	Flag indicating if it is requested to show the value of the barcode or not.
checksum	Boolean	Flag to include the checksum in the barcode.

- The `HTML` set of properties doesn't provide the `append-header` property
- The `Excel` set of properties only provides the `formula` property

Bar-sparkline, line-sparkline, and pie-sparkline

This section is about `bar-sparkline`, `line-sparkline`, and `pie-sparkline` elements. These elements contain exactly the same set of common properties as introduced earlier in the chapter, except for some differences, described as follows:

- The `font` set of properties is not defined for these elements
- `Sparklines` set is introduced here with the following properties:

Name	Type	Description
low-color	String	Sets the color for the lowest slice. No default is provided for the property. Valid for `pie-sparkline` only.
medium-color	String	Sets the color for the medium slice. No default is provided for the property. Valid for `pie-sparkline` only.
high-color	String	Sets the color for the higher slice. No default is provided for the property. Valid for `pie-sparkline` and `bar-sparkline`.
lastcolor	String	Sets the color for the bar/line. No default is provided for the property. Valid for `bar-sparkline` and `line-sparkline`.

- The text set of properties contains only h-align, v-align, text-color, and bg-color
- The text-spacing set of properties is not defined for these elements
- The links set of properties does not provide the pdf-bookmark property
- The excel set of properties is not defined for these elements
- Common properties in Attributes defines also the image-map property as a string, optionally developed in different languages
- Sparklines in the Attributes tab sets is introduced here with the following properties:

Name	Type	Description
spacing	Integer	Sets the spacing (in pixels) between bars for bar/line sparkline. Default is 0.
low-slice, medium-slice, high-slice	Decimal	Angle for the low/medium/high slice in pie-sparkline.
start-angle	Integer	Sets the start angle (in degrees) on pie-sparkline. Possible values are from 1 to 360. Default is 1.
counter-clockwise	Boolean	Sets the plot direction on pie-sparkline. Default is false, which represents clockwise.

- The Encoding set is provided with the same properties as introduced for the image and image-field elements
- The HTML set of properties doesn't provide the append-header property
- The Excel set of properties only provides the formula property

Band

This section is about the band element. This element contains exactly the same set of common properties as introduced earlier in the chapter, except for some differences, described as follows:

- The object set of properties contains only anti-alias and keep-aspect-ratio
- The excel set of properties does not provide formula-override

- The `page-behaviour` set of properties provides the `pagebreak-before` and `pagebreak-after` properties also
- The `Table` set is provided with the same properties as introduced for the `Page Header` and `Page footer` elements
- The `HTML` set of properties doesn't provide the `append-header` property
- The `Excel` set of properties only provides the `formula` property

Sub-report

This section is about the `sub-report` element. This element contain exactly the same set of common properties as introduced earlier in the chapter, except for some differences, described as follows:

- The `excel` set of properties does not provide `formula-override`.
- The `page-behaviour` set of properties provides the `pagebreak-before` and `pagebreak-after` properties also.
- The `Query` set is provided here with the some properties as defined for the `Master Report` element.
- The `Common` properties in attributes has the `sub-report-active` Boolean property. The property contains the flag to *switch-on* or *switch-off* the sub-report.
- The `HTML` set of properties doesn't provide the `append-header` property.
- The `Excel` set of properties only provides the `formula` property.

Table-of-content and index

This section is about the `table-of-content` and `index` elements. These elements contain exactly the same set of common properties as introduced earlier in the chapter, except for some differences, described as follows:

- The `excel` set of properties does not provide `formula-override`.
- The `Query` set is provided here with the same properties as defined for the `Master Report` element.
- The `Common` properties in attributes has the `sub-report-active` Boolean property. The property contains the flag to *switch-on* or *switch-off* the sub-report containing the element.

- Table-of-contents in the Attributes tab sets is introduced here for Table-of-content only, with the following properties:

Name	Type	Description
group-fields	String	Defines both the depth of the data-collection and the fields from where to read the group-value-X values. If the group-field given in the array is empty, the field value will be read from the current relational group, and in the details-processing, the value will be null. If the group-fields list is empty, an automatic mode is activated that collects all the groups, extracting group-value from the relational group.
title-field	String	Defines a field in the master-report that will be read for a valid item-title.
title-formula	String	Defines a formula that is evaluated when a new item has been collected. The formula will only be evaluated if title-field is not set.
collect-details	Boolean	Defines whether detail items should be included in the data-collection.
index-separator	String	Defines the separator text that is used between the index-elements. It defaults to the dot character (.).

- Index in the Attributes tab sets is introduced here for Index only, with the following properties:

Name	Type	Description
data-field	String	Defines the field to be used as item-data or item-key.
data-formula	String	Defines an open formula to be used as item-data or item-key.
condensed-style	Boolean	Defines whether – is used between continuous page numbers; for example, 1, 2, 3, 4 would display as 1-4.
index-separator	String	Defines the separator text that is used between page numbers in the item-pages field in the index sub report. It defaults to the dot character (.).

- The HTML set of properties doesn't provide the append-header property.
- The Excel set of properties only provides the formula property.

Hiding and showing bands

In the previous sections, you learnt much about the report's structure through the report explorer and its hierarchical definition, from the root called Master Report to the first level represented by the bands, and the sub-elements defining the visible content of the report. This section describes the possibility of hiding (or showing) some elements, to customize the final report's layout.

As an example, you can focus your attention to the structure shown in report explorer and the visible bands (and content) in the report canvas. As introduced earlier in the chapter, by default, the report canvas shows the Page Header, Report Header, Details, Report Footer, and Page Footer bands. But taking a look at the report's structure, you can also find the Group element with nested Group Header, Details Header, Details Footer, and Group Footer bands. As you can easily imagine, the last set of bands come hidden by default.

To show the hidden elements (usually bands) or hide the visible ones, right click on the entity in the report element and uncheck (or check) the Hide Element item, as shown in the following image:

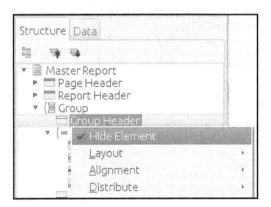

Acting on the Hide Element item, the corresponding band will be shown (or hidden) in the report canvas accordingly.

This behavior of hiding/showing bands is useful for customizing the final report's layout, and is also useful for managing the grouping of results. Grouping the results of a report in a sort of master-detail layout is a powerful feature that you saw an example in chapter 2, Getting started with Report Designer. Use the Group element properties in the report explorer to control and customize this feature in your future advanced developments.

Visual layout in Report Designer

With Pentaho Report Designer, you have pixel level control of your individual elements within a report. Grid and guide lines may appear within each report canvas band, which make it simple to align and configure locations of the elements.

The grid

By default, the report grid is enabled. To hide the grid, disable the menu item **View** | **Grids** | **Show**. The grid presents itself in point units (also known as pixel units), with a light grey grid line displayed every 25 pixels. Grid lines are useful for visual feedback of alignment, as well as for providing a method for snapping elements to the grid. This makes aligning of elements a simple exercise.

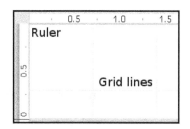

To adjust the ruler unit to centimeters, millimeters, inches, or picas, go to the View | Units sub-menu. The default grid size may be adjusted by launching the grid size dialog. Select the View | Grids | Settings menu item and adjust your grid sizing. You may show or hide the grid by selecting the menu item View | Grids | Show, or by pressing Ctrl+Quote.

Guide lines

Guide lines allow you to specify a custom grid line. To add a new horizontal or vertical guide line, click within the ruler section of the report canvas. A new blue guide line should appear. Guide lines are useful for visual feedback of layout, as well as for snap to grid features that simplify element placement.

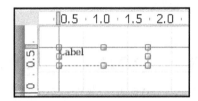

Guide lines may be moved by dragging their location within the ruler. They may also be moved by right-clicking on the line within the ruler and selecting **Properties...**, and then typing in the new value for the guide line.

It is possible to deactivate a single guide line by right-clicking and selecting Deactivate. This causes the guide line to be removed from the report canvas content and appear as a grayed out mark within the ruler section of the canvas. Also, guide lines may be completely removed from the report by right-clicking and selecting **Delete**.

All guide lines may be activated and deactivated together by selecting **View** | **Grids** | **Show Guides**, or by clicking *Ctrl + S*. This is useful if you use many guidelines and want to quickly see the report without all the blue lines running through it.

Additional visual indicators

In addition to grid lines and grid guides, a couple of other handy shortcuts exist to make it easier to lay out your report. By default, when selecting a report element, the style of the selection is considered an **outline selection**. An alternative selection style is **clamp selection**. You may toggle between these two types of selections by selecting **View** | **Outline Selection or View** | **Clamp Selection**.

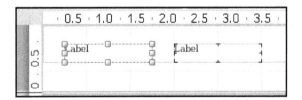

Also, it is possible to show and hide all element frames by selecting **View** | **Guides** | **Show Element Frames**, or by pressing *Ctrl + H*. This is another tool to make it easy to visualize how the elements will be laid out next to each other, and to see potential overlaps that might cause problems when rendering the report.

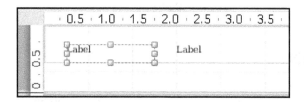

Another visual indicator within Report Designer is the **View** | **Show Overlapping Elements** menu option. With this option selected, any overlapping elements are highlighted, warning that there may be problems when rendering the report.

Finally, another useful capability within the Report Designer is the ability to zoom in and out of the grid. By default, the Report Designer displays the grid rendered at 100 percent. Within the **View** | **Zoom** menu, you may view the report as 50 percent, 100 percent, 200 percent, or 400 percent of its actual size.

As another helpful feature, the **View** | **Element Alignment Hints** menu can help you to place the elements showing some alignment bars on each element. This could help you in alignment, even if the easier **Format** | **Alignment** menu is probably faster.

To complete the item available in the **View** menu, the **Snap to Elements** option lets you easily place elements one close to the other without paying too much attention to the difference of a few pixels in vertical or horizontal distance.

Moving and aligning single elements

In addition to dragging and dropping elements around the report canvas, it is also possible to use shortcut keys and menu items to more easily align and move report elements.

To move an element, first select the element and then drag-and-drop it to the new location within a band. You may also use the arrow keys to move the selected element by individual pixels.

To control the visibility of an element in context to other elements that may overlap, select the element and then select the `Format | Arrange | Send Forward` or `Format | Arrange | Send Backward` option to adjust the order in which the elements appear within a band. `Bring to Front` and `Send to Back` move the element to first visible or last visible respectively. This is also known as **Z ordering**.

Aligning groups of elements

To really sharpen a report, there are two easy-to-use shortcuts available for aligning groups of elements. First, select the elements as a group by holding the *Shift* key and dragging a selection area around the elements, or by holding down the *Shift* key while selecting individual elements.

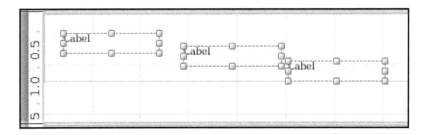

Once you've selected a group of elements, you can easily align all the elements in a group, both horizontally and vertically. If you want to align all the labels in the example to the top, select the menu item **Format | Align | Top**. This will align all the selected elements to the topmost selection in the group. Additionally, you may align these elements in `Middle` or `Bottom`. For elements grouped vertically, you can align them `Left`, `Center`, or `Right`.

Now, assume that you want to evenly distribute all the elements that are selected. This is possible by selecting the menu item Format I Distribute I Equal Horizontal Space. You can do the same vertically by selecting Equal Vertical Space.

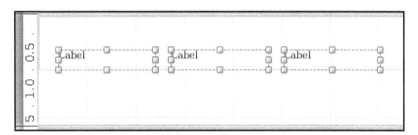

Miscellaneous layout capabilities

There are also some additional layout features that make your life easier when working within the Report Designer. The first feature is the ability for **paste formatting** of an element into another element. Select and copy the element you would like to use to share formatting with. Now, select the additional elements you would like to apply the formatting to and select the menu item Edit I Paste Formatting. All the formatting-related attributes are copied into the selected elements, preserving their data-related properties.

Pentaho Report Designer shortcut keys

The following table shows the list of all the shortcut keys available in Pentaho Report Designer:

Shortcut key	Description	Shortcut key	Description
Ctrl+N	Create a new report	Ctrl+Arrow key	Move element one grid line in direction
Ctrl+Shift+N	Launch the report wizard	Arrow Key	Move element by one pixel in the direction of the arrow key
Ctrl+O	Bring up the Open Report dialog	Ctrl+A	Select all

Shortcut key	Description	Shortcut key	Description
Ctrl+Shift+NumPad/	Bring up the Open Report dialog from the repository	Escape	Clear all selection
Ctrl+F	Close the report	Ctrl+Quote	Show or hide the grids
Ctrl+S	Save the report	Ctrl+1	Font properties
Ctrl+Shift+P	Publish the report in the repository	Ctrl+B	Bold element font
Ctrl+Z	Undo	Ctrl+I	Italicize element font
Ctrl+Y	Redo	Ctrl+H	Bring to front
Ctrl+X	Cut	Ctrl+U	Send forward
Ctrl+C	Copy	Ctrl+D	Send backwards
Ctrl+V	Paste	Ctrl+E	Sent to back
Ctrl+Shift+V	Paste formatting	Ctrl+3	Show or hide the report explorer window
Delete	Delete the current element	Ctrl+2	Show or hide the element properties window

In addition, you have the following shortcut keys to access the menus:

Shortcut key	Description
Alt+F	Opens the **File** menu
Alt+V	Opens the **View** menu
Alt+I	Opens the Insert menu
Alt+O	Opens the Format menu
Alt+D	Opens the Data menu
Alt+E	Opens the Extras menu
Alt+W	Opens the Window menu
Alt+H	Opens the Help menu

Considerations for different output formats

Depending on your output format, there may be differences in the rendering of your designed report. You will cover some of the more common issues faced when rendering to various output formats. When developing your report, make sure to preview the report in the formats you plan to render in, in order to avoid any surprises after the publishing of your report.

Cell output

When rendering to CSV, Excel, RTF, and in some respects to HTML, cell layout becomes an important issue. The Pentaho Reporting Engine does its best to determine the most appropriate cell layout for your report, but certain practices are necessary to ensure a nice looking report.

Alignment of elements is critical when dealing with cell output. Make sure all horizontal and vertical alignments are accurate. Even with subtle differences in horizontal or vertical locations, the report-to-cell-rendering algorithm can experience difficulties.

The following screenshot shows an illustrative example; the elements in the report aren't properly aligned:

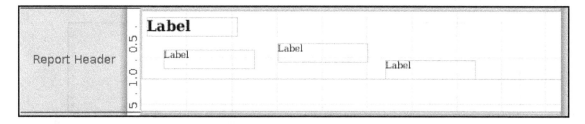

This is how the report will look in Excel:

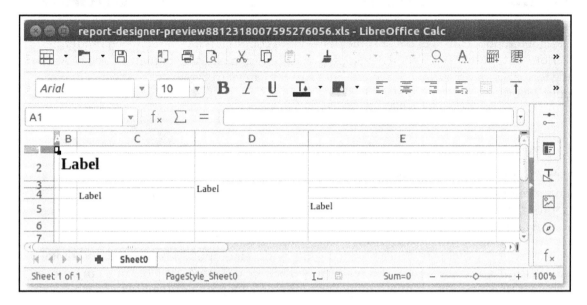

Note how additional cells appear before the labels and make the final result absolutely imprecise and unprofessional. The following screenshot shows a report where the elements are properly aligned:

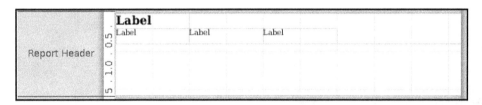

This is what the Excel output will look:

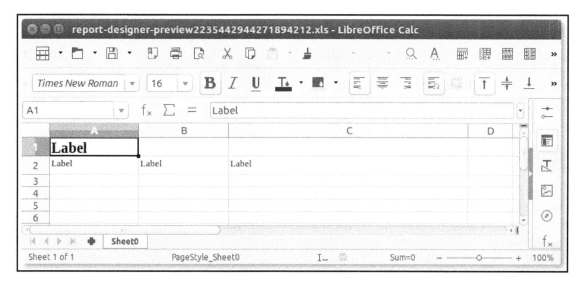

Another consideration when working with cell-based report generators is element overlap. Elements that overlap with one another will not render correctly, so it is important to avoid overlaps.

Paging

Certain output formats, such as HTML, CSV, RTF, and Excel Output, treat the report (no matter how long the report is) as a single page. Use the page header and footer with the knowledge that many output types will not render identically.

In relation to paging, Excel output offers the ability to treat sheets as pages, as long as explicit page breaks are specified in the report bands using the `page-break-before` and `page-break-after` style attributes.

Limits to rich graphics and charts

While certain formats, such as Excel, HTML, and PDF, support images and charts, others such as CSV, Text, and RTF do not have the capability to embed these rich elements. Keep that in mind when designing your reports.

Certain graphical elements, such as ellipses, do not render in most formats. Always verify how a report looks by previewing in the expected format.

Summary

In this chapter, you explored in-depth the ins and outs of design and layout of reports using the Pentaho Report Designer. You first learned about the various user interface components that make up the Report Designer. From there, you dove deep into each reporting band and its properties. You learned that each band may be accessed via the tree structure, and each band may display in the canvas as well as offering properties in the property editor.

You then took an exhaustive look at all the report elements. The chapter introduced you to the common properties seen throughout all the elements, along with displaying the dialogs that the various attributes present when editing. You also walked through utilizing the menu, toolbar, canvas, and shortcut keys to quickly arrange and layout your report. This included introducing shortcuts that make it easy to align and distribute groups of elements.

Finally, the chapter touched on additional details when dealing with common issues with the various output formats that Pentaho Reporting supports.

This chapter was written as a reference manual for developers and information technologists. The goal was to give you a detailed description of what will help you to develop the best reports, with the most accurate details. Now that you have read this chapter, you should feel comfortable with Pentaho Report Designer interface, and you should be able to use it to the best of its capabilities.

In the next chapter, you will discover all the available ways Pentaho Reporting can define data sources. You will go through Pentaho Report Designer again, but you will see in Chapter 12, *Developing Using Data Sources,* how to re-use what you are going to learn in the following topic.

6
Configuring JDBC and Other Data Sources

In `Chapter 4`, *Creating a Report with Report Designer*, you saw how to create a report from scratch using Pentaho Report Designer. As an exercise, you created a data source defining the list of fields requested for viewing results, making charts, calculating formulas, and so on. In this chapter, you will go through the details of the founding concept of the data source, discovering all the available types and their specific features.

In this chapter, you will start with an introduction about data source management using the Pentaho report, diving deep into all the different data sources one by one, and learning how to configure them using Pentaho Report Designer. In particular, you will see:

- The data source for a DBMS using JDBC
- The data source for metadata in XML metadata interchange format
- The data source for MongoDB
- The data source for Pentaho Data Integration transformation
- The data source for an OLAP schema (Mondrian)
- The data source for XML
- The data source for a table structure
- Advanced data sources with Report Designer
- The data source for Pentaho community data access

A similar chapter, covering the data source topic using the Pentaho Reporting SDK, will be `Chapter 12`, *Developing Using Data Sources*, entirely dedicated to the developer experience.

This chapter is written as a reference manual for developers and information technologists. The goal is to share all the relevant and advanced features about data sources in Pentaho Report Designer. At the end of this chapter you will feel comfortable with all the ways it offers to connect to a source. This is the very first step to go through in the development of a simple and complex Pentaho report.

Introducing data sources

We have already introduced the importance of data sources in report development. Indeed, data sources are the very first step in report development, using both the Report Designer and the Pentaho Reporting SDK. In short, data sources are used by Pentaho Reporting to define the dataset available in a report, using a table representation made of fields and rows. Each field is defined by a name and a type (that is, string, integer, and so on), and a row is a collection of values related to the fields. Fields and rows are the real content of a Pentaho report and they can be used for viewing results, making charts, calculating formulas, the definition of parameters and user inputs, and a lot of other things.

Even if the result of a data source is always a table, the types of sources can vary significantly. We can have relational DBMSs, NoSQL databases, different engines (like OLAP, Pentaho Data Integration, and so on), or even different formats of static data structures like XML, metadata, and others. In the following section, you will learn where your data sources can be managed, using the Pentaho Report Designer.

Datasets in report explorer

Starting from the Report Designer user interface, you should already be confident with report explorer (you can find it in the top right panel). Report explorer is composed of two different tabs: **Structure** and **Data**. You used the **Structure** tab a lot in Chapter 5, *Design and Layout in Report Designer*, but now it's the first time you will see the **Data** tab. As an initial introduction, the **Data** tab is where all the data sources live, together with some other types of objects.

Looking at the **Data** tab content, you can see a Data Sets item listing all the defined data sources for the report. In an empty report, the Data Sets item has no children, but in every working report, it has at least one child. The following screenshot shows what the report explorer looks like with two data sources defined:

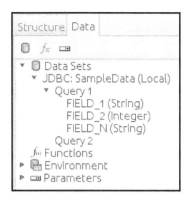

As you can see, each data source is identified with a unique name (`Query 1` and `Query 2` in the example) and each data source contains a list of fields. Even if a report has more than one data source, only one is selected to be used for detail (in this example, `Query 1`). Only the selected data source shows the list of available fields. All the other data sources are used for different purposes: for the listing of parameter values, query in subreports, and so on.

 In case you have more than one data source, right-click on one of them directly in the report explorer panel and click on **Select Query**. This will enable the data source to be used in the details of the current report.

Each field of a data source has a name and a type. The name of a field is nothing more and nothing less than a meaningful label. The type of a field is a Java type, like string, integer, long, date, timestamp, and others. You will see that the field's type will help you during the report development, to set up the format and grouping, and everything is directly connected to presentation. Starting from this panel, you can drag a field and drop it directly into the preferred place in the bands of your report.

Coming back to the data source topic, you can create a new data source by right clicking on the `Data Sets` item and choosing the preferred type. Alternatively, you can click on the database icon (◉) in report explorer or use the upper menu choosing the **Data | Add Datasource** item. In the following sections you will see, one by one, how to create (and manage) all the different available data sources.

The JDBC data source

The first type of data source in the list, and the most used one, is the JDBC data source. JDBC is an API for the Java language, which defines how a client may access a database. It provides methods to query (and update) data in a database and is oriented towards relational databases. See `https://en.wikipedia.org/wiki/Java_Database_Connectivity` for further details.

Once selected, a modal window, similar to the following one, appears:

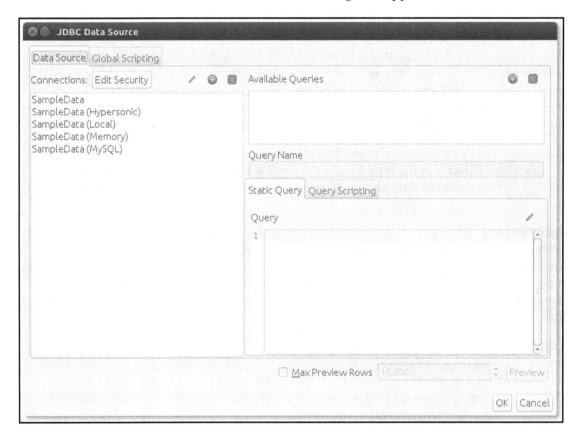

The window contains two main sections: the connections (on the left) and the queries (on the right). The next two sections will introduce all the features for both the panels.

Adding or editing a JDBC connection

Even if the connection panel contains some `SampleData` connections, you can see here how to add a new one or how to edit an existing one. In the connection panel of the window, you can see:

- A pencil icon (✎) used to edit an existing connection
- A green plus icon (⊕) used to add a new connection to the list of the available ones
- A red icon (⊠) used to delete an existing connection

In addition, if you want to provide parameters that contain different authentication credentials for the connections, click the **Edit Security** button in the upper-left corner of the window and then type in the fields or variables that contain the user credentials you want to store as a parameter. A username and password will be available as security parameters when you are creating your report.

The user experience for adding or editing a JDBC connection is mainly the same; a new modal window similar to the following one is shown, containing all the requested fields and parameters to connect to a relational DBMS. The user experience for deleting an existing connection is simpler, as it requires only a confirmation.

The **Database Connection** user interface contains a grouping selector on the left pointing to **General** and **Options**, a **Connection Name** field, a **Connection Type** field, **Settings**, **Access**, and few buttons for actions (**Test**, **OK**, and **Cancel**). Selecting **Options** in the grouping selector, a collection of empty couples of parameter/value can be specified for the connection (they really depend on the database).

The **Connection Name** field is mandatory (in the example, it points to the existing `SampleData (Hypersonic)` connection). The **Connection Type** field lists all the available types of databases supported by the Pentaho Reporting Engine, with more than 40 different types of relational DBMS, from the most famous to the more specific ones, open source or legacy ones, newest, and oldest versions, and so on.

 All the drivers are provided for the supported databases. Even if you are going to use a very common type of relational DBMS, you may need to add the right driver. To check for the existing drivers or to add a new one, look at the `jar` libraries in the `<report-designer>/lib/jdbc` folder. Always remember to restart Pentaho Report Designer after every change to the drivers in the `jdbc` folder.

Once selected a connection type, settings can change accordingly. To be more precise, the number (and types) of settings requested by the user depends on the connection type and access. Access depends on the connection type, and for most of the supported relation databases, it includes `JDBC`, `ODBC`, and `JNDI`.

 The **Open Database Connectivity** (**ODBC**) is a standard API for accessing DBMS. The designers of ODBC aimed to make it independent of database systems and operating systems.

The available buttons are easy to understand: the **Test** button tries to access the database and check the correct connection; the **OK** button confirms the changes to the database connection; and the **Cancel** button, well, you can imagine what this button does.

Once you have added or edited a database connection, select one of the available connection to instruct Pentaho to use it during the query development.

About the JNDI access

The **Java Naming and Directory Interface** (**JNDI**) is a Java API for a directory service that allows Java software clients to discover and look up data and objects using a name. Because of its nature, the settings requested for the JNDI connection is a name only. This unique name should match an existing JNDI connection available in the Pentaho Reporting environment.

To set up a JNDI data source in Pentaho Reporting, edit the `.pentaho/simple-jndi/default.properties` file. The `.pentaho` directory is in the home or user directory of the user account that runs Pentaho Report Designer. If you have multiple copies of Pentaho Report Designer installed in multiple user accounts, each `default.properties` file should be edited.

The following example shows text lines to be added/edited relation to an existing JNDI connection; the JNDI connection to `SampleData` on HyperSQL:

```
SampleData/type=javax.sql.DataSource
SampleData/driver=org.hsqldb.jdbcDriver
SampleData/url=jdbc:hsqldb:hsql://localhost/sampledata
SampleData/user=pentaho_user
SampleData/password=password
```

As you can see, the name of the JNDI connection is used as a prefix for all the settings in the properties file.

Adding or editing a query

Once the connection is added (or updated), the next task is defining the queries. Starting from the **JDBC Data Source** window, the **Available Queries** panel lists all the queries defined for the current data source. In the top-right corner of the panel, you can see:

- A green plus icon (◉) used to add a new query
- A red icon (◪) used to delete an existing query

A query is generally identified by a name and content. The name of a query can be edited in the **Query Name** field and the content can be managed in the bottom panel of the window. The content could be a static string or a script. The static query (widely used) is written in the syntax required for the database type (usually SQL). The SQL string can be enriched with some optional parameters defined using a specific notation (you will see the syntax of the notation in the following chapters).

The query scripting is a source code in ECMAScript or Groovy and you can use it to manipulate the dataset, using a programming language. The query scripting is rarely used and we won't treat it in detail, but it's a collection of functions you can develop to make the dataset exactly as you want. The static query can be specified in the **Query** field of the **Static Query** tab, and the query scripting can be specified in the **Query Script** field of the **Query Scripting** tab.

Click on the **Template** button of the **Query Scripting** tab to see all the available functions, and documentation on how to develop the dataset using the source code instead of a standard query.

The pencil icon (⁄) in the **Static Query** tab is useful to launching SQLeonardo Query Builder, a powerful and easy-to-use GUI that lets you query databases without any relevant knowledge of the SQL syntax. **Max Preview Rows**, if enabled, lets you declare the maximum number of rows retrieved for previewing the data, and the **Preview** button checks that everything is working as expected and shows a bunch of data results as a data table.

As you can see, in the **Available Queries** panel, you can define one or more SQL queries. As introduced at the beginning of the chapter, the definition of multiple queries in a report is useful for the listing of parameter values, to be used in subreports, and so on.

The metadata data source

The metadata data source lets you inquire about a single file in XMI format. The **XML Metadata Interchange** (**XMI**) is an **Object Management Group** (**OMG**) standard for exchanging metadata information via XML. It can be used for any metadata whose metamodel can be expressed in a **Meta-Object Facility** (**MOF**). The most common use of XMI is as an interchange format for UML models, although it can also be used for serialization of models in other languages (metamodels). Some tools of the Pentaho suite (for example, Pentaho Data Integration) can generate XMI files to represent the metadata, and with this data source, they can be used to generate reports.

Once this data source type is selected, a modal window is shown, as follows:

As you can see at the top of the window, in this data source you can also define the dataset using a standard configuration or script. The script is similar to what you saw for the JDBC data source, and for this reason, we will concentrate the discussion on the regular settings.

The first item in the panel (at the top) relates to the definition of an XMI file. As an example, we used the `metadata.xmi` file bundled in the Pentaho Report Designer distribution. In the preceding screenshot, you can check the exact location of the file (in the `report-designer/samples` folder).

In the **Domain Id** field, specify the name of the solution directory this metadata file pertains to. In the **Available Queries** panel, you can see the list of all the queries defined for the current data source. As you saw for the JDBC queries, you can use the green plus icon () to add a new query and you can use the red icon (⊠) to delete an existing query.

In the **Query Name** field, you can enter a meaningful label to identify the query, and at the bottom of the window, you have the query content. Like you saw for the JDBC data source, the query content can be defined using a static query or a script. The script is the same as described for the JDBC data source and the static query is in XML format.

In consideration of the XML format of the query being less easy for users, a metadata **Query Editor** is provided. To access the metadata **Query Editor**, click on the small pencil icon () in the top right-corner of the panel. Once clicked, a window similar to the following one is shown:

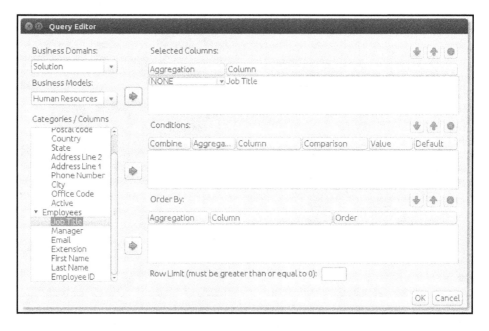

Select an item from the **Business Domains** menu and the **Business Models** menu, and then add one or more of **Categories/Columns** to **Selected Columns** and/or **Conditions** and/or **Order By** to define your query. When done, click on **OK** to confirm the definition.

As you saw for the JDBC data source, the **Max Preview Rows** and the **Preview** buttons enable you to check that everything is working as expected, showing a bunch of data results as a data table.

The MongoDB data source

The MongoDB data source lets you natively connect to the famous NoSQL database. To do this, you must already have MongoDB database connection information, such as host name(s), port number(s), and authentication credentials.

 MongoDB (from humongous) is a free and open source cross-platform document-oriented database program. Classified as a NoSQL database program, MongoDB uses JSON-like documents with schema, stored as content.

Once selected, this data source type shows a modal window with two panels: the query list panel on the left and the query details panel on the right. The query list panel is similar to the one introduced for the JDBC data source, where you can see the icons to add queries () and delete queries (✖). Clicking on the green plus (●) icon, a new Query 1 is added to the available ones, as shown in the following screenshot:

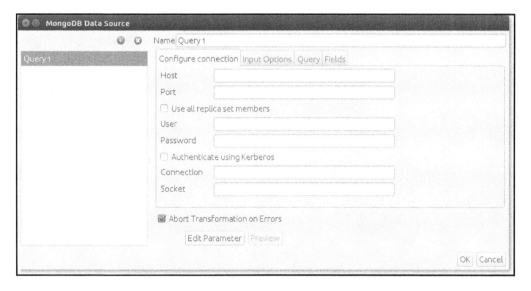

Once a query is selected (or a new one is created), the right panel shows the **Name** field, where you can change the meaningful label for the query and below a set of four tabs to set up the connection to the MongoDB source. Configure connection is the first one where some settings are required. Enter the hostname and port number for your MongoDB database. You can also specify a different port number for each hostname by separating the hostname and port number with a colon and separating each combination of hostname and port number with a comma, like <ip1>:<port1>,<ip2>:<port2>.

Check **Use all replica set members** if you want MongoDB to automatically sense and attempt to connect to available hosts, even if one is down. Type the credentials needed to access the MongoDB database in the **User** field and the **Password** field. Check **Authenticate using Kerberos** if you are using this protocol.

> Kerberos is a computer network authentication protocol that works on the basis of tickets to allow nodes communicating over a non-secure network to prove their identity to one another in a secure manner.

Set **Connection** and **Socket** to define the optional timeout for the source. Moving to the **Input Options** tab, in the following screenshot you can see how the window looks. In this tab, you specify all the settings to point to the correct database, before writing the query:

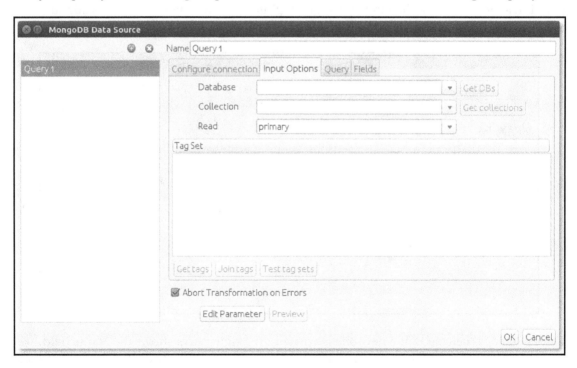

Clicking on the **Get DBs** button will populate the drop-down menu with names of available databases. Select the appropriate one or use the field to enter the database name. The same steps, but in Mongo Collections, are used for the **Get collections** button and the **Collection** field.

A Mongo Collection is a grouping of MongoDB documents. A collection is the equivalent of an RDBMS table. A collection exists within a single database. Collections do not enforce a schema. Documents within a collection can have different fields. Typically, all documents in a collection have a similar or related purpose.

Last but not least, you can indicate the read preference in the **Read** field. If you want to specify a tag set, click the **Get tags** button. Tag sets that have been specified on the MongoDB database appear in the **Tag Set** section of the window. If you want to append tag sets together, so that they are processed at one time, select the tag sets and then click the **Join tags** button. Click the **Test tag sets** button to see a list of nodes that match the tag set criteria.

Moving to the **Query** tab, in the following screenshot, you can see how the window looks:

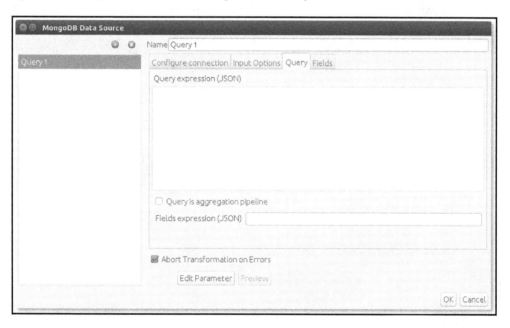

In this tab, you formulate a query using two different methods: creating the query as a JSON query expression or using the Mongo aggregation framework.

 The Mongo aggregation framework processes data records and returns computed results. Aggregation operations group values from multiple documents together, and can perform a variety of operations on the grouped data to return a single result.

Using JSON query expressions is analogous to using the Mongo `find()` command. In order to use the JSON query expression mode, ensure that the **Query is aggregation pipeline** checkbox is not selected. The query argument to find is entered in the **Query expression (JSON)** field and the projection argument is supplied in the **Fields expression (JSON)** text box.

To query MongoDB using the aggregation framework, click the **Query is aggregation pipeline** checkbox and enter a sequence of pipeline operations in the **Query expression (JSON)** field. This mode uses the same syntax as the MongoDB `aggregation()` command. You can parameterize both JSON query expressions and aggregation pipeline queries using simple string replacement (you will see in the following chapters how parameterization looks).

Moving to the **Fields** tab, in the following screenshot, you can see how the window looks. In this tab, you can view the fields that are in the database and collection you specified:

Click the **Get fields** button to ask Pentaho to determine which fields are available and what their data types are. The fields will then be displayed. If desired, you can edit the names of the fields and you can edit the path to the field in the MongoDB database. If an array is returned, you can specify the element in the array by indicating the number of the element in brackets; for example, `$.myArrayElement[0]` (use `$.myArrayElement[*]` for the whole set).

Last but not least, use the **Abort Transformation on Errors** checkbox to request aborting in case of errors, the **Edit Parameters** button to edit the parameters to the transformation, and **Preview** to test the connection and to see what the data will look like when it is brought into the Report Designer.

When complete, click **OK**. Pentaho Report Designer can now access your MongoDB data source.

 During the development of this book, I experienced some problems with this data source for Pentaho Report Designer version 7.0 and 7.1. Version 6.1 seems to work fine. Of course, this can happen in the development of a complex product like Report Designer. In case you are experiencing a similar issue, you can choose to use Pentaho Data Integration data source as an alternative to get the data from MongoDB.

The Pentaho Data Integration data source

Use the Pentaho Data Integration data source option if you want to create a report containing data from any step in a PDI transformation. As you probably know, Pentaho Data Integration is one of the core tools of the Pentaho suite and it is designed and developed to implement a fully featured ETL and data integration solution (for a complete introduction, checkout `Chapter 16`, *Using Reports in Pentaho Data Integration*). This type of data source is particularly useful if you want to create a report that includes data from transformation steps such as Excel input or other PDI steps.

 If you are using this type of data source, remember to copy all the JAR files from `<data-integration>/lib` to `<report-designer>/lib` in order to access it through Pentaho Report Designer.

Once this data source type is selected, a modal window is shown, as follows:

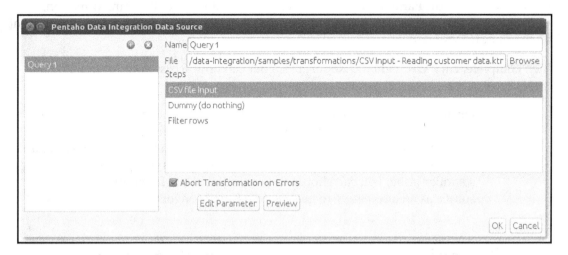

On the left side of the window the list of queries is shown with the well-known green plus icon (●) to add a new query and the red icon (●) to delete an existing one. On the right side of the window, you can find the query definition. As with the previous data sources, the **Name** field specifies a meaningful label for the query. The **File** field points to one .ktr file (the Pentaho Data Integration format for the transformations), with the list of steps defining the transformation listed in the bottom panel. Selecting one step from the list will instruct Pentaho Report Designer to use it as data generator for the data source.

As an example, you can take the CSV Input - Reading customer data.ktr file stored in the <data-integration>/samples/transformations folder of the Pentaho Data Integration distribution.

To complete the description, the **Preview** button is the same as you saw for the previous data sources and the **OK/Cancel** buttons are the standard ones to confirm/cancel the current operation. Last but not least, use the **Edit Parameter** button to set up the call of the PDI transformation with the correct settings.

This type of data source is extremely interesting because of the Pentaho Data Integration features. Pentaho Data Integration has the ability to connect to a wide range of sources, so as a paradox, you could use this data source to only connect to all the possible sources Pentaho suite can connect with. Do you want an example? Open the .ktr file in <reporti-designer>/resources/datasources/MongoDb.ktr and see how it can be used to extract data from a MongoDB instance.

The OLAP data source

The **Online Analytical Processing** (**OLAP**) data source is used in case a multidimensional engine is involved.

 Quoting from Wikipedia about OLAP (`https://en.wikipedia.org/wiki/Online_analytical_processing`): a multidimensional structure is defined as a variation of the relational model that uses multidimensional structures to organize data and express the relationships between data. Even when data is manipulated it remains easy to access and continues to constitute a compact database format. A multidimensional structure is quite popular for analytical databases that use OLAP applications. Analytical databases use these databases because of their ability to deliver answers to complex business queries swiftly.

The Pentaho suite provides an open source multidimensional engine called Mondrian (`http://community.pentaho.com/projects/mondrian`). Mondrian is entirely written in Java and it executes queries written in the **Multidimensional Expressions** (**MDX**) language, reading data from a relational database and presenting the results in a multidimensional format.

 Quoting from Wikipedia about MDX (`https://en.wikipedia.org/wiki/MultiDimensional_eXpressions`): MDX is a query language for OLAP using a database management system. Much like SQL, it is a query language for relational databases. It is also a calculation language, with syntax similar to spreadsheet formulas.

Once accessible to the selection of the data source type, you can see there are two different subgroups available: **OLAP** and **OLAP (Advanced)**. **OLAP (Advanced)** data sources differ from standard OLAP data sources only in the method by which you design and enter the MDX query. Standard OLAP data sources allow for Report Designer's built-in metadata query editor, whereas **OLAP (Advanced)** data sources require you to build a formula to calculate the query, which gives you more power over report parameterization functionality.

Included in both the subgroups, you can find a version of each OLAP data source named as denormalized (the default data sources assume they are normalized). Normalized and denormalized are two possible classifications of MDX queries, depending on the structure of the resulting dataset. It's not within the scope of this book to elaborate over the details of data normalization/denormalization, but the following example can shed some light over the differences between the two.

Here is an example of a normalized form of an MDX query:

[Time].[(All)]	[Time].[Years]	[Measures].[Revenue]	[Measures].[Quantity]
All years	2015	150,000	1,000
All years	2016	170,000	1,100
All years	2017	190,000	1,200

Here is an example of a denormalized form of the same MDX query:

[Time].[(All)]	[Time].[Years]	[Measures].[MeasuresLevel]	Measure
All years	2015	Revenue	150,000
All years	2016	Revenue	170,000
All years	2017	Revenue	190,000
All years	2015	Quantity	1,000
All years	2016	Quantity	1,100
All years	2017	Quantity	1,200

Considering that the normalized and denormalized data sources are defined in exactly the same way, and the only changes are in the resulting formats, in the following description, we won't detail the denormalized ones, assuming they can be defined in exactly the same way.

Pentaho analysis

The Pentaho analysis data source defines the access to the Mondrian multidimensional engine. Once selected, a modal window is shown, as seen in the following screenshot.

As you can see at the top of the window, in this data source you can also define the dataset using a standard configuration or script. The script is similar to what you saw for the JDBC data source, and for this reason, we concentrate the discussion on the regular settings.

The first task in the panel (at the top) is about the Pentaho analysis schema file. The requested schema file is a Mondrian schema in XML format. As an example, we used the `steelwheel.mondrian.xml` file bundled in the Pentaho Reporting Designer distribution. In the following screenshot, you can check the exact location of the file (in the `report-designer/samples` folder):

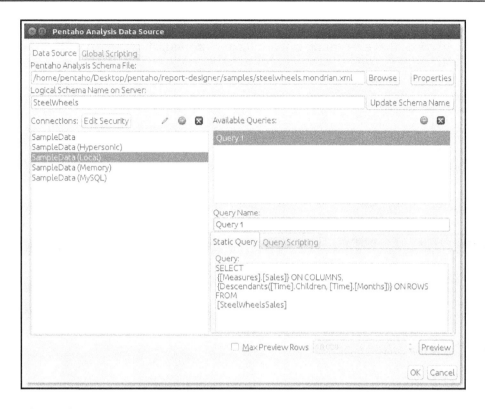

In the **Logical Schema Name on Server** field, specify the name of the OLAP Cube you are interested in inquiring about. Below in the window, you can see the JDBC connection panel (on the left) and the query panels (on the right). Both are similar to the ones you saw for the previous data sources.

The JDBC connection panel is specified here because the Mondrian Engine works on top of a relational DBMS, so it is required. The JDBC connection works as described earlier in the chapter. The **Edit Security** button lets you specify some security parameters, the icons let you edit (✎), add (🌐), and delete (❎) the connections, and the following panel lists the existing connections.

The query panels are again similar to the JDBC data source, except for the fact that the query syntax must be in MDX language. In the query panels, you can see **Available Queries** with the icon (🌐) for creating and the icon (❎) for deleting, the list of defined queries, and the following field named **Query Name**. In the bottom panel, the **Static Query** tab and the **Query Scripting** tab give you the same user experience and content as the JDBC connection. Again, remember that the **Query** field of the **Static Query** tab must contain an MDX query with the possibility to define parameters that will be described in the following chapters.

As you saw for the JDBC data source, the **Max Preview Rows** and the **Preview** buttons enable you to check that everything is working as expected, showing a bunch of data results as a data table.

OLAP4J

The OLAP4J data source defines the access to any OLAP server using a common API. OLAP4J, which is an open Java API for OLAP (http://www.olap4j.org). Think of it like JDBC, but for accessing multidimensional data.

Once selected, a modal window is shown, as follows:

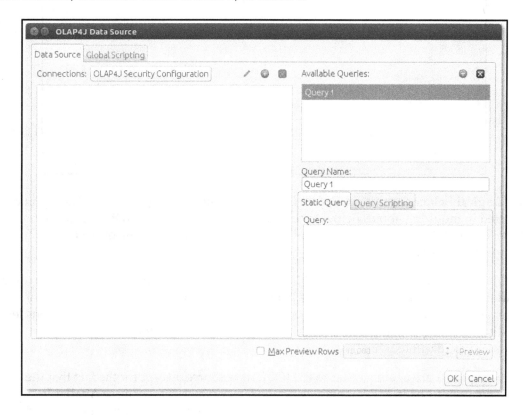

As you can see, the components of the user interface are exactly the same as for a JDBC connection: the **Data Source** tab and the **Global Scripting** tab, and the connection panel (on the left) and the query panels (on the right). All of them have the same meaning and use as the JDBC connection panel, except for the **OLAP4J Security Configuration** button containing different parameters to be used with respect to the JDBC ones. Of course, in this case, the **Query** field is also expected to be in MDX language with the possibility to define parameters.

Note that the connection to set up is a custom JDBC connection with settings similar to the following ones:

```
Custom Connection URL:
jdbc:xmla:Server=http://<server>:<port>;Catalog=FoodMart;Cube=Budget
Custom Driver Class Name: org.olap4j.driver.xmla.XmlaOlap4jDriver
```

Pentaho analysis - custom

The Pentaho analysis (custom) data source is specifically for the OLAP (advanced) group. It defines access to the Mondrian multidimensional engine like Pentaho analysis, with a difference—the query is provided as a dynamic calculation instead of a static query.

Once selected, a modal window is shown, as follows:

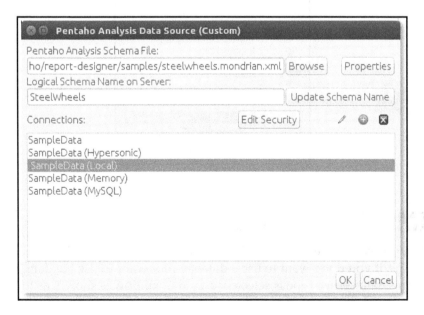

As you can see, the provided fields are a subset of the ones provided for Pentaho analysis. As explained in the introduction to this data source, the query panels are missing. To specify the MDX query, a formula is used directly in the report definition at run time. You can build the formula for your use case in the `name` property of the `Master Report` element, as shown in the following screenshot:

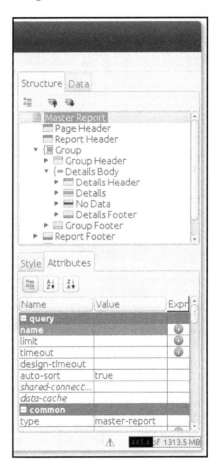

The XML data source

The XML data source is quite easy to understand and can be useful for exported data from external systems, if you don't want to use a database but want to use the data in a report. Once this data source type is selected, a modal window is shown, as follows:

Starting from the top, the first parameter is about pointing to an XML file. In this example, in particular, we are going to use the `steelwheels.mondrian.xml` file stored in the `report-designer/samples` folder.

If you feel that the `steelwheels.mondrian.xml` file has not got a nice data structure and it's probably difficult to inquire, you are right! The `steelwheels.mondrian.xml` file contains the declaration of a Mondrian schema and does not contain data similar to a database export. Unfortunately, this is what we have available bundled in the Pentaho Reporting distribution and it's enough for our purpose to demonstrate an example of use of the XML data source.

Below the selection of the XML file, you can see the list of available queries, with the well known green plus icon ( ) to add a new query and the red icon ( ) to delete an existing one. The **Query Name** field is where you can change the meaningful label for the query. In the **Query** field, you can specify the static string representing the query. The format used in the **Query** field is the **XML Path Language** (**XPath**) format.

XPath is a query language for selecting nodes from an XML document. In addition, XPath may be used to compute values (for example, strings, numbers, or Boolean values) from the content of an XML document.

Last but not least, the **Preview...** button and the **OK/Cancel** buttons are the standard ones described in most of the previous data sources.

The table data source

The table data source is used if you have to manage static and predefined data, not stored in a mass storage or configuration file. Compared to the other data sources, this one defines its structure directly inside the Pentaho Report Designer. For this reason, the first thing to do is to declare before the query and define its structure after, starting with a two column table. The definition of the table is straightforward: you can specify the value for the columns, change the column name, and add (or remove) rows or columns.

Once this data source type is selected, a modal window is shown, as follows:

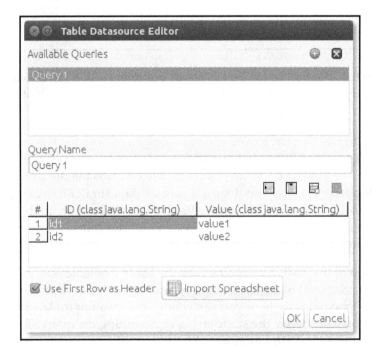

As you can see from the window, you can define the table structure starting from a Microsoft Excel sheet. To complete the features, the **OK/Cancel** buttons are the standard ones to confirm/cancel the current operation.

The advanced data source

Advanced data sources require advanced knowledge and skills, so only a high-level overview of each advanced data source is given in this section.

Scriptable

The scriptable data source lets the developer develop a source code generating a dataset in various languages. As in the previous data sources, you can create multiple queries and manage the addition/deletion of queries.

External

The external data source is used when a report is used in `.xaction`. You can refer to the official documentation for the (few) documents about this data source. Pentaho action sequence XML documents (`.xaction`) define activities such as database queries, report generation, and email actions, and the order in which they occur.

Sequence generator

The sequence generator develops a sequence to be used in your report. As in previous data sources, you can create multiple queries and manage the addition/deletion of queries. For each query, you can define the group (numeric or system), the sequence (depending on group), and some other parameters.

OpenERP data access

The OpenERP data access is a data source for the famous Odoo ERP and CRM system (`https://www.odoo.com`). The interface is quite simple and lets you execute a standard search or a custom function, with the goal to extract data from the open source ERP.

The Pentaho community data access data source

The **Community Data Access** (**CDA**) data source is an interesting type related to the so called Pentaho CDA. Pentaho CDA was designed to allow great flexibility for data sources. Most of the available tools can perform queries over a single data source and there's no easy way to combine data coming from different databases or in different languages (combining data from an SQL query with data from an MDX query). These tasks usually require an independent ETL job to synchronize different data sources and build a new database. Pentaho CDA was developed as an abstraction tool between database connections and **Community Dashboard Framework** (**CDF**), but in this context are used also in reporting.

Once this data source type is selected, a modal window is shown, as follows:

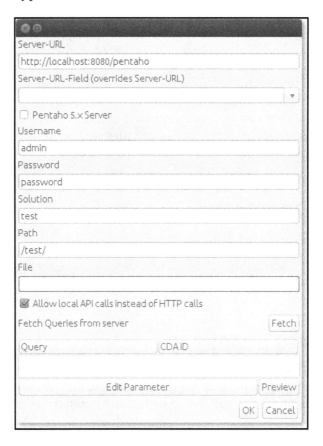

As you can see at the top of the window, a URL pointing to the Pentaho Business Analytics Platform is required (you will learnt more about it in `Chapter 15`, *Using Reports in Pentaho Business Analytics Platform*). After the definition of credentials (**Username** and **Password**), **Solution**, and **Path**, the **Fetch** button lets you extract all the available Pentaho CDA deployed in the Pentaho Business Analytics Platform. Once listed, in the bottom panel you can edit the parameters passed to the data access, using the **Edit Parameter** button.

To complete the description, the **Preview** button is the same as you saw for the previous data sources and the **OK/Cancel** buttons are the standard ones used to confirm/cancel the current operation.

Summary

In this chapter, you learnt everything Pentaho Report Designer can do with data sources, discovering all the available types and their specific features. You started with an introduction to how a data source looks in the user interface and how the fields are used in the layout of the report. Then you moved on to discover how to manage all the possible types of data sources using Report Designer, finding out all about:

- The JDBC data source
- The metadata data source
- The MongoDB data source
- The Pentaho Data Integration transformation data source
- The OLAP data source in various versions (legacy and generic, normalized and denormalized, standard, and custom)
- The XML data source
- The table data source
- The advanced data sources (scriptable, external, sequence generator, and OpenERP)
- The Pentaho community data access data source

Now that you have read this chapter, you should feel comfortable with all the ways Pentaho Report Designer offers to connect to a source. This is the very first step to go through in the development of a simple and complex Pentaho report.

In the next chapter, you will learn everything about including graphics and charts in your Pentaho reports.

7
Including Graphics and Charts in Reports

After the discovery of all the possible data source types, in this chapter you will learn how to incorporate graphics and charts in your Pentaho reports. You will start understanding how to include graphics and charts from the Pentaho Report Designer and then you will move on to the description of all the settings and configurations. Graphics and charts will be described one by one, as we did for the data sources, with the goal to make you a real expert for the best final result; the most useful and appealing report for your customers and manager.

In particular, the charts discussed are bar charts, line charts, area charts, bar line charts, pie charts, multipie charts, ring charts, bubble charts, scatter plot charts, XY bar charts, XY line charts (regular and extended), XY area charts, XY area line charts, waterfall charts, radar charts, thermometer charts, bar-sparklines, line-sparklines, and pie-sparklines.

This chapter is written as a reference manual for developers and information technologists. The goal is to share all the relevant and advanced features about graphics and charts that are available in Pentaho Report Designer.

Including static images in reports

Including static images in your Pentaho report is useful, because in that way you can add logos, and graphics in general, to make the final result more appealing for the users.

To include static images in your report, select the image icon (🖼) from the Report Designer palette and place it into your report. Double-click on the element, or right-click on it by selecting **Edit Content**, to bring up a resource dialog where you can browse to the specific file location. You may select the **Link to** option to link an external resource, or you may select **Embed** to include the image in the .prpt file.

 If you are in doubt, using the embedded image is always a good choice, as you can avoid the bad side effect of a change in the external link. When embedding the image, the dimensions of the .prpt file will be bigger.

Including dynamic images in reports

Including dynamic images in your Pentaho report is useful, because in that way you can add logos, and graphics in general, that may change according to a data source. As an example, we can imagine a report changing its logo depending on the department of the user or the image of a product in a product list.

To add dynamic images to your report, use the image-field icon (🖼) from the Report Designer palette and place it in your report. The content field accepts different types of image inputs for rendering. By double-clicking on the element, you can edit the source pointing to the right field of your dataset. If you have a field that contains a URL or file system location to your image, the image-field element will render the specified image.

Including charts in reports

Including charts in your Pentaho reports makes a difference because of two main reasons: it's powerful and it's easy. Pentaho charts are powerful because they give you the ability to represent complex information in a single image (the chart itself) with many different styles. They are easy because the inclusion of chart in a report can be easily done with a configuration (and not development), starting from a data source.

 Pentaho Reporting relies on JFreeChart. The JFreeChart project was founded in February 2000 and today it is the most widely used chart library for Java, with more than 2.2 million downloads to date.

To add charts to your report, drag the chart icon (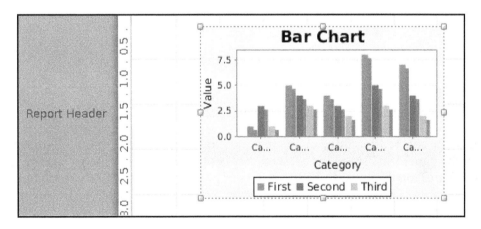) from the Report Designer palette and drop it in the place where you want to see the chart. Usually, a chart is placed in a grouping band like `Report Header` or `Group Header` (and rarely on footers or `Page Header`). This is because a chart makes sense if used on a collection of data and not on single values. In any case, nothing really limits your fantasy and you can place the chart anywhere in the report.

Once dropped in the report canvas, an image similar to the following one is shown:

Double-clicking on the image or right-clicking and selecting chart, the chart editor similar to the following screenshot is shown:

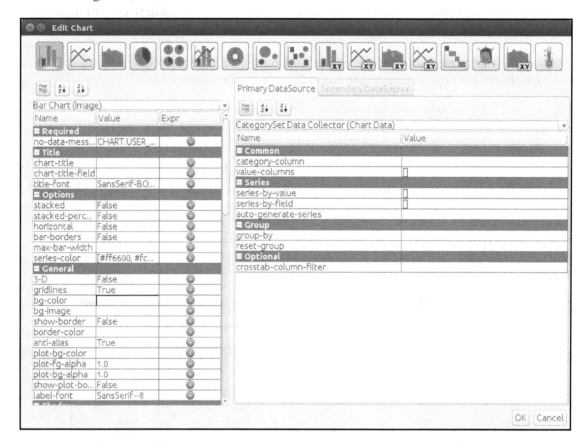

Looking at the chart editor, three main areas appear when editing a chart. The first area is on top of the panel and lists all the available types of charts (17 in Pentaho Reporting 8.0). The second area, on the left side, contains a set of properties related to chart rendering. The third tabbed area of properties, on the right side, is related to the data that populates a chart.

Selecting one type of chart, the property panel is updated according to the selection, as well as the panel of data properties. In the following sections, you will see in detail all the available properties for all the types of charts.

As you can expect, the different types of charts are suitable for different use cases. If you want to show the strength of a trend for a single value over time, the best chart types are:

- Line
- Area
- XY line area
- XY line

If you are directly comparing two or more related values, the best chart types to choose are:

- Pie
- Ring
- Bar
- Line
- Area
- Radar

If you want to show how one set of values directly affects another, the best chart types are:

- Bar line combination
- Waterfall

If you are comparing a large number of data points, the best chart types are:

- XY dot (scatter plot)
- Bubble
- Pie grid (multipie)

Types of datasets

All chart types receive their data from different types of datasets. Each chart can be compliant with one or more dataset types. Dataset types can be selected and managed in the chart editor through the right panel.

Following are sections on each type of dataset, describing in detail their properties and their meanings. During the description, you will also discover the chart types compliant with each type of dataset. Also, in case of dataset types, the properties are grouped for better management and understanding.

Category dataset

The first type of dataset is known as a **category dataset**, where the dataset series and values are grouped by categories. A series is like a subgroup. If the exact category and series appear, the chart will sum the values into a single result. The following table is a simple example of a category dataset:

Category	Series	Sale price
Store 1 sales	Cash	14
Store 1 sales	Credit	12
Store 2 sales	Cash	100
Store 2 sales	Credit	200

The charts that use the category dataset are: bar chart, line chart, area chart, bar line chart, waterfall chart, and radar chart.

Pentaho Reporting builds a category dataset using `CategorySetDataCollector`. Also available is `PivotCategorySetCollector`, which pivots the category and series data. Collector classes implement Pentaho Reporting's function API. You can view (and change) the collector from the chart editor, in the data properties panel, as the first drop-down menu in the tabs.

In the following section, you can see listed the set of properties defined to control the category dataset using the chart editor. The properties are grouped in the same way as they are grouped in the element properties panel.

Common properties

In the following table you can see listed, the set of properties defined for common properties:

Name	Type	Description
category-column	String	Field name of the data source representing the category
value-column	Array of strings	Field names of the data sources representing the values

Series properties

In the following table you can see listed, the set of properties defined for series properties:

Name	Type	Description
series-by-values	Array of strings	Specifies the values you are charting. Series are usually placed in the chart legend.
series-by-fields	Array of strings	Specifies the fields you are charting. Series are usually placed in the chart legend.
auto-generate-series	Boolean	If true, then when the items advance, no action is taken to accumulate data. This should only be used with a group specified so that when the groups advance, the data can be properly accumulated.

Group properties

In the following table you can see listed, the set of properties defined for group properties:

Name	Type	Description
group-by	Selection	This property defines the group level at which the data should be collected
reset-group	Selection	This property defines the group level at which the data should be reset

Optional properties

In the following table you can see listed, the set of properties defined for optional properties:

Name	Type	Description
cross-tab-column-filter	Selection	This property defines the group level at which the data should be filtered in cross tab

Pie dataset

Differently from the category dataset, the **pie dataset** defines the dataset series and values (categories are not defined). A series is like a subgroup. If the exact series appears, the chart will sum the values into a single result. The following table is a simple example of a pie dataset:

Series	Sale price
Cash	14
Credit	12
Cash	100
Credit	200

The groups of charts that use the pie dataset are pie charts and ring charts.

Pentaho Reporting builds a pie dataset using `PieDataSetCollector`. Considering that the pie dataset is a sort of simplified version of the category dataset, in the following list we describe the differences in the set of properties defined to control the pie dataset:

- In the common properties, the pie dataset has only the `value-column` property containing the field name of the data source representing the values. Note that differently from the category dataset, this field is not an array of strings but a string.
- In the series properties, the pie dataset has only `series-by-field` and `auto-generate-series`. Check the category dataset for the meaning of these two properties.
- Group properties and optional properties are the same as those of the category dataset. Check the category dataset for a detailed explanation of the properties included in the groups.

XY series and XYZ series dataset

Another two similar types of datasets are known as **XY series dataset** and **XYZ series dataset**. Both types of datasets are dimensional groups of values that may be plotted in various forms. In these datasets, the series may be used to draw different lines, and so on. The following is a simple example of an XY series dataset:

Series	Cost (X)	Sale price (Y)
Cash	10	14
Credit	11	12
Cash	92	100
Credit	105	200

As you can figure out, the XYZ series dataset is a three dimensional group of values, different from XY series dataset, which is a bidimensional group of values (all the rest is the same). The groups of charts that use the XY series dataset are scatter plot charts, XY bar charts, XY line charts, XY area charts, extended XY line charts, and XY area line charts. The groups of charts that use the XYZ series dataset are the same that use the XY series dataset, plus bubble chart.

Pentaho Reporting builds a XY series dataset using XY-SeriesCollector and builds a XYZ series dataset using XYZ-SeriesCollector. Both the datasets define a set of properties not so different from the category dataset. They are described in detail, as follows:

- In the common properties, the XY series dataset and the XYZ series dataset define x-value-columns and y-value-columns as the field names of the data source representing the values for the *x* axis and the *y* axis respectively. Only for the XYZ series dataset is the z-value-columns property also provided.
- The series properties, group properties, and optional properties are the same as of the category dataset. Check the category dataset for a detailed explanation of the properties included in the groups.

 If you take a look at Pentaho Reporting 8.0 (as an example), another collector is provided with the name IntervalXY-SeriesCollector. Unfortunately, Report Designer does not work for this type of dataset, so we can only suppose that it will be something closed to the datasets detailed here.

Time series dataset

Another type of dataset is known as the **time series dataset**, which is a two dimensional group of values that are plotted based on time and date. The time series dataset is more like an XY series than a category dataset, as the time scale is displayed in a linear fashion with appropriate distances between the different time references. The following is a simple example of time series dataset:

Time	Series	Sale price
Jun 02, 2017 11:05 pm	Cash	14
Jun 04, 2017 12:42 pm	Credit	12
Jun 05, 2017 04:25 pm	Cash	100
Jun 07, 2017 01:52 pm	Credit	200

The groups of charts that use the time series dataset are scatter plot charts, XY bar charts, XY line charts, XY area charts, extended XY line charts, and XY area line charts (exactly like the XY series dataset).

Pentaho Reporting builds a time series dataset using `TimeSeriesCollector`. The Time series dataset defines a set of properties not so different from the category dataset. They are described in detail, as follows:

- In the common properties, the time series dataset `category-time-column` defines the field name of the data source representing the time, and `time-period-type` lets you define the granularity, from second, minute, hour, day, week, month, quarter, or year. The property `value-column` is provided and it has the same meaning (and type) as of the category dataset.
- The series properties, group properties, and optional properties are the same as those of the category dataset. Check the category dataset for a detailed explanation of the properties included in the groups.

Thermometer dataset

Last but not least, the thermometer dataset is used to implement a variation of the typical *traffic light* indicator. The dataset requires only a single value to work, and if you have more than one row of data per grouping, the chart collector will aggregate all values together as one big sum.

Due to its specific nature, the dataset is used by only one chart, called thermometer, and Pentaho Reporting builds a thermometer dataset using `ThermometerDataSetCollector`. The thermometer dataset defines a limited set of properties, composed of `value-column` (containing the field name of the data source representing the single value) and the same group properties as of the category dataset. Check the category dataset for a detailed explanation of the properties included in the group.

Style and layout common properties

As you saw in `Chapter 5`, *Design and Layout in Report Designer*, for the report bands, and also in the case of charts, the style and layout properties are grouped for better management and understanding. In the case of charts, the style and layout properties can be managed in the left panel of the chart editor. The groups of properties are managed in exactly the same way as the element properties panel: same behavior and same user experience. Of course, the properties are different with different meanings and behaviors, and here in this section, you will learn more about them, discovering all the relevant details.

As we saw for the report bands, most charts share a common set of properties. The following properties are common across all the charts. Any exceptions are mentioned as part of the specific chart type.

Required properties

A set of properties defined as mandatory for the correct behavior of the chart:

Name	Type	Description
`no-data-message`	String	The message to display if no data is available to render the chart

Title properties

A set of properties defined to control the (optional) title of the chart:

Name	Type	Description
`chart-title`	String	The title of the chart, which is rendered in the report
`chart-title-field`	String	A field of the data source representing the chart title
`title-font`	String	The chart title's font family, size, and style

General properties

A set of properties defined to control the general properties of the chart:

Name	Type	Description
3-D	Boolean	If set to true, renders the chart in a 3D perspective. The default value is set to false.
bg-color	String	The background color for the chart.
bg-image	String	Path to the background image for the chart.
show-border	Boolean	Flag indicating if the border of the entire chart is requested to be shown. Default is false.
border-color	String	The color for the chart's border.
plot-bg-color	String	Sets the plot's background color to the specified color. If not set, defaults to white.
plot-fg-alpha	Decimal	Sets the alpha value of the plot foreground color relative to the plot background. The default value is set to 1.0.
plot-bg-alpha	Decimal	Sets the alpha value of the plot background color relative to the chart background color. The default value is set to 1.0.
anti-alias	Boolean	If set to true, renders chart fonts as anti-aliased. The default value is set to true.

Legend properties

A set of properties defined to control the legend of the chart:

Name	Type	Description
show-legend	Flag	Flag controlling the view/hide of the legend. Default value is true.
location	Selection	Position of the legend with respect to the chart. Possible values are: north, west, south, east, top, left, bottom, and right.
legend-bg-color	String	Background color. The color picker discussed in Chapter 5, *Design and Layout in Report Designer* is available in this property.

Name	Type	Description
legend-border	String	Flag indicating if the border of the legend should be visible or not. Default value is true.
legend-font	String	Font used in the legend.
legend-font-color	String	Font color. The color picker discussed in Chapter 5, *Design and Layout in Report Designer* is available in this property.

Scripting properties

A set of properties defining the scripts that to control the processing of the chart:

Name	Type	Description
Chart Post-Processing Script Language	Selection	Language of scripting used in the field. Possible values are: beanshell, groovy, netrexx, javascript, xslt, jacl, and jython.
Chart Post-Processing Script	String	Source code for post-processing the chart rendering.

Bar chart

Starting from here, you will see all the details related to the different types of charts. The bar chart is the first one, displaying individual bars broken into individual categories and series. Bar charts are useful for comparing relative sizes of data across categories. The bar chart utilizes the category dataset (previously introduced), together with the common properties defined earlier.

In the following description are listed all the differences in terms of available properties:

- The options set is introduced here with the following properties:

Name	Type	Description
stacked	Boolean	If set to true, the series values will appear layered on top of one another instead of being displayed relative to one another.

Name	Type	Description
stacked-percent	Boolean	If set to true, determines the percentages of each series, and renders the bar height based on those percentages. The property stacked must be set to true for this property to have an effect.
horizontal	Boolean	If set to true, the chart's x and y axis are rotated horizontally. The default value is set to false.
bar-borders	Boolean	If set to false, clears the default rendering value of the chart border.
max-bar-width	Decimal	The maximum width of a bar in pixels. Unless set, bars will generally expand to the available space within the chart.
series-color	Array of strings	The color in which to render each series. The default for the first series colors are defined but you can change it using a color editor.

- The shadow set is introduced here with the following properties:

Name	Type	Description
shadow-visible	Boolean	If set to true, displays the shadow for the chart. This value is set to false by default.
shadow-color	String	Color of the shadow.
shadow-x-offset	Integer	Distance of the shadow on the x axis in pixels. This value is set to 0 by default.
shadow-y-offset	Integer	Distance of the shadow on the y axis in pixels. This value is set to 0 by default.

- The general set has the same properties as described in the general common set, and some additional properties listed as follows:

Name	Type	Description
gridlines	Boolean	If set to true, displays category grid lines. This value is set to true by default.
show-plot-border	Boolean	If set to false, clears the default rendering value of the chart border. This value is set to false by default.

- The *X* axis set is introduced here with the following properties:

Name	Type	Description
x-axis-title	String	Sets the title for the primary numeric data axis; typically the *x* axis in a horizontally-oriented chart.
x-font	String	Font used for the *x* axis. The property uses a font picker for a friendly user experience.
x-tick-font	String	Font used for the range ticks in the chart. The property uses a font picker for a friendly user experience.
x-tick-format	String	The label format used for displaying category items within the chart. This property is required if you would like to display the category item values. The following parameters may be defined in the format string to access details of the item: 0 to access the series name detail of an item; 1 to access the category detail of an item 2 to access the item value details of an item.
x-axis-label-width	Decimal	Sets the maximum category label width ratio, which determines the maximum length each category label should render in. This might be useful if you have really long category names. The invisible default value is 20.0. If your labels are being truncated, try increasing this value.
x-axis-label-rotation	Decimal	If set, adjusts the category item label rotation value. The value should be specified in degrees. If not specified, labels are rendered horizontally.
category-margin	Decimal	If set, adjusts the category margin in pixels.
lower-margin	Decimal	Specifies the space (in pixels) between the *y* axis and the first bar in the chart.
upper-margin	Decimal	Specifies the space (in pixels) between the last bar and the outer edge of the chart.
item-margin	Decimal	If set, adjusts the item margin in pixels.

- The *Y* axis set is introduced here with the following properties:

Name	Type	Description
y-axis-title	String	Sets the title for the primary numeric data axis; typically the *y* axis in a horizontally-oriented chart.
y-font	String	Sets the font for the range axis title.
y-sticky-0	Boolean	If the range includes zero in the axis, making it sticky will force truncation of the axis to zero, if set to true. The default value of this property is true.
y-incl-0	Boolean	If set to true, the range axis will force zero to be included in the axis.
y-auto-range	Boolean	If set to true, the range axis will be automatically adjusted depending on the content.
y-min	Decimal	The minimum value to render in the range axis.
y-max	Decimal	The maximum value to render in the range axis. The font to render the range tick value in.
y-scale-factor	Decimal	Scaling factor for the range axis.
y-tick-interval	Decimal	The numeric interval value to separate range ticks in the chart.
y-tick-font	String	The font to render the range tick value in.
y-tick-ftm-str	String	The DecimalFormat string to render the numeric range tick value.
y-tick-period	Selection	Specifies the *y* axis tick intervals if the y (range) dataset returns date or time data.
enable-log-axis	Boolean	If set to true, displays the y-axis as a logarithmic scale.
log-format	Boolean	If set to true, will present the logarithmic scale in a human readable view.

- The values set is introduced here with the following properties:

Name	Type	Description
show-item-labels	Selection	If set to Show Labels, will present the item labels.
item-label-font	String	Font used for the item label.
item-label-rotation	Decimal	The degree of the angle of rotation for the item labels. Possible values are from 0 to 360.
text-format	String	Determines the content of the domain plot labels. There are three possible values, any or all of which may be used: 0 represents the series name; 1 represents category; 2 represents the plotted value.
numeric-format	String	Determines the content of the domain plot labels. Must be in the Java number format.
date-format	String	Determines the content of the domain plot labels. Must be in the Java date format.
url-formula	Selection	Formula available in a drop-down menu to determine the content of the domain plot labels in case of URLs.
tooltip-formula	Selection	Formula available in a drop-down menu to determine the content of the tooltips of the domain plot labels.

Bar chart example

To try what you have learnt about the bar charts, let's build here a concrete example to see it in action. Starting from an empty report, as you learnt in Chapter 4, *Creating a Report with Report Designer*, create a JDBC data source, as you saw in Chapter 6, *Configuring JDBC and Other Data Sources*. The data source uses the SampleData (Local) connection and it is defined as shown in the following screenshot:

Once done, select **File** | **Page Setup** and check **Landscape** in the **Orientation** panel. Then press the **OK** button and check the **Do not change the layout** option. Once confirmed, drag on the chart (⊚) icon from the report element palette and drop it into the Report Header band. Stretch the chart element to cover the whole width of the page, and set to 450 the height property of the size & position group in the element properties panel. This setup will give to your chart a bigger space, so as to be correctly visible on the page.

By double-clicking on the chart element, the chart edit window will be presented, with the bar chart type selected by default. Set the `category-column` property to PRODUCTLINE and the `value-columns` property to BUYPRICE, directly in the `Common` group of the dataset panel. In the property panel, set to true the `3-D` property in the `General` group, set to false the `show-legend` property in the `Legend` group, and set to `Show Labels` the `show-item-labels` property in the `Values` group. Then press the **OK** button and preview the resulting report by pressing the eye () icon. The following screenshot shows how the preview looks like for your first bar chart:

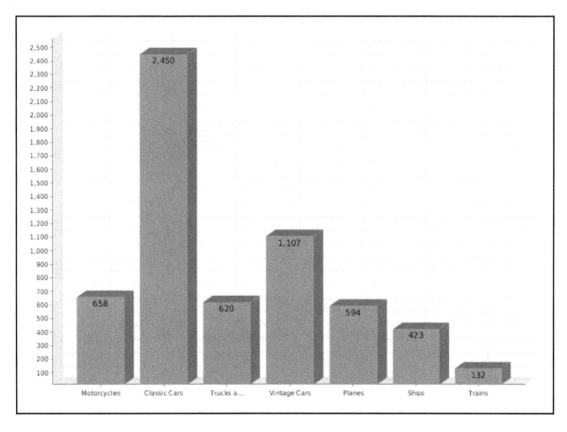

It is always good practice to experiment by yourself with how the resulting chart changes according to different values of one (or more) property. As an exercise, try to change one (or more) property and see what happens to the Pentaho report using the preview. Don't worry about trying advanced settings, nothing bad can happen and you can only learn.

Line chart

The line chart displays connected lines between categories for each series provided. This chart is useful for visualizing trends. The line chart utilizes the category dataset (previously introduced), together with the common properties defined earlier. In the following description are listed all the differences in terms of available properties:

- The options set of properties is provided with a specific content for this chart type:

Name	Type	Description
line-style	Selection	Sets the style of line series lines. Possible values are: `solid`, `dash`, `dot`, `dashdot`, and `dashdotdot`. Default value is `solid`.
line-size	Decimal	Sets the width of line series lines. Default value is `1.0`.
show-markers	Boolean	Sets the point markers visible in applicable charts. Default value is false.
horizontal	Boolean	If set to true, the chart's x and y axis are rotated horizontally. The default value is set to false.
series-color	Array of strings	A comma-separated list of hexadecimal color values. The colors are used in order, starting with the first value returned by the dataset.

- The general set has the same properties as described for the bar chart (the general common set, and `gridlines`, `show-plot-border` in addition)
- The X axis set has the same properties as described for the bar chart (`item-margin` excluded)
- The Y axis and values sets are also provided here with the same properties as described for the bar chart

Line chart example

As an example, let's reuse the same data source we described for the bar chart. Starting from an empty report, select **File** | **Page Setup** and check Landscape in the **Orientation** panel. Then press the **OK** button and check the **Do not change the layout** option. Once confirmed, drag the chart (⊚) icon and drop it into the `Report Header` band. Stretch the chart element to cover the whole width of the page, and set to `450` the `height` property of the `size & position` group in the element properties panel.

By double-clicking on the chart element, the chart edit window will be shown. Select the line chart icon from the upper panel and set the `category-column` property to `PRODUCTLINE` and the `value-columns` property to `BUYPRICE`, directly in the `Common` group of the dataset panel. In the property panel, set to true the `show-markers` property and set to true the `horizontal` property, both available in the `Options` group. Last but not least, set to false the `show-legend` property in the `Legend` group, then press the **OK** button, and then preview the resulting report by pressing the eye (👁) icon. The following screenshot shows what the preview looks like for your first line chart:

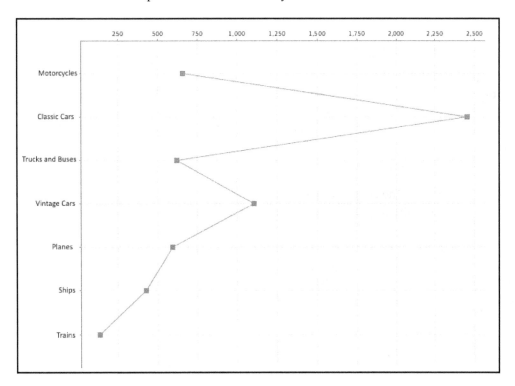

Area chart

The area chart displays a category dataset as a line, with the area underneath the line filled in. Multiple areas may appear depending on the number of series provided. The area chart is useful for visualizing the differences between two or more sets of data. The area chart utilizes the category dataset (previously introduced), together with the common properties defined earlier. In the following description are listed all the differences in terms of available properties:

- The options set of properties is provided with the same properties as described for the bar chart (`bar-borders` and `bar-max-width` excluded)

- The general set has the same properties as described for the bar chart (the general common set, and `gridlines`, `show-plot-border` in addition)

- The X axis, Y axis, and values sets are also provided here with the same properties as described for the bar chart

Area chart example

As an example, let's reuse the same data source we described for the bar chart. Starting from an empty report, select **File | Page Setup** and check **Landscape** in the **Orientation** panel. Then press the `Ok` button and check the **Do not change the layout** option. Once confirmed, drag the chart (🖻) icon and drop it into the `Report Header` band. Stretch the chart element to cover the whole width of the page, and set to `450` the `height` property of the `size & position` group in the element properties panel.

By double-clicking on the chart element, the chart edit window will be shown. Select the area chart icon from the upper panel and set the `category-column` property to `PRODUCTLINE` and the `value-columns` property to `QUANTITYINSTOCK`, `BUYPRICE`, directly in the `Common` group of the dataset panel. In the property panel, set to false the `show-legend` property in the `Legend` group and set to `Show Labels` the `show-item-labels` property in the `Values` group. Then press the **OK** button and preview the resulting report by pressing the eye (👁) icon. The following screenshot what how the preview looks like for your first area chart:

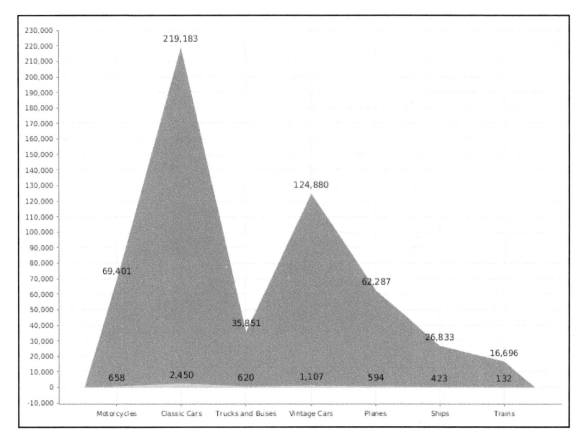

As an exercise, try to invert the suggested order of the `value-columns` property from `[QUANTITYINSTOCK,BUYPRICE]` to `[BUYPRICE,QUANTITYINSTOCK]`. Previewing the report, you will see two main changes: the color of the highest area changes from orange to yellow, and the second area (the lowest one) is not visible anymore. This behavior tells us that the order of the values is relevant and should be considered during the report's design.

Pie chart

The pie chart displays a sliced, multi-colored pie with individual slices that consist of individual series information. The pie chart utilizes the pie dataset (previously introduced), together with the common properties defined earlier. In the following description are listed all the differences in terms of available properties:

- The required set of properties is provided with a couple of additional properties for this chart type:

Name	Type	Description
ignore-nulls	Boolean	Specifies whether nonexistent data points should be referenced in the chart. Default value is true.
ignore-zeros	Boolean	Specifies whether a data value of zero should be referenced in the chart. Default value is true.

- The options set of properties is provided with a specific content for this chart type:

Name	Type	Description
slice-colors	Array of strings	A comma-separated list of hexadecimal color values. The colors are used in order, starting with the first value returned by the dataset.
show-labels	Selection	Defines if labels in correspondence of the value of the chart should be presented or not. Two possible values are defined: Show Labels and Hide Labels. Default value is Hide Labels.
label-font	String	Sets the font for the labels on the pie sections.
label-format	String	Determines the content of the domain plot labels. There are three possible values, any or all of which may be used: 0 represents the series name; 1 represents the value; 2 represents the percentage value.
rotate-clockwise	Boolean	Specifies whether the values returned by the dataset are ordered from left to right (clockwise) or right to left (counterclockwise). Default is true (clockwise).

Name	Type	Description
explode-slice	String	A list of series names to explode in the pie chart. Pie slices will not explode on a 3D pie chart. The possible values are integers representing the data points returned by your dataset, starting at zero.
explode-pct	Decimal	A decimal value that represents the percentage by which you want to expand the radius of the chart, to make room for the exploded pie piece. The larger the value, the further out the piece will be exploded. Possible values are between 0.0 and 100.0.

- The general set of properties is provided with some additional properties:

Name	Type	Description
shadow-paint	String	The color of the chart shadow; this is the area behind the chart. Press the ... button to display available colors.
shadow-x-offsetshadow-y-offset	Decimal	Coordinates relative to the chart for background shadow. Negative values are acceptable.
url-formula	String	Associates a link to the series key and category name.
tooltip-formula	String	Defines the tooltip (hover text) for the url-formula.

- The legend set of properties is provided with some additional properties:

Name	Type	Description
legend-label-format	String	Determines the content of the legend labels. There are three possible values, any or all of which may be used: 0 represents the series name; 1 represents the value; 2 represents the percentage value.

Pie chart example

As an example, let's reuse the same data source that we described for the bar chart. Starting from an empty report, select **File | Page Setup** and check **Landscape** in the **Orientation** panel. Then press the **OK** button and check the **Do not change the layout** option. Once confirmed, drag the chart (🖸) icon and drop it into the `Report Header` band. Stretch the chart element to cover the whole width of the page, and set to `450` the `height` property of the `size & position` group in the element properties panel.

By double-clicking on the chart element, the chart edit window will be shown. Select the pie chart icon from the upper panel and set the `value-column` property to `BUYPRICE` and the `series-by-field` property to `PRODUCTLINE`, directly in the dataset panel. In the property panel, set the `location` property to `left` in the `Legend` group and set to true the `3-D` property in the `General` group. Then press the **OK** button and preview the resulting report by pressing the eye (👁) icon. The following screenshot shows what the preview looks like for your first pie chart:

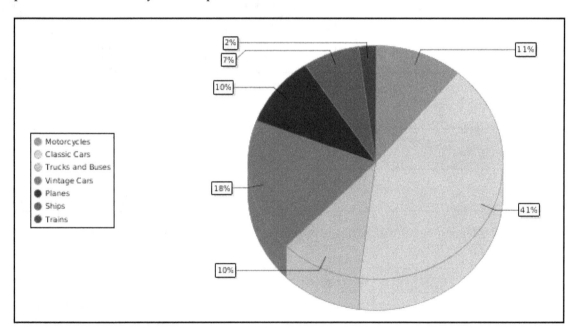

Multipie chart

The multipie chart renders a group of pie charts, based on a category dataset. This meta-chart renders individual series data as a pie chart, each broken into individual categories within the individual pie charts. The pie chart utilizes the category dataset (previously introduced), together with the common properties defined earlier. In the following description are listed all the differences in terms of available properties:

- The title set of properties is provided with one additional properties:

Name	Type	Description
pie-title-font	String	Sets the font for the pie title for the chart

- The options set of properties is provided with a specific content for this chart type:

Name	Type	Description
by-row	Boolean	Switches the category and series result sets. Default value is true.
series-color	Array of strings	A comma-separated list of hexadecimal color values. The colors are used in order, starting with the first value returned by the dataset.
show-labels	Selection	Defines if labels in correspondence of the value of the chart should be presented or not. Two possible values are defined: Show Labels and Hide Labels. Default value is Hide Labels.
label-font	String	Sets the font for the labels on the pie sections.
label-format	String	Determines the content of the domain plot labels. There are three possible values, any or all of which may be used: 0 represents the series name; 1 represents the value; 2 represents the percentage value.
pie-no-data-message	String	Message shown if the pie chart has no data.

- The general set has the same properties as described for the pie chart (the general common set and `shadow-paint`, `shadow-x-offset`, `shadow-y-offset`, `url-formula`, and `tooltip-formula` in addition)
- The legend set has the same properties as described for the pie chart (the legend common set and `legend-label-format` in addition)

Multipie chart example

As an example, let's reuse the same data source we described for the bar chart. Starting from an empty report, select **File | Page Setup** and check **Landscape** in the **Orientation** panel. Then press the **OK** button and check the **Do not change the layout** option. Once confirmed, drag the chart (⬛) icon and drop it into the `Report Header` band. Stretch the chart element to cover the whole width of the page, and set to `450` the `height` property of the `size & position` group in the element properties panel.

By double-clicking on the chart element, the chart edit window will be shown. Select the area chart icon from the upper panel and set the `category-column` property to `PRODUCTVENDOR`, the `value-columns` property to `BUYPRICE`, and the `series-by-field` property to `[PRODUCTLINE]`, directly in the dataset panel. In the property panel, set the `show-legend` property to false in the `Legend` group and set to `{0}` the `label-format` property in the `Options` group. Then press the **OK** button and preview the resulting report by pressing the eye (👁) icon. The following screenshot shows what the preview looks like for your first pie chart:

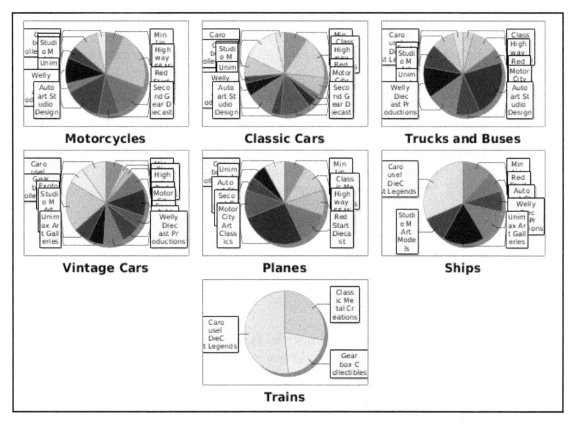

The result is not the best in terms of labels, but it gives you an idea of the potential use cases you can cover using the multipie chart.

Bar line chart

The bar line chart combines the bar and line charts, allowing visualization of trends with categories, along with comparisons. The bar line chart is unique in that it requires two category datasets to populate the chart: the first dataset populates the bar chart and the second dataset populates the line chart.

Note that the bar line chart is one of the two chart types that have activated the second tab named **Secondary DataSource** in the dataset panel. The tab named **Primary DataSource** controls the bar chart dataset and the tab named **Secondary DataSource** controls the line chart dataset.

The bar line chart utilizes the common properties defined earlier, including the category dataset properties. This chart also inherits the properties from both the bar chart and the line chart. In the following description are listed all the differences in terms of available properties:

- The bar options set defines the same properties as described for the options set in the bar chart, with one property added: `ctgry-tick-font` (string), defining the font used for the range ticks in the chart
- The line options set defines the same properties as described for the options set in the line chart, with some differences, described as follows:
  - The horizontal property is not available here

  - `series-color` is renamed as `line-series-color`. If not defined, `line-series-color` uses the `series-color` property in the bar options set

  - `lines-label-font` (string) defines the font used for the labels of the line

- The general set has the same properties as described for the bar chart (the general common set, and `gridlines` and `show-plot-border` in addition)

- The shadow, *x* axis, and *y* axis sets are also provided here with the same properties as described for the bar chart
- The *Y2* axis set is introduced here with the following properties:

Name	Type	Description
y2-same-as-y-axis	Boolean	Sets the *Y2* axis (the right side axis) to the same tick intervals as the *Y1* (left side) axis.
y2-axis-title	String	Sets the title for the *Y2* (right-side) numeric data axis.
y2-font	String	Sets the font for the *Y2* (right side) axis title.
y2-sticky-0	Boolean	If the range includes zero in the *Y2* (right side) axis, making it sticky will force truncation of the axis to zero, if set to true. The default value of this property is true.
y2-incl-0	Boolean	If set to true, the *Y2* (right side) axis will force zero to be included in the axis.
y2-auto-range	Boolean	If set to true, the *Y2* (right side) axis will be automatically adjusted depending on the content.

Name	Type	Description
y-2min	Decimal	The minimum value to render in the Y2 (right side) axis.
y2-max	Decimal	The maximum value to render in the Y2 (right side) axis.
y2-tick-interval	Decimal	The numeric interval value to separate Y2 (right-side) ticks in the chart.
y2-tick-font	String	The font to render the range tick value in, for the Y2 (right-side) axis.
y2-tick-ftm-str	String	The DecimalFormat string to render the numeric range tick value for the Y2 (right side) axis.
y2-tick-period	Selection	Specifies the Y2 (right side) axis tick intervals if the Y2 (range) dataset returns date or time data.

- The values set has the same properties as described for the bar chart, where show-label is used (with the same meaning, type, values, and behavior) instead of show-item-labels

Bar line chart example

As an example, let's reuse the same data source we described for the bar chart. Starting from an empty report, select **File | Page Setup** and check **Landscape** in the **Orientation** panel. Then press the **OK** button and check the **Do not change the layout** option. Once confirmed, drag the chart () icon and drop it into the Report Header band. Stretch the chart element to cover the whole width of the page, and set to 450 the height property of the size & position group in the element properties panel.

By double-clicking on the chart element, the chart edit window will be shown. Select the bar line chart icon from the upper panel and set the `category-column` property to `PRODUCTLINE` and the `value-columns` property to `BUYPRICE`, directly in the `Common` group of the dataset panel. Now press on the **Secondary DataSource** tab and set the `category-column` property to `PRODUCTLINE` again, with the `value-columns` property set to `QUANTITYINSTOCK`. In the property panel, set to `[#2a0cd0]` the `line-series-color` property in the `Line Options` group, set to false the `show-legend` property in the `Legend` group, and set to `Show Labels` the `show-labels` property in the `Values` group. Then press the **OK** button and preview the resulting report by pressing the eye (👁) icon. The following screenshot shows what the preview looks like for your first bar line chart:

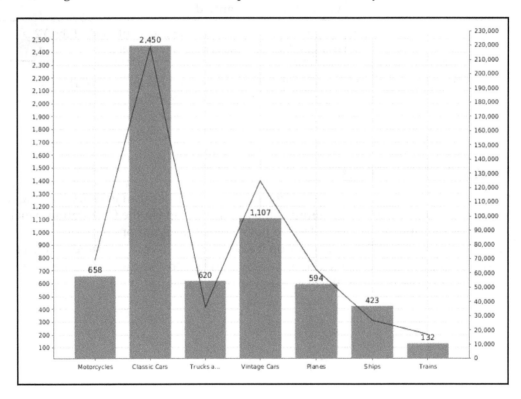

Ring chart

The ring chart is identical to the pie chart, except that it renders as a ring as opposed to a complete pie. In addition to sharing all the properties similar to the pie chart, it also defines the `section-depth` property (decimal) in the options set.

The `section-depth` property defines the percentage of the circle that will be filled with the ring chart. The larger the value, the less space there is in the center of the ring. Possible values are between 0.1 and 1, where 1 is equivalent to a pie chart.

Ring chart example

As an example, let's reuse the same data source we described for the bar chart. Starting from an empty report, change the orientation to landscape and set the chart element as described in the previous examples.

By double-clicking on the chart element, the chart edit window will be shown. Select the ring chart icon from the upper panel and set the `value-column` property to BUYPRICE and the `series-by-field` property to PRODUCTLINE, directly in the dataset panel. In the property panel, set the `show-legend` property (in the `Legend` group) to false , the `section-depth` property to 0, 4, and `label-format` to {0} - {2} (both in the `Options` group). Then press the **OK** button and preview the resulting report by pressing the eye (👁) icon. The following screenshot shows what the preview looks like for your first ring chart:

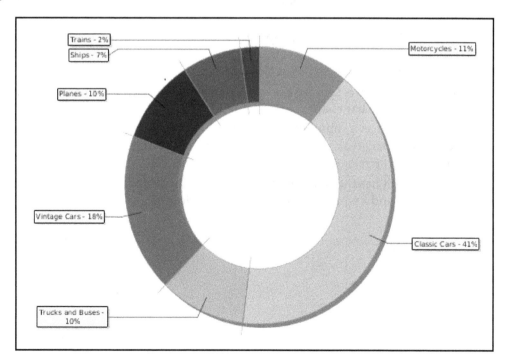

Bubble chart

The bubble chart allows you to view three dimensions of data. The first two dimensions are your traditional x and y dimensions, also known as domain and range. The third dimension is expressed by the size of the individual bubbles rendered. The bubble chart utilizes the common properties defined previously, including the XYZ series dataset properties. In the following description are listed all the differences in terms of available properties:

- The title set of properties is provided with one additional property:

Name	Type	Description
pos-title	Selection	Sets the position to display the chart title. Possible values are: north, west, south, east, top, left, bottom, and right

- The options set of properties is provided with some of the properties previously introduced: horizontal, series-color, and label-font. In addition, there is the max-bubble-size property (decimal) defining the preferred maximum bubble size, as a percentage of the bubble value represented. Possible values are integers between 1 and 100.
- The general set has the same properties as described for the pie chart (the general common set, and shadow-paint, shadow-x-offset, shadow-y-offset, url-formula, and tooltip-formula in addition).
- The X axis and y axis sets are also provided here with the same properties as described for the bar chart.
- The values set has a subset of the properties described for the bar chart (particularly: show-item-labels, item-label-font, url-formula, and tooltip-formula).
- The legend set has the same properties as described for the pie chart (the legend common set and legend-label-format in addition).

Bubble chart example

As an example, let's reuse the same data source we described for the bar chart. Starting from an empty report, change the orientation to landscape and set the chart element as described in the previous examples.

By double-clicking on the chart element, the chart edit window will be shown. Select the bubble chart icon from the upper panel and set the `x-value-columns` property to `BUYPRICE`, the `y-value-columns` and `z-value-columns` properties to `QUANTITYINSTOCK`, and the `series-by-field` property to `PRODUCTLINE`, directly in the dataset panel. In the property panel, set the `max-bubble-size` property (in the `Options` group) to `100`, then press the **OK** button and preview the resulting report by pressing the eye (👁) icon. The following screenshot shows what the preview looks like for your first ring chart:

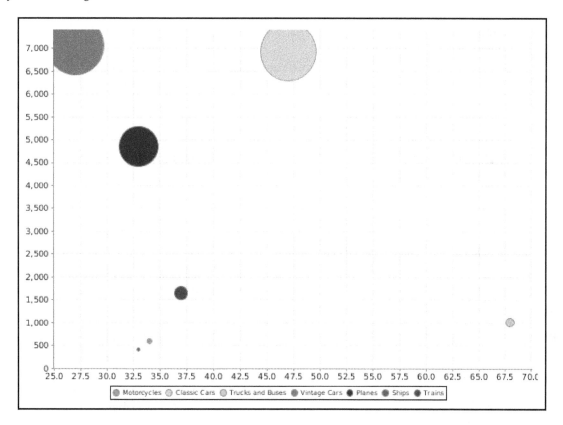

Scatter plot chart

The scatter plot chart renders all items in a series as points within a chart. This chart type utilizes the common properties defined earlier, including the XY series dataset properties as default. As alternative datasets, you can also decide to use the XYZ series dataset or the times series dataset. You can change the dataset using the drop-down menu in the upper part of the **Primary DataSource** tab. Concerning the available properties, in the following description are listed all the differences from the common list introduced in the beginning of the chapter:

- The title set of properties is provided with the same properties as described for the bubble chart (the title common set and `pos-title` in addition).
- The options set of properties is provided with some of the properties previously introduced: `stacked`, `horizontal`, and `series-color`. In addition are provided the `dot-height` and `dot-width` properties (integer), which define the height/width of the marker that represents a series point (in pixels), are additionally provided.
- The general set has the same properties as described for the common set, and in addition, it has `show-plot-border` and `label-font` (see bar chart for their definitions).
- The X axis and *y* axis sets are also provided here with the same properties as described for the bar chart.
- The values set has a subset of the properties described for the bar chart (more in detail: `show-item-labels`, `item-label-font`, `url-formula`, and `tooltip-formula`).

Scatter plot chart example

As an example, even if it's not perfect for this case, let's reuse the same data source introduced for the bar chart. Starting from an empty report, change the orientation to landscape and set the chart element as described in the previous examples.

By double-clicking on the chart element, the chart edit window will be shown. Select the bubble chart icon from the upper panel and set the `x-value-columns` property to BUYPRICE, the `y-value-columns` property to QUANTITYINSTOCK, and t he `series-by-field` property to PRODUCTLINE, directly in the dataset panel. Then press the **OK** button and preview the resulting report by pressing the eye (👁) icon. The following screenshot shows what the preview looks like for your first scatter plot chart:

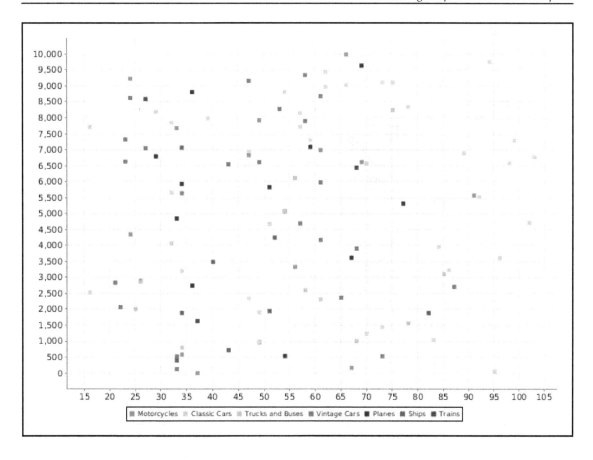

XY bar chart, XY line chart, and XY area chart

The XY bar, XY line, and XY area charts graph an XY series dataset as a bar, a line, or an area chart. These chart types utilize the common properties defined earlier, including the XY series dataset properties as default. As alternative datasets, you can also decide to use the XYZ series dataset or the times series dataset. You can change the dataset using the drop-down menu in the upper part of the **Primary DataSource** tab.

Concerning the available properties for the XY bar chart, in the following description are listed all the differences from the common list introduced in the beginning of the chapter:

- The title set has the same properties as described for the bubble chart (the title common set and `pos-title` in addition)
- The options set has the same properties as described for the bar chart, excluding `max-bar-width`

- The general set has the same properties as described for the bar chart, excluding `gridlines`
- The shadow set has the same properties as described for the bar chart, excluding `shadow-color`
- The X axis set is composed of different properties, as follows:

Name	Type	Description
x-axis-title	String	Sets the title for the domain axis, if it exists. In a typical 2D horizontal chart, this is the categorical or *x* axis.
x-font	String	Sets the font for the range axis title.
x-sticky-0	Boolean	If the range includes zero in the axis, making it sticky will force truncation of the axis to zero, if set to true. The default value of this property is true.
x-incl-0	Boolean	If set to true, the range axis will force zero to be included in the axis.
x-auto-range	Boolean	If set to true, the range axis will be automatically adjusted depending on the content.
x-min	Decimal	The minimum value to render in the range axis.
x-max	Decimal	The maximum value to render in the range axis.
x-tick-interval	Decimal	The numeric interval value to separate range ticks in the chart.
x-vtick-label	Decimal	Sets the orientation of the tick labels on the domain axis; true for vertical and false for horizontal. Default is false.
x-tick-font	String	The font to render the range tick value in.
x-tick-ftm-str	String	The `DecimalFormat` string to render the numeric range tick value.
x-tick-period	Selection	Specifies the *x* axis tick intervals if the *x* (range) dataset returns date or time data.

- The Y axis set has the same properties as described for the bar chart, excluding `y-scale-factor`
- The values set is a subset of the properties described for the bar chart, limited to `show-item-labels`, `item-label-font`, `url-formula`, and `tooltip-formula`

Concerning the available properties for the XY line chart, in the following description are listed all the differences from the common list introduced in the beginning of the chapter:

- The title set has the same properties as described for the bubble chart (the title common set and `pos-title` in addition)
- The options set has the same properties as described for the line chart, excluding `show-markers` and including `stacked` (introduced in the options group for the bar chart)
- The general set has the same properties as described for the bar chart, excluding `gridlines`
- The *X* axis set has the same properties as described for the XY bar chart
- The *Y* axis set has the same properties as described for the bar chart, excluding `y-scale-factor`
- The values set is a subset of the properties described for the bar chart, limited to `show-item-labels`, `item-label-font`, `url-formula`, and `tooltip-formula`

Concerning the available properties for the XY area chart, in the following description are listed all the differences from the common list introduced in the beginning of the chapter:

- The title set has the same properties as described for the bubble chart (the title common set and `pos-title` in addition)
- The options set has the same properties as described for the bar chart, excluding `stacked-percent` and including `stacked` (introduced in the options group for the bar chart), `line-style`, `line-size`, and `show-markers` (introduced in the options group for the line chart)
- The general set has the same properties as described for the bar chart, excluding `gridlines`
- The *X* axis set has the same properties as described for the XY bar chart
- The *Y* axis set has the same properties as described for the bar chart, excluding `y-scale-factor`
- The values set is a subset of the properties described for the bar chart, limited to `show-item-labels`, `item-label-font`, `url-formula`, and `tooltip-formula`

XY bar chart, XY line chart, and XY area chart examples

As an example, even if it's not perfect for this case, let's reuse the same data source introduced for the bar chart. Starting from an empty report, change the orientation to landscape and set the chart element as described in the previous examples.

By double-clicking on the chart element, the chart edit window will be shown. Select the XY bar chart icon from the upper panel and set the x-value-columns property to BUYPRICE, the y-value-columns property to QUANTITYINSTOCK, and the series-by-field property to PRODUCTLINE, directly in the dataset panel. In the property panel, set the stacked property (in the Options group) to true, then press the **OK** button and preview the resulting report by pressing the eye (👁) icon. The following screenshot shows what the preview looks like for your first XY bar chart:

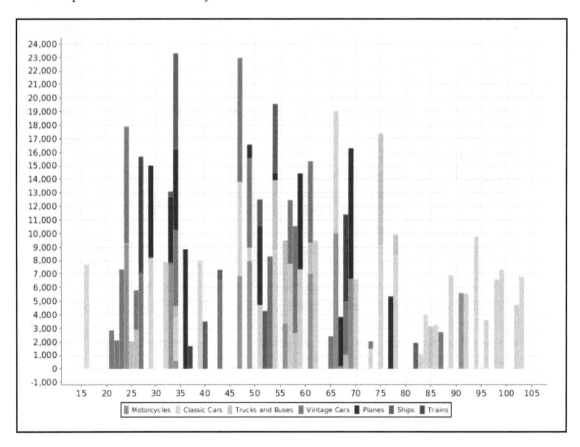

Now edit the chart element again and change the chart type from XY bar chart to XY line chart (from the upper panel, select the icon representing the target chart type). Press the **OK** button and preview the resulting report using the eye (👁) icon. The following screenshot shows what the preview looks like for your first XY line chart:

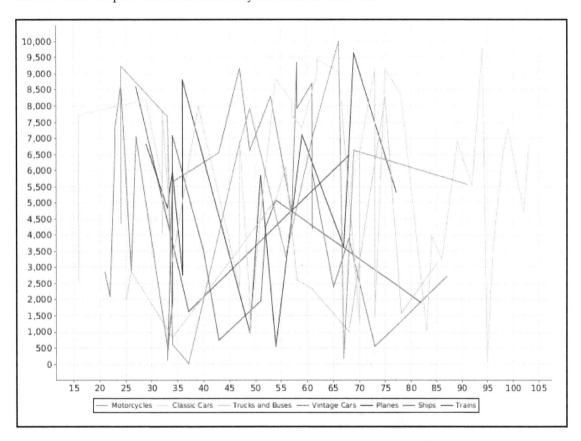

As the last example, edit the chart element again and change the chart type from XY line chart to XY area chart (from the upper panel, select the icon representing the target chart type). In the property panel, set the `stacked` property (in the options group) to false, then press the **OK** button and preview the resulting report by pressing the eye (👁) icon. The following screenshot shows what the preview looks like for your first XY area chart:

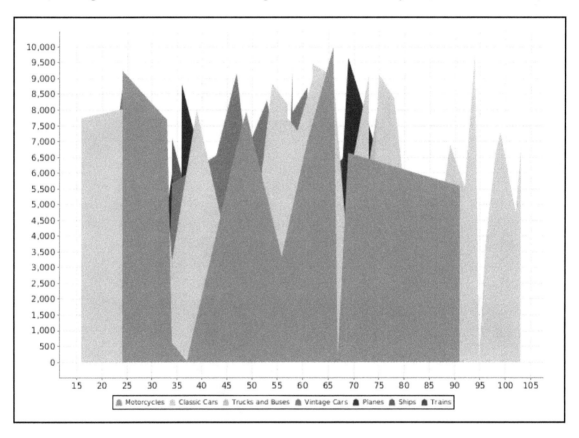

 The resulting charts, using the sample query, are not the best, but they are functional to our goal of showing the technical setup and behavior of Pentaho Reporting. This could be a great exercise if you could find a more appealing result, defining a better query on your data or on `SampleData` database.

Extended XY line chart

The extended XY line chart allows the rendering of three additional chart types: step area charts, step charts, and difference charts. The step chart types display an XY series dataset as a set of steps, and the difference chart renders two XY series and highlights the differences between the two. These chart types utilize the common properties defined earlier, including the XY series dataset properties as default. As alternative datasets, you can also decide to use the XYZ series dataset or the times series dataset. You can change the dataset using the drop-down menu in the upper part of the **Primary DataSource** tab.

Concerning the available properties for the extended XY line chart, in the following description are listed all the differences from the common list introduced in the beginning of the chapter:

- The title set has the same properties as described for the bubble chart (the title common set and `pos-title` in addition)
- The options set has the same properties as described for the line chart, including `ext-chart-type` (with possible values `StepChart`, `StepAreaChart`, and `DifferenceChart`) and `stacked` (introduced in the options group for the bar chart)
- The general set has the same properties as described for the bar chart, excluding `gridlines`
- The X axis set has the same properties as described for the XY bar chart
- The Y axis set has the same properties as described for the bar chart, excluding `y-scale-factor`
- The values set is a subset of the properties described for the bar chart, limited to `show-item-labels`, `item-label-font`, `url-formula`, and `tooltip-formula`

Extended XY line chart example

As an example, start from the previous example (XY bar chart, XY line chart, or XY area chart) and edit the chart element, changing the chart type to extended XY line chart (from the upper panel, select the icon representing the target chart type). In the property panel, set the `ext-chart-type` property (in the `Options` group) to `StepChart` and press the **OK** button. Then preview the resulting report by using the eye (👁) icon. The following screenshot shows what the preview looks like for your first extended XY line chart:

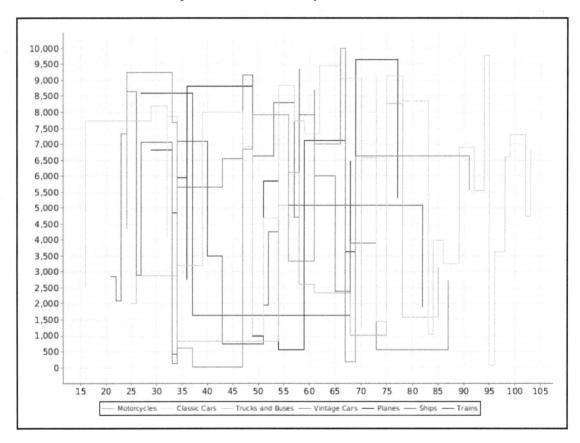

Repeat the exercise by changing the value of the `ext-chart-type` property (in the `Options` group) to `StepAreaChart`, and then preview. Later on, change the value to `DifferenceChart` and preview again. Also, in these cases you could find a more appealing result, defining a better query in your data or directly on the `SampleData` database.

Waterfall chart

The waterfall chart displays a unique stacked bar chart that spans categories. This chart is useful when comparing categories to one another. The last category in a waterfall chart normally equals the total of all the other categories to render appropriately, but this is based on the dataset, not the chart rendering. In the following description are listed all the differences in terms of available properties:

- The options set has a subset of the properties described for the bar chart, limited to `horizontal` and `series-color`
- The *X* axis set has the same properties as described for the bar chart, excluding `item-margin`
- The general, *y* axis, and values sets have the same properties as described for the bar chart

Waterfall chart example

As an example, let's reuse the same data source introduced for the bar chart. Starting from an empty report, change the orientation to landscape and set the chart element as described in the previous examples.

By double-clicking on the chart element, the chart edit window will be shown. Select the waterfall bar chart icon from the upper panel and set the `category-column` property to `PRODUCTLINE` and the `value-columns` property to `BUYPRICE`, directly in the dataset panel. In the property panel, set the `show-legend` property (in the `Legend` group) to false and the `show-item-labels` property (in the `Values` group) to `Show Labels`. Then press the **OK** button and preview the resulting report by pressing the eye ( ) icon. The following screenshot shows what the preview looks like for your first waterfall chart:

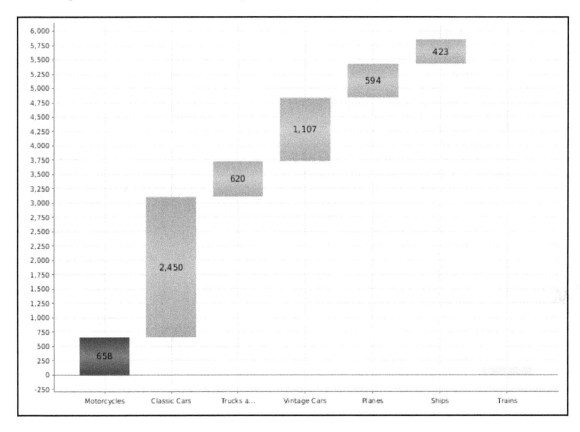

Radar chart

The radar chart renders a web-like chart that displays a categorical dataset. The radar chart utilizes the category dataset (previously introduced), together with the common properties defined earlier. In the following description are listed all the differences in terms of available properties:

- The options set of properties is provided with the following properties:

Name	Type	Description
line-width	Decimal	Sets the width of line series lines. Default value is 2.0.
head-size	Decimal	The size of the oval drawn where the value line and grid line intersect the category grid line.
series-color	Array of strings	List of colors to apply (in order) to the series in the chart.
gridline-interval	Percentage	Determines how many grid lines are drawn, in terms of line spacing. For instance, 20% will show 5 grid lines and 10% will show 10 grid lines. Default is 25.0% or four lines.
radar-web-filled	Boolean	Determines whether the web layers are filled in with solid colors or left as outlines.

- The general set has the same properties as described for the general common set, with the following additional properties: url-formula, tooltip-formula (from the values set in bar chart), and gridlines (from the general set in bar chart)
- Items set is introduced here with the following property:

Name	Type	Description
label-font	String	Sets the font for the labels on the items

Radar chart example

As an example, start from the previous example (waterfall chart) and edit the chart element by changing the chart type to radar chart (from the upper panel, select the icon representing the target chart type). Then press the **OK** button and preview the resulting report by using the eye (👁) icon. The following screenshot shows what the preview looks like for your first radar chart:

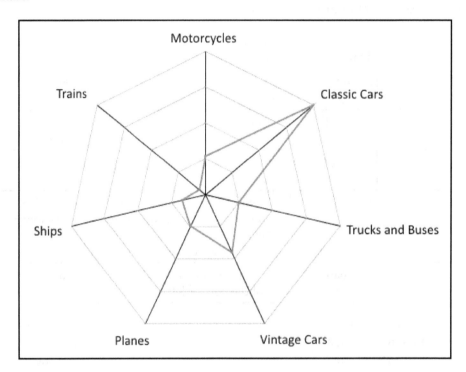

XY area line chart

The XY area line combines the XY area and XY line charts, allowing visualization of trends, along with comparisons. The XY area line chart is unique in that it requires two XY series datasets to populate the chart: the first dataset populates the XY area chart and the second dataset populates the XY line chart. In the same way that you saw for the bar line chart, in this case also both the **Primary DataSource** tab and the **Secondary DataSource** tab are available.

The XY area line chart utilizes the common properties defined earlier, including the XY series dataset properties. This chart also inherits the properties from both the XY area chart and the XY line chart. In the following description are listed all the differences in terms of available properties:

- The title set has the same properties as described for the XY bar chart (the title common set and `pos-title` in addition).
- The options set has the same properties as described for the bar chart, excluding `max-bar-width`.
- The line options set is composed of different properties, introduced as follows:

Name	Type	Description
line-series-color	Array of string	List of colors to apply (in order) to the line series in the chart
lines-label-font	String	Specifies the font of both the labels above the line at each data point
line-tick-fmt	String	Specifies the Java `DecimalFormat` string for rendering the line axis labels
line-tick-font	String	Defines the Java font to use when rendering the line axis labels

- The Ggneral set has the same properties as described for the bar chart, excluding `gridlines`.
- The values set is a subset of the properties described for the bar chart, limited to `show-item-labels`, `item-label-font`, `url-formula`, and `tooltip-formula`.
- The X axis set has the same properties as described for the XY area chart.
- The Y axis set has the same properties as described for the bar chart, excluding `y-scale-factor`, `enable-log-axis`, and `log-format`, but including the `y-vtick-label` property (decimal) defining the orientation of the tick labels on the *y* axis; true for vertical, false for horizontal. Default is false.
- The Y2 axis set has the same properties as described for the bar line chart, excluding the `y2-tick-ftm-str` property.

Thermometer chart

The thermometer chart displays a single value in an obvious format, described by its name. Thermometer is a variation of the known "traffic light" indicator and it's useful if you have to quickly show if a single number is within a range. The thermometer chart utilizes the thermometer dataset (previously introduced), together with the common properties defined earlier. In the following description are listed all the differences in terms of available properties:

- The options set is composed of different properties, introduced as follows:

Name	Type	Description
show-labels	Selection	Defines if labels in correspondence of the value of the chart should be presented or not. Two possible values are defined: Show Labels and Hide Labels. Default value is Hide Labels.
label-fonts	String	Sets the font for the labels.
bulbRadius	Integer	Radius of the bulb of the thermometer.
columnRadius	Integer	Radius of the column of the thermometer.
thermometerUnits	Selection	Possible selection is None, Fahrenheit, Celsius, and Kelvin. Default is None.
criticalRageHigh	Integer	Higher limit of the possible values.
criticalRageLow	Integer	Lower limit of the values defined as critical.
criticalRageColor	String	Color of the mercury in case the value is in the critical range. The color picker discussed in Chapter 5, *Design and Layout in Report Designer* is available in this property.
warningRangeHigh	Integer	Higher limit of the values to be in the warning range.
warningRangeLow	Integer	Lower limit of the values to be in the warning range.
warningRangeColor	String	Color of the mercury in case the value is in the warning range. The color picker discussed in Chapter 5, *Design and Layout in Report Designer* is available in this property.
normalRangeHigh	Integer	Higher limit of the values to be in the normal range.
normalRangeLow	Integer	Lower limit of the possible values.

Name	Type	Description
normalRangeColor	String	Color of the mercury in case the value is in the normal range. The color picker discussed in Chapter 5, *Design and Layout in Report Designer* is available in this property.
thermometerPaint	String	Color of the thermometer. The color picker discussed in Chapter 5, *Design and Layout in Report Designer* is available in this property.
mercuryPaint	String	Default color of the mercury. The color picker discussed in Chapter 5, *Design and Layout in Report Designer* is available in this property.

Thermometer chart example

As an example, let's reuse the same data source as introduced for the bar chart. Starting from an empty report, change the orientation to landscape and set the chart element as described in the previous examples.

By double clicking on the chart element, the chart edit window will be shown. Select the thermometer chart icon from the upper panel and set the value-column property to BUYPRICE, directly in the dataset panel. In the property panel, in the Options group, set criticalRageHigh to 10000, criticalRageLow to 75000, warningRageHigh to 7500, warningRageLow to 3000, and normalRageHigh to 3000. Then press the **OK** button and preview the resulting report by pressing the eye (👁) icon. The following screenshot shows what the preview looks like for your first thermometer chart:

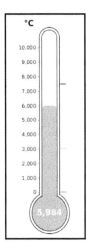

Including sparkline charts in reports

If you need to show a trend among a small number of related numerical data points, a sparkline chart may be appropriate. Different from charts and used mainly in the headers or grouping bands, the sparkline charts are often used in the details of a Pentaho report, of course if it makes sense to do so.

 Sparkline charts require comma-separated values for input, so if your data is not in that format, you must create a function to pull it from your data source and put commas between each data point.

Pentaho Reporting provides three different sparkline charts: `bar-sparkline` represented by the 🔲 icon, `line-sparkline` represented by the 🔲 icon, and `pie-sparkline` represented by the 🔲 icon. As usual, to use the sparkline chart, drag the icon from the Report Designer palette and drop it in the place where you want to see the chart. All the configurations and settings can be managed from the element properties panel, as you saw in `Chapter 5`, *Design and Layout in Report Designer*, in the section dedicated to the `bar-sparkline`, `line-sparkline`, and `pie-sparkline` elements.

Summary

In this chapter, you learned how to incorporate many chart types in your reports in many different ways. You learned how to configure a chart's dataset as well as how to customize how each chart type looks in a report. You learned how to populate a category series dataset, a pie dataset, an XY (and XYZ) series dataset, a time series dataset, and a thermometer dataset. You saw in detail all the dozens of properties of 17 different chart types. You also learned how to include static and dynamic images, as well as sparkline charts, in your reports.

Now that you have read this chapter, you should feel comfortable with all the ways Pentaho Report Designer offers to render a chart (and graphics in general). This is an advanced task in developing complex Pentaho reports and makes you an expert in dealing with practical use cases.

In the next chapter, you will learn more about parameterization, functions, variables, and formulas in a Pentaho report.

8
Parameterization, Functions, Variables, and Formulas

In the previous chapters, you learned about Pentaho Report Designer, layout and design, and you saw the available elements and the different types of data sources. In this chapter, you will start off by learning how to parameterize a report. You will then learn about all the predefined functions and expressions available for use within a report. From there, you will learn about Pentaho Reporting's environment variables and formula capabilities, including the correct syntax and available formula methods.

This chapter is written as a reference manual for developers and information technologists. The goal is to share all the relevant and advanced features about parameterization, functions, variables, and formulas, there are available in Pentaho Report Designer.

Report parameterization

Report parameterization allows the end users to customize results of Pentaho reports, by entering values that limit report datasets or trigger rendering decisions. Report parameterization is also useful to develop user filtering through the user interface.

In the following sections, you are going to see how to use the report parameterization, get acquainted with all the different types of report parameters, and learn how to create and use them, using the Pentaho Report Designer. During the description of the creation and use of report parameters, a practical example about a report filter will be presented.

Using report parameters

As presented in Chapter 6, *Configuring JDBC and Other Data Sources*, there are many different options for providing data to Pentaho Reporting. All of them are grouped under the name *data sources* and each different type of data source has its own features, syntax, and reasons to be used.

Because of the different syntax and features, each data source type uses its underlying method for parameterizing queries. For instance, the default syntax for XPath, Kettle, and MDX are supported through their respective DataFactory implementations. Each data source query syntax defines how to specify parameters, and Pentaho Reporting provides those parameters via the DataRow API. The two exceptions from the default management of parameters include SQL and static data. When specifying a SQL statement in JDBC, you would normally specify a question mark to denote which parameters should be specified.

Pentaho Reporting requires that you specify the parameters by name, so some parsing is done on the SQL query before passing the query to JDBC. You may specify parameters as ${PARAM}, and SQLReportDataFactory will replace each named parameter with a question mark (?) before making the prepared JDBC call. NamedStaticDataFactory allows for Java class methods with parameters to be executed. The names provided when configuring DataFactory are used when resolving the values from provided DataRow.

The following is an example of a SQL query containing one parameter named productLine, which filters the products' line on the PRODUCTS table of the SampleData schema:

```
SELECT
  *
FROM
  PRODUCTS
WHERE
  PRODUCTLINE = ${productLine}
```

Be aware that the parameters are defined together with a collection of properties (you will see this better in the following sections). This means that the automatic replacement of the parameter's value really depends on those properties, and this should be considered during the development of the query string. If not done so, the query could fail; for example, a multi-value parameter is provided where a SQL command defines a single value WHERE condition.

The available report parameter types

Pentaho Reporting provides a rich collection of different parameters, which each render differently within Pentaho Report Designer or any other frontend tool (you will see an example in `Chapter 15`, *Using Reports in Pentaho Business Analytics Platform*). The following list shares all the parameter types available in Pentaho Reporting 8.0:

- **Drop-down**: Defining a typical drop-down list and allowing a single value selection
- **Single value list**: Defining a panel containing the list of values and allowing a single value selection
- **Multi-value list**: Defining a panel containing the list of values and allowing multiple selections
- **Radio button**: Defining a panel containing the list of values and allowing a single value selection in radio button style
- **Checkbox**: Defining a panel containing the list of values and allowing selections in check button style
- **Single selection button**: Defining a panel containing the list of buttons (one for each value) and allowing a single selection
- **Multi-selection button**: Defining a panel containing the list of buttons (one for each value) and allowing multiple selections
- **Textbox**: Defining a text field
- **Text area**: Defining a text area field
- **Date picker**: Defining a user friendly interface picking a single date/time value

When embedding Pentaho Reporting into a custom application, it is the embedded program's responsibility to render parameters, as demonstrated in the following example. All parameter types may specify a data source for population of possible selections, as well as for validation. It is possible to nest parameters by parameterizing the data sources, which are used to populate selections. For example, a top level drop-down parameter, such as country, could drive a secondary radio button parameter, such as region. Queries are executed in the order in which they appear in the data source list.

Multi-value list, checkbox, and multi-selection button parameter types allow the selection of multiple types. These parameter types return an array of values rather than a single value. Data sources, including SQL, have special logic that maps the array of values in the generated query.

Creating parameters

Starting from the Report Designer user interface, you should be already confident with report explorer (you can find it as the top-right panel). Report explorer is composed of two different tabs: **Structure** and **Data**. In the previous chapters, you have already used both the tabs, and the **Data** tab is where all the parameters live. The following screenshot shows how the report explorer looks with two parameters defined:

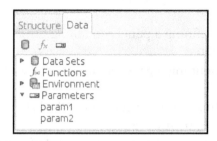

You can create a new parameter by right-clicking on the `Parameters` item and choosing **Add Parameter...**. As an alternative, you can click on the parameter icon (⊡) in report explorer or use the upper menu, choosing the **Data | Add Parameter...** item.

Once selected, a modal window similar to the following one appears:

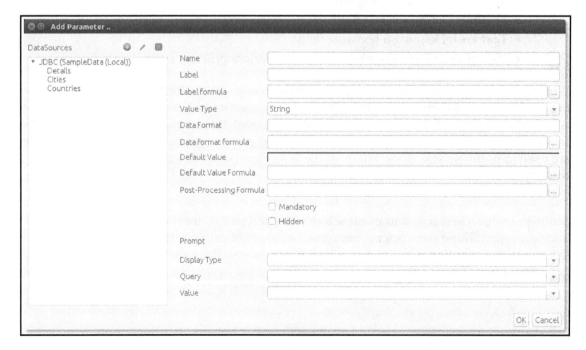

As you can see in the left panel, you can manage the report data sources as you saw in Chapter 6, *Configuring JDBC and Other Data Sources*, because they could be used in the parameter definition. The right panel lists a collection of fields defining all the properties of the parameter. The panel is grouped in the upper part related to the properties and the **Prompt** group is used to setup the presentation of the parameter. In the following table, all the properties are introduced for better understanding:

Name	Type	Description
Name	String	Name of the parameter. This property will be used in data source definition, so define with attention.
Label	String	Label shown in the user interface to request the field value.
Label Formula	String	Formula defining the label's value dynamically.
Value Type	Selection	Datatype of the parameter. Possible values are: String, Boolean, Number, Date, Date (SQL), Time, Timestamp, Double, Float, Integer, Long, Short, Byte, Biginteger, BigDecimal, TableModel, and Object.
Data Format	String	Format string of the data used in case of numbers, dates, timestamps, and so on.
Data format formula	String	Formula defining the format's value dynamically.
Default Value	String/array of strings	Default value for the parameter. If the parameter is multi-value, the values can be specified as arrays.
Default Value Formula	String	Formula defining the default's value/values dynamically.
Post-Processing formula	String	Formula defining the post-processing action to the value of the parameter.
Mandatory	Boolean	If set to true, the parameter cannot be empty. Default value is false.
Hidden	Boolean	If set to true, the parameter is not visible to the user (but it is defined). Default value is false.
Display Type	Selection	Parameter's type, selected from the list of possible parameter types.

Name	Type	Description
Query	Selection	Data source used to define the possible values of the parameter.
Value	Selection	Field of the data source used to define the possible values of the parameter.
Display Name	Selection	Field of the data source used to define the possible display names of the parameter. This property is available only if a display name is provided.
Display Value Formula	String	Formula defining the display name of the parameter. This property is available only if a display name is provided.
Visible items	Integer	Number of visible items. Available for multi-value parameters only. Default value is 0.

Once all the requested properties are defined, click on the **OK** button to create the parameter and see it listed in the **Data** tab of the report explorer.

Creating a report using parameters

In this section, let's see a practical example to show in practice how the report parameters can be created and used. As usual, this is only an example of what can be done, but this is a very common need that you will reuse for sure in the future. This example shows how to develop two cascade parameters, one depending on the other's value.

In more detail, let's develop a very simple report describing the list of customers available in the CUSTOMERS table of the SampleData schema. As you learnt in Chapter 6, *Configuring JDBC and Other Data Sources*, the very first step is defining an empty report (using the new empty report icon (⬜)). Once done, create three new data sources (named Details, Cities, and Countries), as shown in the following screenshot:

The `Details` query defines the details of the report and depends on two parameters: the `country` and `city` parameters. The `Cities` query defines the list of possible cities in one country in particular. As you can see, the query uses the `country` parameter to filter the existing cities in a given country. This use of the `country` parameter defines a dependency in the two parameters that will be defined. The `Countries` query defines the list of possible countries. Once the queries are defined, remember to select the `Details` query, by right-clicking on it in the **Data** tab (in report explorer) and clicking on **Select Query**.

Now that the data sources are correctly setup, let's drag the `COUNTRY`, `CITY`, and `CUSTOMERNAME` fields from the `Details` query and drop it in the `Details` band, as shown in the following screenshot. Pay attention to stretch the `CUSTOMERNAME` field to cover the entire space till the right margin of the page.

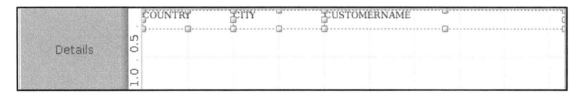

To complete the report, let's create the two parameters. As introduced earlier, click on the parameter icon (▭) in report explorer and fill the modal window as described in the left side of the following screenshot. This task will create the country parameter. Repeat for the creation of the city parameter by clicking on the parameter icon (▭) in report explorer again and filling the modal window as described on the right side of the following screenshot:

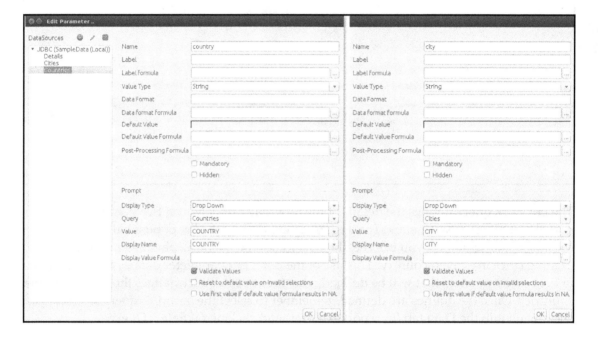

Once done, preview the report by using the eye icon () and you will see two interactive parameters appear at the top of the panel. Take your time to play with them, changing the value of the `country` parameter and checking how the `city` parameter changes accordingly. Selecting a value for the `city` parameter, will change the resulting report accordingly. The following screenshot shows how the report parameters look in the report's preview:

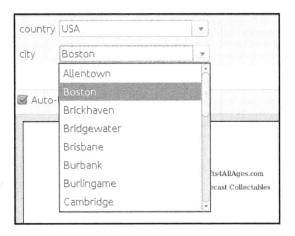

In the `https://github.com/fcorti/pentaho-8-reporting-for-java-developers` repository, specifically, in the `Chapter 08 - Parametrization, functions, variables and formulas/my_reports` path, you can find the `sample_with_parameters.prpt` report that develops exactly the example described here. Feel free to open it with Report Designer and play with settings and parameters to understand all the advanced features and advanced behaviors.

Functions and expressions

Pentaho Reporting provides many functions and expressions that may be used during report creation. A function in Pentaho Reporting is used to calculate a computed value, while an expression in Pentaho Reporting is a function whose scope is limited to the current dataset row. A function may maintain state, having access to many rows of data.

Functions and expressions in Report Designer

Starting from the Report Designer user interface, functions and expressions live in two different places because their scope is different. Functions can be found in report explorer, in particular, in the **Data** tab under the `Functions` group. The following screenshot shows how the report explorer looks with two functions defined:

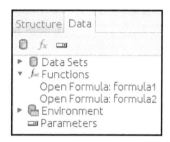

Expressions, being related to the dataset, live in a different place: in the element properties panel. In particular, expressions live on each property of the panel, in the fourth column of the table showing an icon. There are two possible icons: the green plus icon ( ), indicating that no expression is defined, and the pencil icon ( ), indicating that an expression is already defined. The following example shows two properties: the `text-color` property with the static value filled and the expression empty, and the `bg-color` property with the static value empty and the expression filled.

 In case an expression is defined for a property, the third column, containing the static value, will be ignored. This behavior is relevant during report development and could cause pain if you are not aware of it.

Creating and using functions

Starting from the Report Designer user interface, specifically, in the **Data** tab of the report explorer, you can create a new function by right clicking on the `Functions` item and choosing **Add Function...**. As an alternative, you can click on the function icon (*fx*) or use the upper menu, choosing the **Data | Add Function...** item.

Once function creation is selected, a modal window, similar to the following one, appears. The window contains a list of the available types of functions, grouped for better understanding. Expanding the right group, you can pick the function type to use in your report.

Once the correct function type for your needs is selected, a brand new function appears in the list of the **Data** tab of the report explorer. Selecting the new function, the element property panel will show all the available properties, as a regular element of the report. In the following sections, all the properties will be introduced for each type of function.

To use the function in your report, it is exactly as you saw for the other report elements in previous chapters: drag the function from the **Data** tab and drop it in the preferred place, directly into the bands of the report.

Example of function

As an example, let's reuse a report developed in `Chapter 4`, *Creating a Report with Report Designer*, named `report_01.prpt`. If you followed the suggestion, you should have the report in your `my_report` folder on your development environment. If not, you can download it from the `https://github.com/fcorti/pentaho-8-reporting-for-java-developers` repository, from the `Chapter 04 – Creating a report with Report Designer/my_reports` path.

The goal is to add page numbering to this report. This example is really basic, but it will be really useful in your future development.

Once the report is opened in the Report Designer, create a new function as explained earlier in the chapter: select the **Data** tab in the report explorer and then click on the function icon (f_x). As for the function type, expand Common and select Page. Once the **OK** button is clicked, a new function named PageFunction1 will be created.

Take your time to check the properties in the element properties panel when you select the new function from the **Data** tab in the report explorer. At this stage, you should be more confident with the meaning of the properties and you can easily predict their goals and supposed behaviors.

Now that the new function named PageFunction1 is available, drag it from the **Data** tab in report explorer and drop it in the center of the page footer. To reach perfection, you should also center the alignment of the content by clicking the 🔲 icon on the upper toolbar. Once done, preview the report by using the eye icon (👁) and you will see the page numbers as shown in the following screenshot. Use the arrow icons ⏮ ◀ ▶ ⏭ in the toolbar to change the pages and check the result.

CTO	405,985	459,650
VP Engineering	383,242	443,405
Senior Engineer	770,272	719,855
Engineer	695,925	666,750
QA Manager	374,863	437,420
1		

In the https://github.com/fcorti/pentaho-8-reporting-for-java-developers repository, specifically in the Chapter 08 – Parametrization, functions, variables and formulas/my_reports path, you can find the sample_with_page_numbering.prpt report, which develops exactly the example described here. Feel free to open it with Report Designer and play with settings and parameters to understand all the advanced features and advanced behaviors.

Creating and using expressions

Starting from the Report Designer user interface, specifically, in the element properties panel, you can create a new expression for a property by clicking on the green plus icon (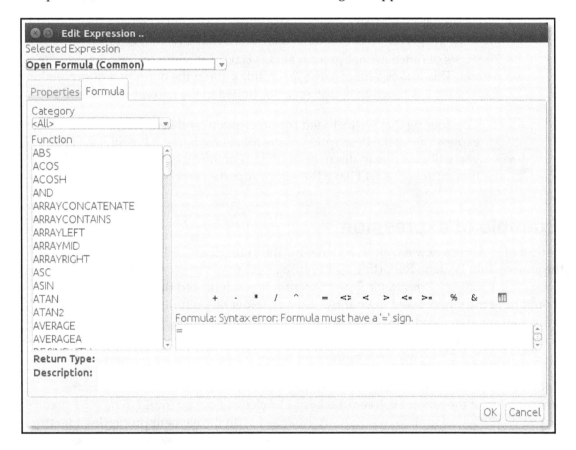). Once pressed, a modal window similar to the following one appears:

In the modal window, you can recognize on top a drop-down menu selecting the type of expression you want to define and below that a panel with the available properties to set up (in case of `Open Formula`, you also have the **Formula** tab). Taking a look at the available types of expressions, they are exactly a subset of the type of functions introduced earlier. About this, we can observe that:

- The types with the same name between expressions and functions have exactly the same properties with the same name and behavior.
- The types of functions not present also as type of expression are not related to a dataset. This makes a lot of sense if you think about the definition of expression (expression is a function whose scope is limited to the current dataset row).

Considering that we included the description (and behavior) of expressions in the description of the functions, in the following sections you will continue to discover the details of the functions, only assuming that expressions will have the same properties and behavior.

Example of expression

Instead of creating a new example, let's review the example we did at the very beginning of the journey into Pentaho Reporting. Let's reuse `report_02.prpt`, which we saw in `Chapter 4`, *Creating a Report with Report Designer*. If you followed the suggestion, you should have the report saved in your `my_report` folder on your development environment. If not, you can download it from the `https://github.com/fcorti/pentaho-8-reporting-for-java-developers` repository, from the `Chapter 04 - Creating a report with Report Designer/my_reports` path.

Once the report is opened in the Report Designer, select the `Details` element in the **Structure** tab of the report explorer (the `Details` element can be found in `Master Report` | `Group: DEPARTMENT` | `Details Body` | `Details`). In the element properties, identify the `bg-color` property and click on the pencil icon (✎). The following you can see the resulting expression, defined to instruct Pentaho Reporting Engine to set a different background color if the row is even or odd:

```
= IF ( ISEVEN(ROWCOUNT()); "#d2e8f4"; "white" )
```

The available function types

In this section, you will learn about all the available function types. As introduced earlier in the chapter, every function available in Report Designer is categorized according to the group it belongs to. Following you will find a section for each group, with a brief introduction of the content and a full list of properties and settings.

Before describing the specific properties for each group, let's introduce the common properties of all the groups:

Name	Type	Description
Function name	String	Used to reference the function or expression in elements, formulas, and other functions
Dependency level	Integer	Used to determine the order in which to execute the functions

 The functions included in groups named `Deprecated` and `Internal Function (Do not use)` will not be described. The reason is quite obvious—you should not use them.

Common functions

The common functions include the most commonly used functions within Pentaho Report Designer:

Name	Description
Open Formula	This function evaluates a `LibFormula` formula defined later in this chapter. The following are properties of this function: | Name	Type	Description
------	------	-------------
Formula	String	Formula to evaluate. By clicking on the ... button, the formula editor is shown. Check the section dedicated to the formula topic for details.
Dependency level	Integer	Used to determine the order in which to execute the function.	

Name	Description
Page	This function returns the current page number. The following are properties of this function: <table><tr><th>Name</th><th>Type</th><th>Description</th></tr><tr><td>Page increment</td><td>Integer</td><td>The number by which to increase the count for each page</td></tr><tr><td>Start Page Number</td><td>Integer</td><td>The page from which to start counting</td></tr><tr><td>Reset on Group Name</td><td>String</td><td>If this value is set, the page total value is reset when the named group appears</td></tr></table>
Total Page Count	This function calculates the total number of pages in a report. The properties defined for this function are the same as introduced previously: Page increment, Start Page Number, and Reset on Group Name.
Page of Pages	This function returns a string that displays the current page and the total page count. The properties defined for this function are described in the following table, in addition to Page increment, Start Page Number, and Reset on Group Name: <table><tr><th>Name</th><th>Type</th><th>Description</th></tr><tr><td>Format Pattern</td><td>String</td><td>The format string to render the current page and total pages into. The default value is {0} / {1}: {0} to render the current page; {1} to render the total page count.</td></tr></table>

Report functions

Report functions are related to the rendering of a report:

Name	Description
Is Export Type	This function returns true if the export type of the report string begins with the export type property provided. The following a property of this function:
	<table><tr><td>**Name**</td><td>**Type**</td><td>**Description**</td></tr><tr><td>Export Type ID</td><td>String</td><td>The string to compare to the report export type string</td></tr></table>
Row Banding	The row banding function manages changing background colors for rows in a report. The properties defined for this function are described in the following table, in addition to Reset on Group Name:
	<table><tr><td>**Name**</td><td>**Type**</td><td>**Description**</td></tr><tr><td>Number of Rows</td><td>String</td><td>The number of rows to render before changing the banding color</td></tr><tr><td>Active Banding Color</td><td>String</td><td>The primary banding color</td></tr><tr><td>Inactive Banding Color</td><td>String</td><td>The secondary banding color</td></tr><tr><td>State On New Groups</td><td>Boolean</td><td>If set to true, resets the banding color for each new group</td></tr><tr><td>State On New Pages</td><td>Boolean</td><td>If set to true, resets the banding color for each new page</td></tr><tr><td>Ignore Crosstab</td><td>Boolean</td><td>If set to true, does not apply to cross tab</td></tr></table>

Name	Description			
Hide Repeating	This function hides repeated elements of a specified field in the item band. The properties defined for this function are described in the following table.			
	Name	**Type**	**Description**	
	Field Name	String	The field to watch for changes	
	Apply to Element(s) Named	String	The element to hide in the item band	
	Ignore All Group Breaks	Boolean	If set to false, this function will reset itself on group breaks	
	Ignore All Page Breaks	Boolean	If set to false, this function will reset itself on page breaks	
Hide Page Header & Footer	This function hides the page header and footer if the export type is not pageable. The properties defined for this function are described in the following table:			
	Name	**Type**	**Description**	
	Export Descriptor	String	This property is used to determine whether the current report export type should disable page headers and footers. Its default value is `table`.	
	Hide Page Bands	Boolean	If set to true, hides page bands.	
	Disable Repeating Headers	Boolean	Disables any repeating group headers and footers.	
Show Page Footer	This function hides the page footer except for the last page. It has no additional properties.			

Summary functions

Summary functions calculate values during the first phase of report processing and make those values available during report rendering:

Name	Description
Sum	This function sums a field within a group during the prepare run stage of a report, making available the total group sum in later stages of report generation. The properties defined for this function are described in the following table, in addition to `Field Name` and `Reset on Group Name`: <table><tr><th>Name</th><th>Type</th><th>Description</th></tr><tr><td>Crosstab Column Filter</td><td>String</td><td>The field to use to filter in cross tab</td></tr></table>
Count	This function counts the rows within a group during the prepare run stage of a report, making available the total group count in later stages of report generation. The properties defined for this function are the same as introduced previously: `Reset on Group Name` and `Crosstab Column Filter`.
Count for Page	This function is identical to the `Count` function, but also resets at the beginning of each page.
Group Count	This function counts the occurrence of groups within a report during the prepare run stage of a report, making available the total group count in later stages of report generation. The properties defined for this function are described in the following table: <table><tr><th>Name</th><th>Type</th><th>Description</th></tr><tr><td>Group Name to Count</td><td>String</td><td>The name of the group that should be counted. If set to empty, counts all groups within a parent group.</td></tr><tr><td>Reset on Parent Group Name</td><td>String</td><td>The name of the group which resets the count. If set to empty, counts the subgroups of the entire report.</td></tr></table>

Name	Description
Minimum	Determines the global minimum value of a specified field in a report. The properties defined for this function are the same as introduced earlier: `Field Name`, `Reset on Group Name`, and `Crosstab Column Filter`.
Maximum	Determines the global maximum value of a specified field in a report. The properties defined for this function are the same as introduced earlier: `Field Name`, `Reset on Group Name`, and `Crosstab Column Filter`.
Sum Quotient	This function sums a dividend and a divisor, and then divides the two for the result value, using the `Sum` function to sum the values. The properties defined for this function are described in the following table, in addition to `Reset on Group Name` and `Crosstab Column Filter`: <table><tr><th>Name</th><th>Type</th><th>Description</th></tr><tr><td>Dividend Field</td><td>String</td><td>The field that holds the dividend of this division calculation.</td></tr><tr><td>Divisor Field</td><td>String</td><td>The field that holds the divisor of this division calculation.</td></tr><tr><td>Rounding Mode</td><td>Integer</td><td>Java's BigDecimal rounding mode. See Java's documentation for values.</td></tr><tr><td>Scale</td><td>Integer</td><td>The scale of the quotient returned. The default value is 14.</td></tr></table>
Sum Quotient Percent	This function is an extension of the `Sum Quotient` function, and simply multiples the final result by 100. It shares the same properties as the `Sum Quotient` function.
Calculation	This function stores the result of a field calculated during the prepare run stage of report generation, allowing access later on in the report. The properties defined for this function are the same as introduced earlier: `Field Name`, `Reset on Group Name`, and `Crosstab Column Filter`.
Sum for Page	This function is identical to the `Count` function, but also resets at the beginning of each page.

Name	Description
Count for Page (Running)	This function is identical to the Count function, but maintains the value of the current number of rows in a dataset and resets at the beginning of each page.

Running functions

Running functions calculate values during report rendering, allowing for incremental aggregation information throughout a report.

Name	Description
Sum (Running)	Calculates the sum total value of a specified field over the number of rows in a report. The properties defined for this function are the same as introduced earlier: Field Name, Reset on Group Name, and Crosstab Column Filter.
Count (Running)	Maintains the value of the current number of rows in a dataset. The properties defined for this function are the same as introduced earlier: Reset on Group Name and Crosstab Column Filter.
Group Count (Running)	This method counts the occurrence of groups within a report. The properties defined for this function are the same as introduced earlier: Group Name to Count and Reset on Parent Group Name.
Count Distinct (Running)	This method counts the distinct occurrences of a value within a specified field. The properties defined for this function are described in the following table, in addition to Field Name, Reset on Group Name, and Crosstab Column Filter:

	Name	Type	Description
	Ignore Null Values	Boolean	If true, the counter will not consider the null values. Default value is false.

Name	Description
Average (Running)	Calculates the average value of a specified field over the number of rows within a report. The properties defined for this function are the same as introduced earlier: Field Name, Reset on Group Name, Rounding mode, and Scale.

Name	Description
Minimum (Running)	Determines the minimum value of a specified field over the number of rows in a report. The properties defined for this function are the same as introduced earlier: `Field Name` and `Reset on Group Name`.
Maximum (Running)	Determines the maximum value of a specified field over the number of rows in a report. The properties defined for this function are the same as introduced earlier: `Field Name` and `Reset on Group Name`.
Percent of Total (Running)	Calculates the percentage value of a specified field, by summing all the data rows and dividing the current row by the total sum. The properties defined for this function are described in the following table, in addition to `Field Name`, `Reset on Group Name`, `Crosstab Column Filter`, `Rounding mode`, and `Scale`:

Name	Type	Description
Scale Result To 100	Boolean	If true, it multiplies the value by `100`

Advanced functions

Advanced functions include functions that are specialized and are not generally used:

Name	Description
Message Format	Formats a message, based on the current data row. The properties defined for this function are described in the following table:

Name	Description		
	Name	**Type**	**Description**
	Message Pattern	String	A string pattern to render, with row data referenced by ${FIELD}
	Encoding	String	Use this encoding if URL encode properties are set
	URL-Encode all Values	Boolean	To encode the individual row data rendered within the message
	URL-Encode the result	Boolean	To encode the final result
	Null-String	String	What value to render if the field referenced is null
Resource Message Format	Returns a formatted message from a resource bundle. The properties defined for this function are described in the following table, in addition to Null-String:		
	Name	Type	Description
	ResourceBundle Identifier	String	The name of the resource bundle
	Resource-Key of Pattern	String	The format string to render, which may contain references to the current row fields, using the ${FIELD} syntax

Name	Description
Lookup	This function allows you to choose between different strings, a value based on key matching. The properties defined for this function are described in the following table, in addition to `Field Name` and `Null Value`:

Name	Type	Description
`Fall Back Value`	String	If no keys match the field value, return this value.
`Key Values`	Array of strings	Values to compare with the field. Each key should have a corresponding text value.

Name	Type	Description
`Text Values`	Array of Strings	It is a list of strings. A string is chosen from the list depending on which key matches the field value.
`Ignore Case When Matching`	Boolean	If set to true, ignores the case when making key comparisons.

Name	Description
Indirect Lookup	This function allows you to choose between different columns, a value based on key matching. The properties defined for this function are described in the following table, in addition to `Field Name`, `Key Values`, `Null Value`, and `Ignore Case When Matching`:

Name	Type	Description
`Fallback Forward-Field`	String	If no keys match the field value, return this field's value.
`Forwarding Field List`	Array of Strings	It is a list of fields. A field is chosen from the list depending on which key matches the field value.

Name	Description
Resource Bundle Lookup	Returns a value from a resource bundle, based on the key provided by a field. The properties defined for this function are described in the following table, in addition to `Field Name`: | Name	Type	Description
------	------	-------------
Resource-Bundle Identifier	String	The name of the resource bundle	
Open Formula (Advanced)	This function is a stateful version of the formula expression. The properties defined for this function are described in the following table, in addition to `Formula`: | Name	Type	Description
------	------	-------------
Initialization Formula	String	If specified, this formula will be evaluated when the `Formula` function is called for the first time, instead of evaluating the default formula	

Chart data and value data functions

Chart related functions have been covered in detail in a previous chapter, so there is no need to restate them in this list, where the properties and behavior are exactly the same. Value related functions contain mainly `Thermometer DataSet Collection`, already covered in a previous chapter.

Image functions

As introduced for chart and value data functions, image related functions have been covered in detail in the previous chapter, so there is no need to restate them in this list, where the properties and behavior are exactly the same.

Script functions

Scripting functions make it easy to customize your report through various scripting languages:

Name	Description
Bean-Scripting Framework (BSF)	This function uses Apache's Bean Scripting Framework to generate a result. See `http://jakarta.apache.org/bsf` for more information on the Bean Scripting Framework. The properties defined for this function are described in the following table: <table><tr><th>Name</th><th>Type</th><th>Description</th></tr><tr><td>Expression</td><td>String</td><td>An expression defined in the specified programming language</td></tr><tr><td>Expression Programming Language</td><td>String</td><td>The programming language used in the expression</td></tr><tr><td>Initialization Script</td><td>String</td><td>A script defined in the specified programming language, which is executed during the initialization of the scripting language environment</td></tr></table>
BeanShell (BSH)	This function uses the BeanShell framework to generate a result. See `http://www.beanshell.org` for more information on BeanShell. The properties defined for this function are the same as introduced earlier for `Expression`.

Table of contents functions

Table of content and index were introduced in `Chapter 5`, *Design and Layout in Report Designer* as a report element. Here are described the functions related to the same topic:

Name	Description
`Index Text Generator`	It produces a text as a collection of strings defining a nice table of contents. The properties defined for this function are described in the following table: <table><tr><th>Name</th><th>Type</th><th>Description</th></tr><tr><td>CollectDetails</td><td>Boolean</td><td>Defines whether detail items should be included in the data collection.</td></tr><tr><td>indexSeparator</td><td>String</td><td>Defines the separator text that is used between the index elements. It defaults to ..</td></tr><tr><td>Depth</td><td>Integer</td><td>Defines the number of levels of the table of content.</td></tr><tr><td>Condensed Style</td><td>Boolean</td><td>Define whether a - is used between continuous page numbers; for example, 1, 2, 3, 4 would display as 1-4.</td></tr></table>
`Index Number Generator`	It produces an integer array defining a nice table of contents. The properties defined for this function are the same as introduced earlier: `Collect Details` and `Depth`.
`Index Generator`	The index generator function has been covered in detail in `Chapter 5`, *Design and Layout in Report Designer*, so there is no need to restate it here, as the properties and behavior are exactly the same.
`Table of Contents Generator`	The table of content generator function has been covered in detail in `Chapter 5`, *Design and Layout in Report Designer*, so there is no need to restate it here, as the properties and behavior are exactly the same.

Environment variables

If you are publishing your Pentaho reports to the Business Analytics Platform (see Chapter 15, *Using Reports in Pentaho Business Analytics Platform* for an introduction), you can use certain environment variables to customize and control the behavior. The environment variables are available by default in a Pentaho report when it's created, and they live in the **Data** tab of the report explorer. The following screenshot shows how the report explorer looks with the environment variable expanded:

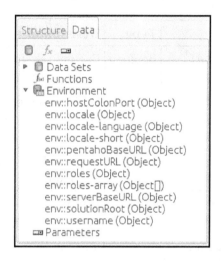

Environment variable can be used as usual, by dragging and dropping it into the right place of the report. The following is a list of the variables with brief descriptions of their meanings:

Name	Description
env:hostColonPort	The hostname and port number for the Business Analytics Platform.
env:locale	Info about locale of the client requesting the report. env:locale-language and env:locale-short are other two variables available.
env:pentahoBaseURL	The complete URL to the Business Analytics Platform, as set in the base URL property.
env:requestURL	The complete URL to the request for the resource.

Name	Description
env:roles	Returns a comma-separated list of roles that the Business Analytics Platform user, who is currently running this report, belongs to.
env:roles-array	Returns a Java array of strings containing the roles that the Business Analytics Platform user, who is currently running this report, belongs to.
env:serverBaseURL	The URL to the Business Analytics Platform, minus the Business Analytics Platform application context name (the default context is /pentaho/).
env:solutionRoot	The path to the top-level Pentaho solution directory.
env:username	Returns the Business Analytics Platform username of the person currently running the published report.

Working with formulas

In addition to providing functions within reports, formulas may also be used to generate dynamic content in a report. Formulas may be used to derive element property and style values. Also, the Open Formula and Open Formula (Advanced) functions defined earlier may be used to combine the formula and function mechanisms in a report.

Formulas in Pentaho Reporting are based on the Open Formula standard. This standard is similar to Excel formula support, and is used in OpenOffice as well as other tools such as Pentaho Metadata. This formula system is often referred to as LibFormula, which is the library name for reporting's formula subproject.

Creating a formula

As you learnt in the section about functions and expressions, there are two places where `Open Formula` and `Open Formula (Advanced)` can be used: in the **Data** tab of report explorer and in each property expression in the element properties panel. Once `Open Formula` or `Open Formula (Advanced)` is requested, the formula editor is shown accessing the `Formula/Initialization formula` property.

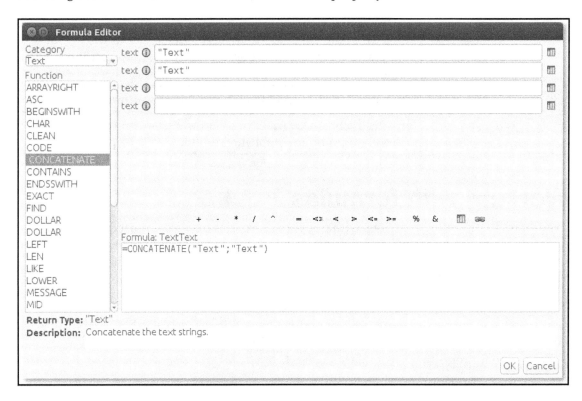

As you can see from the preceding screenshot, the formula editor is very intuitive. Looking at the window, you can recognize: on the left, the list of available functions with a category selector on top; on the right, the helping panel to support the composition of the formula with the formula text area; and at the bottom, a description as reference.

Use the field selection (▥) icon to use an available element in the formula. With *fields*, the formula editor defines the fields of the data sources, the custom functions, and the environment variables. As you will see, using this feature, Pentaho Reporting identifies a field using the syntax [NAME].

Take your time to play a bit with the formula editor. You will see that its use is straightforward. As an example, you can try to develop the formula to show the date of execution of the report in the `Page Footer` band (as a suggestion, try to check the `NOW()` function).

The formula syntax

A formula evaluates to a final value. Formulas support a standard set of datatypes, along with operators and functions that may be used to derive new values. The following is a simple example of a formula:

```
IF([COL1] > 10; "Big"; "Small");
```

This formula uses the `IF` function with parameters separated by semicolons. The first parameter is a comparison, resulting in true or false. To reference an outside data column or named function, reference the column in brackets, as shown for `COL1`. If the comparison example evaluates to true, the second parameter in the `IF` function is returned. To specify a string, use double quotes, shown with `"Big"` and `"Small"`. If the statement evaluates to false, the third parameter is returned. Also, the term null may be used to denote a null reference.

Formula datatypes

Column data, as well as literal values, all get mapped to a formula datatype. The following datatypes are supported. Different types may inherit from one another. The *any* type indicates each one of the available types.

Name	Description
`Array`	Arrays may be declared in a formula, or generated by functions. You may specify one or two dimensional arrays with the following syntax: `{ROW1|ROW2|ROW3...}`. Also, a row may be broken into multiple columns by semicolons. Here is an example: `{1;2;3|4;5;6|7;8;9}`.
`Date`	The date type inherits from the `Numeric` type. This type is represented as a `java.util.Date` object within Java, and represents the date portion of a complete date.
`DateTime`	The date time type inherits from the `Numeric` type, as well as the date and time types. This type is represented as a `java.util.Date` object within Java. Functions such as `DATEVALUE()` are available to generate a `date` object.

Name	Description
Error	Various formula functions may fail. When this occurs, an error is created. Certain functions are available to determine if an error has occurred.
Logical	The `Logical` type inherits from the `Numeric` type. The values of this type are `Boolean`, either true or false. You may specify a logical value through the functions `TRUE()` and `FALSE()`.
Numeric	A numeric value, represented in Java as a `BigDecimal` object. Literal values of this type may take the following forms: `123`, `123.456`, `123e10` or `456E-10`, and `-1.2`.
Text	A text value, represented in Java as a `String` object. Literal values of this type must be quoted with double quotes, as `"Text Here"`. To place a double quote within a string, reference it twice, as `" Here is a "" quote"`.
Time	The time type inherits from the `Numeric` type. This type is represented as a `java.util.Date` object within Java and represents the `Time` portion of a complete date.

Formula operators

The following operators may be used within a formula expression. Note that all operators live in the formula editor as buttons, in the right panel immediately on top of the formula text area.

Name	Description
+	Adds two numbers together.
−	Subtracts two numbers.
*	Multiplies two numbers.
/	Divides two numbers.
^	Returns the first value powered to the second value.
=	Returns true if both values are equal.
<>	Returns true if values are not equal.
<	Returns true if the first value is less than the second value.
>	Returns true if the first value is greater than the second value.

Name	Description
<=	Returns true if the first value is less than or equal to the second value.
>=	Returns true if the first value is larger than or equal to the second value.
%	Divides a number by 100, converting it to percent. For instance, 100 percent will become 1.
&	Concatenates two strings.

The available formula categories

Pentaho Reporting defines many functions available for use within the formula system. As introduced when explaining the formula editor, the available functions are grouped in categories for better understanding. Following is the exhaustive list, along with detailed information about each function. The description is grouped in different sections, each one fully dedicated to a provided category. A unique exception is the all category that includes all the functions from all the categories.

Date or time formulas

These functions allow for creation and manipulation of Date, Time, and DateTime objects:

Name	Description
DATE	Creates a Date object based on the year, month, and day.
DATEDIFF	Returns the difference between two dates, depending on the format code, which may be one of the following: • y: This means the difference in years • m: This means the difference in months • d: This means the difference in days • yd: This means the difference in days, ignoring the years • ym: This means the difference in months, ignoring the years • md: This means the difference in days, ignoring the months and years
DATETIMEVALUE	Parses a string into a date. The string must match one of the supported formats. By default, the following formats are supported: m/d/yy and yyyy-mm-dd.
DATEVALUE	Returns an internal number for text that has a possible date format.

Name	Description
DAY	Returns the day of the month.
DAYS	Calculates the number of days between two dates.
HOUR	Returns the hour of the time.
MINUTE	Returns the minute of the time.
MONTH	Returns the numeric month of the year, where 1 for January, and so on.
MONTHEND	Returns the date at month end.
NOW	Creates a `DateTime` object with the current time.
PREVWEEKDAY	Determines the date of the previous working day.
SECOND	Returns the second of the time.
TIME	Creates a `Time` object, based on the hour, minute, and second value.
TIMEVALUE	Returns a sequential number for a text shown in a possible time entry format.
TODAY	Creates a `Date` object with the current date.
WEEKDAY	Returns the day of the week, where 1 for Sunday, and so on.
YEAR	Returns the year.
YESTERDAY	Determines yesterday's date.

Database formulas

This category of functions implements some SQL like functions, returning a logical type result:

Name	Description
BEGINSWIDTH	Returns true if a string begins with another string
CONTAINS	Returns true if a string contains another string
ENDSWIDTH	Returns true if a string ends with another string
EQUALS	Returns true if two strings are equal
IN	Returns true if any of the subsequent arguments match the first argument

Name	Description
LIKE	Acts like the SQL LIKE function, comparing the first value to a regular expression

Information formulas

Many additional functions are available that offer rich capabilities within Pentaho Reporting:

Name	Description
CHOOSE	Returns the parameter referenced by the index.
COUNT	Returns the number of values. This function counts individual elements within arrays as well.
COUNTA	Returns the number of non-empty values within an array or arrays. This function counts non arrays always, even if they are empty.
COUNTBLANK	Returns the number of empty values within a reference that represents an array of values.
DASHBOARDMODE	Checks whether dashboard-mode is enabled. dashboard-mode is active if body-fragment creation is set to true and if the export type is any HTML export.
DOCUMENTMETADATA	Returns a value from the Document Meta-Data collection.
ENV	Returns a value from the Meta-Data attributes of the given field.
ERROR	Raises an evaluation error with the given message.
EXPORTTYPE	Returns the current export type descriptor for the report.
HASHCHANGED	Returns true if the field with the name of text has changed.
IN	Returns true if any of the subsequent arguments match the first argument.
INDEX	Returns the value at the specified array index.
ISBLANK	Returns true if the value is null.
ISEMPTYDATA	Checks whether the current result set is empty.
ISERR	Returns true if the value is an error, but not the NA error.

Name	Description
ISERROR	Returns true if the value is an error.
ISEVEN	Returns true if the value is even.
ISEXPORTTYPE	Checks whether the current export type matches the specified target type.
ISLOGICAL	Returns true if the value is a logical type.
ISNA	Returns true if the expression has generated the NA error object.
ISNONTEXT	Returns true if the value is not text.
ISNUMBER	Returns true if the value is a number.
ISODD	Returns true if the value is odd.
ISREF	Returns true if the value is a reference.
ISTEXT	Returns true if the value is a text type.
LOOKUP	Looks up an external value. This is the same as the square bracket operator as a result of the field selection (▦) icon.
METADATA	Returns a value from the Meta-Data attributes of the given field.
NA	Returns the error NA, or Not Available.
ROWCOUNT	Returns the current row number of the given group.
VALUE	Converts a text string to a numeric value.

Logical formulas

These functions perform various Boolean logic operations:

Name	Description
AND	If all expressions evaluate to true, returns true; otherwise, returns false. Note that any number of expressions may be AND together.
EQUALS	Returns true if two strings are equal.
FALSE	Returns the Boolean value false.
IF	If the first parameter evaluates to true, returns the second parameter, otherwise returns the third parameter.

Name	Description
IFNA	Returns the first parameter, unless it is an NA, in which case returns the second parameter.
NOT	Returns false if the expression is true, true if the expression is false.
OR	Returns true if any of the expression evaluates to true. Note that any number of expressions may be ORed together.
TRUE	Returns the Boolean value true.
XOR	Returns true if an odd number of expressions evaluate to true.

Mathematical formulas

These functions offer various forms of numeric calculations:

Name	Description
ABS	Returns the absolute value.
ACOS	Returns the arccosine of a number.
ACOSH	Returns the inverse hyperbolic cosine of a number.
ASIN	Returns the arcsine of a number.
ATAN	Returns the arctangent of a number.
ATAN2	Returns the arctangent for the specified coordinates.
AVERAGE	Returns the average value of all the parameters. These values may also be arrays. Each element of an array is evaluated to calculate the average.
AVERAGEA	Returns the average value of all the parameters. These values may also be arrays. Each element of an array is evaluated to calculate the average. Text and logical values are included in the calculation too.
COS	Returns the cosine of a number.
EVEN	Rounds the number up to the nearest even integer.
EXP	Calculates the exponent for basis *e*.
LN	Calculates the natural logarithm of a number.
LOG10	Calculates the base 10 logarithm of a number.

Name	Description
MAX	Returns the maximum value of all the parameters. These values may also be arrays. Each element of an array is evaluated, and the largest value is returned.
MAXA	Returns the maximum value of all the parameters. These values may also be arrays. Each element of an array is evaluated, and the largest value is returned. Text and logical values are included in the calculation too.
MIN	Returns the minimum value of all the parameters. These values may also be arrays. Each element of an array is evaluated, and the smallest value is returned.
MINA	Returns the minimum value of all the parameters. These values may also be arrays. Each element of an array is evaluated, and the smallest value is returned. Text and logical values are included in the calculation too.
MOD	Calculates the remainder of division for *value 1* divided by *value 2*.
N	Returns the number of a value.
ODD	Rounds the number up to the nearest odd integer.
PI	Returns the value of the number pi.
POWER	Computes a number raised to the power by another number.
SIN	Returns the sine of a number.
SQRT	Returns the square root of a number.
SUM	Sums two or more values. These values may also be arrays. Every element of a one or two-dimensional array will be summed together.
SUMA	Sums two or more values. These values may also be arrays. Every element of a one or two-dimensional array will be summed together. Text and logical values are included in the calculation too.
VAR	Calculates the variance based on a sample.

Rounding formulas

These functions offer various forms of numeric calculations:

Name	Description
INT	Rounds a number down to the nearest integer

Text formulas

These functions work with strings and manipulate them:

Name	Description
ARRAYRIGHT	Returns the last element or elements of an array.
ASC	Converts full width to half width ASCII and Katakana characters.
BEGINSWITH	Returns true if a string begins with another string.
CHAR	Converts a code number to a ASCII character or letter.
CLEAN	Removes all non-printable characters from the given text.
CODE	Returns the numeric code for the first character in a text string.
CONCATENATE	Concatenates the text strings.
CONTAINS	Returns true if a string contains another string.
ENDSWIDTH	Returns true if a string ends with another string.
EXACT	Returns true if two text values are exactly equal.
FIND	Returns the index of the first occurrence of the search string in the text, starting at the index specified. The index parameter is optional.
DOLLAR	Rounds up the number to a specified number of decimals and formats the result as a text.
LEFT	Returns the left portion of a string up to length characters.
LEN	Returns the length of the text.
LIKE	Acts like the SQL LIKE function, comparing the first value to a regular expression.
LOWER	Returns the text in all lowercase.

Name	Description
MESSAGE	Formats the values using the given message format.
MID	Returns a substring within the Text, starting at Start and having the length of Length.
PROPER	Returns the input string with the first letter of each word converted to an uppercase.
QUOTETEXT	Quotes a text.
REPLACE	Replaces a portion of the Text, starting at Start and ending at Length, with New text provided.
REPT	Returns the Text Count times. For instance, if the Text was test and the Count was 3, the result would be testtesttest.
RESOURCELOOKUP	Returns the right portion of the string up to Length characters.
RIGHT	Returns the last character or characters of a text.
SEARCH	Looks for a string of text within another (not case sensitive).
STRINGCOUNT	Counts the occurrences of new text in a string.
SUBSTITUTE	Replaces the Old substring with the New substring in Text. If the Which index is provided, only the Nth old substring will be replaced.
T	If the value is of type Text, returns the value, otherwise returns an empty string.
TEXT	Converts the value to Text. Boolean values are converted to true and false.
TRIM	Trims any whitespace at the beginning and end of the text.
UNICHAR	Converts a code number into a unicode character or letter.
UNICODE	Returns the numeric code for the first unicode character in a text string.
UPPER	Returns the text in all uppercase.
URLENCODE	Encodes the text-based on the encoding specified. If no encoding is specified, ISO-8859-1 is used.

User-defined formulas

In this category are all the functions developed with some kind of external contributions:

Name	Description
ARRAYCONCATENATE	Concatenates the arrays.
ARRAYCONTAINS	Checks whether all given values are contained in the array.
ARRAYLEFT	Returns the first element or elements of an array.
ARRAYMIND	Returns a partial array of a given array.
CVSARRAY	Converts a CSV-text into an array.
CVSTEXT	Generates a comma-separated value list. If DoQuoting is set to true, quotes all the strings. By default, the separator is a comma. This can be overridden by setting the Separator parameter. By default, the strings are quoted using a double quote. This can be overridden by setting the Quote parameter.
DRILLDOWN	Creates a drill-down link to another report. This function implements the same as the link (🔗) icon of the formula editor. The user interface of this function is more complex than the others and will enable you to define a drill-down with a URL, a Pentaho repository, or the report itself. Parameters can be passed to the target resource to customize the data.
ENGINEERINGNOTATION	Returns the value in an engineering notation.
MPARAMTERTEXT	Returns a text representing the value suitable for use as multi-selection parameter.
MULTIVALUEQUERY	Returns a single value from the first row of a dataset query.
NORMALIZEARRAY	Converts an array, database, or sequence into a flat array.
NULL	Returns a null value (Deprecated: use NA() instead).
OPENINMANTLETAB	Conditionally generates code to open a URL in a new Mantle tab.
PARAMETERTEXT	Returns a text representing the value suitable for use as a parameter.

Name	Description
PARSEDATE	Converts text into date using `SimpleDateFormat`.
SEQUENCEQUOTER	Converts an array into quoted text for presentation purposes. Do not use this code to construct queries.
SINGLEVALUEQUERY	Returns a single value from the first row of a dataset query.
URLPARAMETERSEPARATOR	Checks whether the given URL fragment contains a parameter `Separator`, and prints either a `?` or a `&`.

Summary

In this chapter, you learned the details involved in report parameterization. You also learned about the various ways to dynamically render a report, including learning all the available functions and expressions, as well as learning the environment variables and the `LibFormula` syntax and function list.

Now that you have read this chapter, you should feel comfortable with all the ways Pentaho Report Designer offers to manage parameters and functions in general (bundled and customized). This is an advanced task in developing complex Pentaho reports and makes you an expert in dealing with complex reports and behaviors.

In the next chapter, you will learn everything about internationalization and localization, to create your Pentaho reports in multi-languages.

9
Internationalization and Localization

After the description of Pentaho Reporting parameterization, functions and expressions, environment variables, and formulas, in this chapter you will learn everything about, internationalization and localization of a Pentaho report. This Pentaho Reporting capability will enable you to manage reports for the best multi-language support, without any dependency on a specific language or alphabet, instead, using a generic approach with labels for texts and strings and some properties to be used for their replacement.

This chapter is written as a reference manual for developers and information technologists. The goal is to share all the relevant and advanced features about internationalization and localization available in Pentaho Report Designer. After reading this chapter, you should feel comfortable with all the ways Pentaho Reporting can enable you to define reports in all the different languages you may need.

Internationalization and localization

As per every modern software, Pentaho Reporting is developed following all the best practices and patterns to support internationalization, so that it can be adapted to various languages, and regions without engineering changes.

Localization is the process of adapting internationalized software for a specific region or language by adding locale-specific components and translating text. Localization (which is potentially performed multiple times, for different locales) uses the infrastructure or flexibility provided by internationalization (which is ideally performed only once, or as an integral part of ongoing development).

This description is mainly a quotation of the Wikipedia definition of internationalization and localization that you can find at `https://en.wikipedia.org/wiki/Internationalization_and_localization`. Even if the description is quite generic, it fits perfectly with Pentaho Reporting being developed as a standard (and modern) Java application.

To internationalize a Pentaho report, you must use the resource elements available within Pentaho Reporting when creating your report. Each resource element defines a resource base and a resource key reference. Normally, the resource base refers to the name of the message properties file in which localized names are kept. The resource key reference is a list of couples (`key` and `value`) where `key` identifies the unique identifier of the content and `value` identifies the content to be presented. The syntax used for the resource key is `key=value`.

For default handling of resource bundles in Java, refer to Java's *i18n* tutorial on resource bundles, at `http://java.sun.com/docs/books/tutorial/i18n/resbundle/concept.html`.

Using resources to localize elements

In Pentaho Report Designer, there are three different elements available to be used for localization: `resource-label`, `resource-field`, and `resource-message`. All of them are available in the report element palette and can be used as usual-by dragging and dropping the element in the chosen place of the right band, directly in the report canvas.

The main idea behind the resource elements is that these kind of elements contain the key value for the resource and not directly the value to show. Once the key value is declared and used in a report element, a property file contains the association key/value and will be used at run time to show the final content to the user.

Using the `resource-label` element within your report allows you to localize labels with static texts. As introduced previously, this element contains the static resource key that will be resolved at runtime using the resource bundles detailed in the following paragraphs.

Using the `resource-field` element within your report allows you to localize dynamic data to a certain extent. Instead of providing a static resource key, this element type specifies the field data source where the key is generated from. For a complete solution to dynamic localization, you may want to investigate using the `Indirect Lookup` function (introduced in `Chapter 8`, *Parameterization, Functions, Variables, and Formulas*), in order to dynamically choose different localized columns in a database for populating a specific dynamic field.

Using the `resource-message` element within your report allows you to localize messages writing multiple datatypes (text, string field, date field, and numeric field) into one object. Also, in this case, this element contains the static resource key that will be resolved at runtime using the resource bundles detailed in the following sections.

Resources for localization

As introduced previously in the chapter, the localization of a Pentaho report requires some resources to resolve the keys declared in the report elements. Starting from the Report Designer user interface, you can access the resources from the upper menu, in **File | Resources...**. Once selected, the **Resource Editor** will appear as shown in the following screenshot:

In few words, the **Resource Editor** is nothing more and nothing less than a manager of property files. By default, it contains the default file (`translations.properties`), but you will soon learn how to add and remove other property files. The property files defined here are part of the Pentaho report and for this reason are stored directly in the `.prpt` file.

Using the buttons on the right, you can create, edit, remove, and even import/export property files. We will not detail the behavior of each button here, because it is supposed to be easy to understand, considering that it is nothing less and nothing more than a well known management of property files.

Instead of this, we would like to discuss how to manage the key/value pairs for a specific resource file. As an example, select the `translations.properties` resource and click on the **Edit** button. Once clicked, the **Edit Property** window is shown, as in the following screenshot:

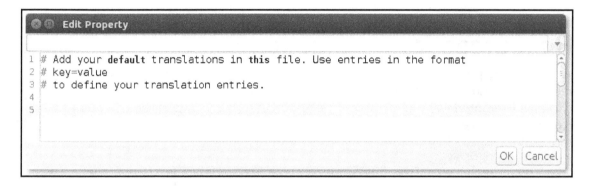

Starting from here, the task is a simple editing of a property file, where you can add, modify, or delete the entries in the format `key=value`. As an example, you can check the following pairs:

```
title=My report
companyName=ACME, Inc.
```

Always double-check the keys you will manage in the resource files. Keys are case sensitive and must be exactly the same as those used into the report elements. If you misspell even a digit, the final content will not be shown and it's always a relevant loss of time to identify these kind of bugs.

Managing resource bundles

To complete the topic about resources for localization, let's give some color to the practical use and impact of the *i18n* management (where *18* stands for the number of letters between the first *i* and the last *n* in the word internationalization).

As described in the Java's *i18n* tutorial on resource bundles, the correct key/value pair to be used in a report is defined by the resource bundle, followed by the language code and the country code. For example, the `translations_en_GB.properties` file contains the resource key reference for English (`en`) in Great Britain (`GB`). You can define generic resource bundles for a specific language and all the countries (in our example, `translations_en.properties`) or all the languages and countries (in our example, `translations.properties`).

 It is highly recommended to define a default resource bundle for all the languages and countries (in our example, `translations.properties`). Then, you can optionally add more resource bundles, specifically for languages and countries. However, be aware that the key/value pairs should be replicated into every resource bundle, otherwise a partial localization will appear to the final user.

Last but not the least, you can localize a Pentaho Report by using external property files. This enables you to share property files among multiple `.prpt` reports. To use external message bundles (the `.properties` files), define the key/value pairs as described previously, but place the bundles on the class path for the Reporting Engine. If you are in Pentaho Report Designer, add the files to the `/resources` directory. For them to be recognized in the Pentaho Analytics Platform, put the files in the `pentaho/WEB-INF/classes` directory.

Testing the localization

After the correct setup of the localization of your Pentaho report, you may want to test it in all the possible languages and countries (in one word, called locale). To achieve that goal, Pentaho Report Designer can be configured to be used with one locale instead of another.

Starting from the Report Designer user interface, you can access the Pentaho Report Designer settings from the upper menu, in **File** | **Configuration...**. Once selected, the report configuration is shown as in the following screenshot.

In the `core-module` settings, you can recognize the `.environment.designtime.Locale` property, not defined with a default value. To set up the requested locale, check the property and fill the text field on the right, that will become editable. Then click the **OK** button and refresh the report to make the configuration active.

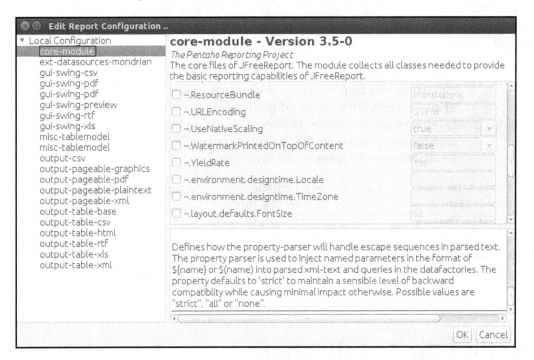

An example of report localization

To see how the localization works in practice, let's develop an example of localized Pentaho Report that you can use in your future tasks. The idea is to reuse a previous example, replacing some static labels with `resource-label`, and see how the report looks in a couple of different languages (we will use English and Spanish as examples).

For this purpose, let's reuse `report_02.prpt` we saw in `Chapter 4`, *Creating a Report with Report Designer*. If you followed the suggestion, you should have the report saved in your `my_report` folder in your development environment. If not, you can download it from the `https://github.com/fcorti/pentaho-8-reporting-for-java-developers` repository, from the `Chapter 04 - Creating a report with Report Designer/my_reports` path.

Once the report is opened in the Report Designer, select the `label: Actuals per position title` element in the **Structure** tab of the report explorer (you can find it under **Master Report | Report Header**). To replace the label with a `resource-label` element, let's click the **Format | Morph | resource-label** item from the upper menu. This feature will transform the type of element, maintaining the same common properties. To complete the task, let's set the `value` property (in the common set) with `report.title`.

In exactly the same way (using the morph feature), change the three labels under **Master Report | Group: DEPARTMENT | Details Body | Details Header**. In case of the position title's header, set the `value` property to `header.positiontitle`. In case of the actual header, set the `value` property to `header.actual`. In case of the budget's header, set the `value` property to `header.budget`.

Now that the report is correctly updated, it's time to set up the resource bundles with the correct key/value pairs. To set up the resources, select **File | Resources...**, and then select `translations.properties` and click on the **Edit** button. Once done, fill the property file with the default values (in our case, in English), described as follows:

```
report.title = Actuals per position title
header.positiontitle = Position title
header.actual = Actual
header.budget = Budget
```

Click on the **OK** button when done. To add a new translation file, press the **Create** button and fill the **Entry Name** field with `translations_es.properties`. After pressing the **OK** button, you will see a new property file will be created with the Spanish locale. Select the new property file and click **Edit**. Once done, fill the property file with the Spanish key/values pairs, described as follows:

```
report.title = Título real por posición
header.positiontitle = Título del puesto
header.actual = Real
header.budget = Presupuesto
```

Disclaimer

I hope Google provided me with the correct translation in Spanish. If not, I apologize in advance to my Spanish friends. It is not my native language, but I thought Spanish would be a good alternative language, considering it is widely used and the Pentaho community is huge in Spanish speaking countries.

Now that the report is correctly localized (in English as default language and in Spanish), let's preview it by clicking on the eye (👁) icon on the toolbar. The following screenshot shows the preview with the default language (English):

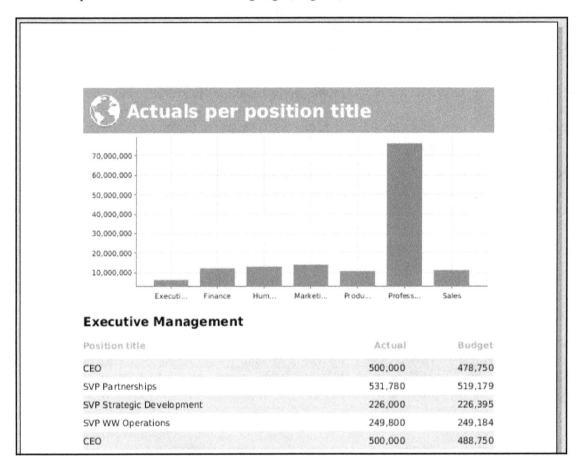

As you can see, the report title and the three header labels for the fields are the same as in the static version. To change the locale, let's click on **File | Configuration...** from the upper menu and check the `.environment.designtime.Locale` property. Once done, fill the right text field with `es` (the *i18n* code for Spanish) and press the **OK** button.

Now that the Report Designer configuration is updated to use the Spanish locale, let's preview the report again by pressing the eye (👁) icon on the toolbar. The following screenshot shows the preview with the Spanish language:

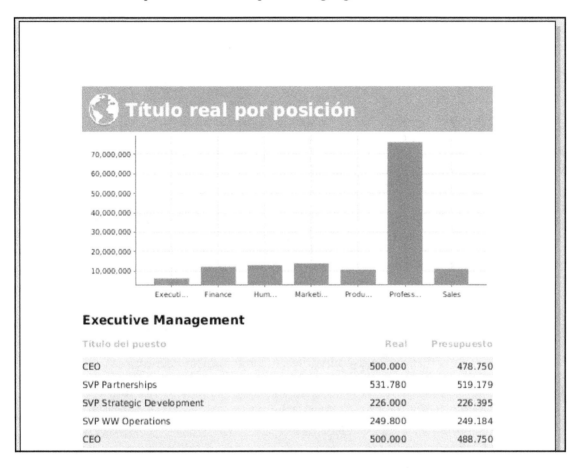

Now it's your turn to deal with it. For example, you could add the localization for French language (fr is the *i18n* code) or play with more detailed countries, like for example, the Spanish for Argentina (es_AR is the *i18n* code), the Spanish for Chile (es_CL is the *i18n* code), and so on.

In the `https://github.com/fcorti/pentaho-8-reporting-for-java-developers` repository, specifically in the `Chapter 09 - Internationalization and localization/my_reports` path, you can find the `report_multilanguage.prpt` report developing exactly the example described here. Feel free to open it with Report Designer and play with settings and parameters to understand how to add and customize internationalization and localization.

Summary

In this chapter, you learnt everything about internationalization and localization using Pentaho Report Designer. You started with the definition of internationalization (and *i18n*) and then you saw what localization means in case of a Pentaho report. To make everything practical, you saw how to include resource elements (`resource-label`, `resource-field`, and `resource-message`) and how to resolve the content using the resource bundles. At last, you also saw how to test the various localizations for your Pentaho report.

To complete the description, for future reference, you also saw how to localize an existing report in English and Spanish (but other translations could be developed in the same way).

Now that you have read this chapter, you should feel comfortable with all the ways Pentaho Report Designer offers to manage internationalization and localization. This is an advanced task in developing complex Pentaho reports and makes you an expert in dealing with complex reports that can be used in different languages and countries.

In the next chapter, you will learn how to add subreports and cross tabs to you Pentaho reports.

10
Subreports and Cross Tabs

In this chapter, you will learn the ins and outs of two advanced reporting topics: subreports and cross tabs. Subreports allow you to embed reusable reports within a master report. As you will see, with the help of examples, subreports can take on many forms, from multi-page detail reports to summary subreports that include charts. As two specific types of subreports, you will learn about table of content element and index element. Along with subreports, you will learn how to incorporate cross tabs in your reports. Cross tabs allow you to compare multiple variables in a single table of data values.

This chapter is written as a reference manual for developers and information technologists. Reading this chapter, you should feel comfortable with all the advanced features of subreports and cross tabs available in Pentaho Report Designer. This is the last chapter dedicated to Report Designer and it covers the last advanced features of this front-end tool of Pentaho Reporting.

Subreports in Pentaho Report Designer

Subreports in Pentaho Reporting may be included in any band of a report, except for the page header and page footer bands. Subreports receive a `DataRow` of parameters, determined by the current state of their parent report when rendering the subreport. These parameters may be used when executing a subreport query or referenced directly in the subreport. Within subreports, you define named queries that may reference the `DataRow` of parameters passed in, allowing a subreport to query only the currently scoped data and not the entire data set available to the parent report.

Subreports may be of any length, may be included in other subreports in a nested fashion, and may also be presented alongside one another in their parent report. When spanning multiple pages, special considerations must be made, including how to handle the master report's page header, page footer, and group headers. This chapter will cover all these topics in the following examples.

Subreport example

In this example, you will build a report which includes a very classical use case scenario: a master-detail report where the master is represented from orders (with order number and date) and detail is represented by a subreport containing products, quantity, and price. To begin with, let's start with an empty report (clicking on the blank report icon (▯) of the Report Designer) and a JDBC data source created as described in Chapter 6, *Configuring JDBC and Other Data Sources*. The JDBC data source is supposed to be defined on the SampleData (Local) connection and the following content:

```
SELECT
  "PUBLIC"."ORDERS"."ORDERNUMBER",
  "PUBLIC"."ORDERS"."ORDERDATE"
FROM
  "PUBLIC"."ORDERS"
```

From here, drag the ORDERNUMBER and ORDERDATE fields and drop them into the Details band of the empty report. Change ORDERNUMBER style to bold and stretch ORDERDATE to cover the remaining width of the page.

Till now, nothing is really different from what you learnt in the previous chapters. Let's now add a subreport representing the details of the order. To add the subreport, drag the subreport icon (▦) from the element palette and drop it below the fields, in the Details band. Once dropped, a modal window will open with the question: do you want to include an inline-subreport or a banded-subreport? Choose an inline-subreport if you want to cover a customizable rectangular area to put the content inside or choose the banded-subreport if you want to place the content in sub-band included in the report's band. Click on the **Inline** button and another tab with a subreport icon (▦) will open, similar to a brand new report.

The new tab contains the subreport and it's really a new report inside the master report. The subreport is made of data sources, layout, elements, and everything you have seen until now while reading this book. Being a real report, a window asks you to specify the data source. In our example, will will create a brand new JDBC data source, using the SampleData (Local) connection and the following query. To create the data source, press the well-known plus green icon (⊕) and follow the same path as described in Chapter 6, *Configuring JDBC and Other Data Sources*.

```
SELECT
  "PUBLIC"."ORDERDETAILS"."PRODUCTCODE",
  "PUBLIC"."ORDERDETAILS"."QUANTITYORDERED",
  "PUBLIC"."ORDERDETAILS"."PRICEEACH"
FROM
  "PUBLIC"."ORDERDETAILS"
WHERE
  "PUBLIC"."ORDERDETAILS"."ORDERNUMBER" = ${ORDERNUMBER}
ORDER BY
  "PUBLIC"."ORDERDETAILS"."ORDERLINENUMBER" ASC
```

Before defining the content of the subreport, go back the master report (click on the report tab in the report canvas) and move the subreport element immediately under the ORDERDATE field. Stretch it to cover the entire width of the ORDERDATE element, until the right edge of the page.

Back to the subreport tab, drag the three fields and drop them into the Details band of the empty subreport. First, place the QUANTITYORDERED and PRICEEACH fields on the right of the band and then place the PRODUCTCODE field on the left, stretching it to cover the entire free space.

Lastly, let's manage the ORDERNUMBER parameter used in the subreport or, more precisely, used in the subreport's data source. With this example of use of the subreport in the Details band of the report, each subreport instance depends by one order in particular. To pass the order number from the master report to the subreport, a parameter must be configured.

As you learnt in Chapter 8, *Parameterization, Functions, Variables, and Formulas*, the report parameters live in the report explorer, in particular, in the **Data** tab. Also, in case of subreports, the parameters can be managed from the same place, with two main differences. The first difference is that the subreport parameters are always used to move values from/to the master report and not asked to the user. The second difference is that the subreport parameters are grouped in import parameters and export parameters. As you can expect, import parameters are used to pass values from the master report to the subreport, and export parameters are used to pass values from the subreport to the master report.

In our example, you need an import a parameter to use the ORDERNUMBER values in the subreport. To define the parameter, right click on the Parameters item in report explorer and fill the **Import Parameter** section, as described in the following screenshot. To add the new input parameter, click on the green plus icon (●) and fill **Outer Name** with the name of the field in the master-report. Use **Inner Name** to name the local parameter in the subreport (in our case, we are going to use the same name for both).

Now that the master-report and the subreport are defined, the Details band of your report should look like the following screenshot:

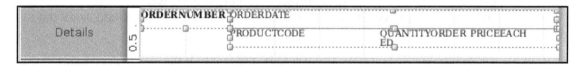

If you are repeating the exercise of creating the report in your development environment, you can see that the available space in the subreport is reduced. Indeed, you cannot drop the element on the left side of the bands, and this space has a grey background with a white grid. This means that the width of the subreport in the master report does not cover the entire page width and only the right portion of the bands can be used. If you go into the master report and enlarge (or reduce) the width of the subreport element, you will see the subreport will be enlarged (or reduced) accordingly. Have this in mind when you use the subreports, because it will affect the available space you will be able to fill with elements.

Click the eye icon (⊙) in the report canvas and the resulting report should look like the following screenshot:

10,100	Mon Jan 06 00:00:00 CET 2003		
	S24_3969	49	34
	S18_2248	50	68
	S18_1749	30	172
	S18_4409	22	87
10,101	Thu Jan 09 00:00:00 CET 2003		
	S18_2795	26	145
	S24_2022	46	54
	S24_1937	45	31
	S18_2325	25	151
10,102	Fri Jan 10 00:00:00 CET 2003		
	S18_1367	41	50
	S18_1342	39	123
10,103	Wed Jan 29 00:00:00 CET 2003		
	S24_2300	36	102
	S18_2432	22	54
	S32_1268	31	104
	S10_4962	42	129

In the `https://github.com/fcorti/pentaho-8-reporting-for-java-developers` repository, more precisely, in the `Chapter 10 - Sub-reports and cross tabs/my_reports` path, you can find the `subreport.prpt` report developing exactly the example described here. Feel free to open it with Report Designer and play with settings and parameters.

Other subreport examples

Before leaving the subreport examples, let's list some use cases where subreports can help a lot; the intention here is to share a practical reference, not an exhaustive and final list:

- **Details in a report**: The first and an easy example of subreport is a portion of the space of the report where some details about an entity are presented. As an example, you can think about the sender of a letter or the company details in an invoice.

- **Multi-page subreports**: Quite similar to the example described earlier, you can think about a report that includes a large subreport that may span multiple pages. As an example, you can think about a catalog of products or an inventory list. In this case, the subreport will be defined in the `Report Header` band instead of the `Details` band, but everything else would work in exactly the same way as you saw here. The difference is that the data source in the subreport could retrieve a long list of data, that may span multiple pages.

- **Chart subreports**: There are no limitations to the elements you can use in subreports. For example, you can use a chart, having an appealing result.

- **Side by side subreports**: Another capability of subreports is to be able to place two or more subreports horizontally, beside one another, within a report band. Using this capability, you can specialize subreports with dedicated data sources, extracting data from different tables or sources (not necessarily one source only).

- **Multiple subreports**: There are no limitations to the number of subreports that you can use. Combining the examples shared in this section, you can create very complex reports with a modular approach. This approach can be suggested if you have to develop changes after a long period of time or in a team with different developers.

 As you are learning here, subreports are very powerful, but there is a disadvantage that you should be aware of: subreports can be very expensive in terms of consuming resources. Do not abuse their use.

Table of contents and index elements

There are two special types of subreports not explained yet: table of contents and index. The **table of content** (**TOC**) feature allows you to generate a TOC based on the groups you have mapped inside the report or to specify the subreports you want included in your TOC. The index feature allows you to generate an index based on the fields (or groups) in your report. When the index is generated, it displays the instances and page numbers in which the field name appears.

Example of index

As an example, let's see how to include the index to an existing report, of course assuming the report is *big*, defined by a lot of pages (otherwise, the index doesn't make a lot of sense). The report used to add the index is a basic report, built on a JDBC data source with the following query:

```
SELECT
  "PUBLIC"."ORDERFACT"."ORDERDATE",
  "PUBLIC"."ORDERFACT"."ORDERNUMBER",
  "PUBLIC"."CUSTOMERS"."CUSTOMERNAME",
  "PUBLIC"."ORDERFACT"."TOTALPRICE"
FROM
  "PUBLIC"."CUSTOMERS" INNER JOIN "PUBLIC"."ORDERFACT" ON
"PUBLIC"."CUSTOMERS"."CUSTOMERNUMBER" =
"PUBLIC"."ORDERFACT"."CUSTOMERNUMBER"
ORDER BY
  "PUBLIC"."ORDERFACT"."ORDERDATE" ASC
```

Talking about the layout, the `Details` band defined for the basic report is developed as shown in the following screenshot:

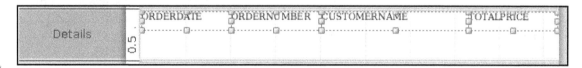

Previewing the report by using the eye icon (👁) in the report canvas, you can see that it is defined by 97 pages. The goal of this example is to add an index at the end of the report, referring to all the customers.

To add the index, drag the index icon (🖹) from the report palette and drop it into the `Report Footer` band. Once dropped, the same question that you saw for the subreport will be raised: do you want to define an inline-subreport or a banded-subreport? In case of index and TOC, the use of a banded subreport is suggested, as it will use 100 percent of the report page width.

Once selected, point to the element properties panel and set the `data-field` property in the index to `CUSTOMERNAME`. This instructs Report Designer to build the index on the customer name. When you double-click on the index element, another tab, containing the index subreport, will open. Here, exactly as you saw for subreports, you have a fully featured layout with only one specific difference in the data source.

Looking at the **Data** tab in the report explorer, the default data source is called `design-time-data` and it's defined as the `Table` type. This specific data source is automatically defined for the index element (and the TOC element too, with few differences in the fields) to be used in the index definition. The following screenshot shows how the data source looks:

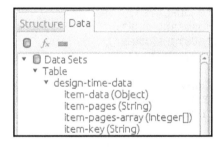

Use the `item-data` and `item-pages` fields to generate the index data field name and page numbers.

To build your own index, drag the fields and drop them in the report bands, exactly in the same way as you learnt in the previous chapters. In our case, we would like to also add a title using a `label` element; the index layout is defined as shown in the following screenshot:

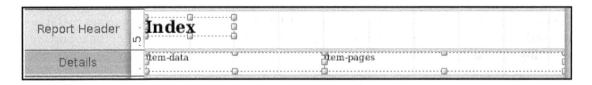

Now that the master-report and the index are defined, let's preview it by pressing the eye icon (👁) in the report canvas. In the following screenshot, you can see the final result of the page number 97, where the index starts. As you can see, customer called **AV Stores, Co.** is quoted in pages 4, 60, 61, 69, and 70, the customer called **Alpha Cognac** is quoted in pages 10, 24, and 87, and so on.

Index

AV Stores, Co.	4.60.61.69.70
Alpha Cognac	10.24.87
Amica Models & Co.	53.57.58
Anna's Decorations, Ltd	14.21.79.80.85.86
Atelier graphique	7.59.73
Australian Collectables, Ltd	29.49.91
Australian Collectors, Co.	6.8.38.71.72.73
Australian Gift Network, Co	15.23.81
Auto Associés & Cie.	36.59.60
Auto Canal+ Petit	35.45.88.89

In the `https://github.com/fcorti/pentaho-8-reporting-for-java-developers` repository, more precisely, in the `Chapter 10 - Subreports and cross tabs/my_reports` path, you can find the `example_of_index.prpt` report developing exactly the example described here. Feel free to open it with Report Designer and play with settings and layout.

Cross tabs in Pentaho Report Designer

A cross tabulation (or cross tab) allows you to view dimensional data in a report. Using cross tabs, you can easily view two or more fields and how they relate based on a measure. Cross tabs summarize the information in your database and they lay out in a grid, with rows representing dimensions (for example, country, date, or salesperson), columns representing another dimensions, and the intersection containing the aggregations (usually sums). Cross tabs are similar to pivot tables in Microsoft Excel.

Pentaho Reporting offers the ability to create cross tab based reports. These are special type of reports that render differently than most standard reports. These reports also expect the data to be in a particular format. Cross tab reports can be driven by multidimensional queries (as highlighted in Chapter 6, *Configuring JDBC and Other Data Sources*, Pentaho Reporting offers a Mondrian and OLAP4j data source for providing multidimensional data to a report), or SQL queries can be used, if the structure of the columns/rows is MDX-like.

Cross tab examples

As a couple of examples, let's show two basic reports using cross tabs: the first using an MDX query showing sales per year and market, and the second using a SQL query showing actual, budget, and variance per region and department. To show a different type of cross tab report, the second example will show multiple measures.

To begin with the first example, using the MDX query, let's start with an empty report (click on the blank report icon (🗋) in the Report Designer) and a Pentaho Analysis data source created as described in Chapter 6, *Configuring JDBC and Other Data Sources*. The Pentaho Analysis data source is supposed to be defined on the steelwheel.mondrian.xml file, bundled in the Pentaho Reporting Designer distribution (in the <report-designer>/samples folder), the SteelWheels logical schema, and the SampleData (Local) JDBC connection. Following is the MDX query to edit in the Static Query field:

```
SELECT
  CrossJoin([Markets].Children, [Time].Children) ON ROWS,
  [Measures].[Sales] ON COLUMNS
FROM
  [SteelWheelsSales]
```

Once done, point on the `Master Report` element in the **Structure** tab of report explorer. In particular, right-click on the `Master Report` element and select the **Add Crosstab** item, as shown in the following screenshot:

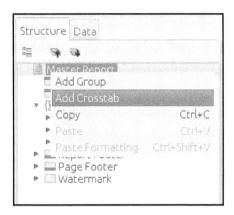

After clicking the item, a cross tab wizard will be shown, as in the next screenshot. Fill in the fields, paying attention to changes the **Aggregation** function to `Sum` for `[Measures].[Sales]`:

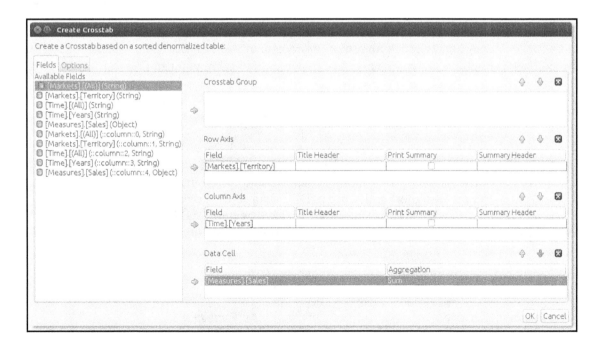

After pressing the **OK** button, you will see that a new band is added to the report layout: the new band is called `Crosstab`. In the `Crosstab` band, you can find all the elements defining the cross tab, very similar to the regular ones introduced in the previous chapters. From there, you can work on the layout (for example, formatting the numbers, highlighting the titles, and so on), exactly in the same way as you learned in the previous chapters.

At this stage, the report is ready in a very simple and basic version, so you can click the eye icon (👁) in the report canvas to get the preview. The following screenshot shows how the preview looks:

[Markets].[Territory]	[Time].[Years] 2003 [Measures].[Sales]	[Time].[Years] 2004 [Measures].[Sales]	[Time].[Years] 2005 [Measures].[Sales]
#null	0	0	0
APAC	343081.6200000002	601606.0900000001	337018.1799999999
EMEA	1681987.4600000007	2396407.8699999973	929828.9900000002
Japan	292557.54000000004	168479.1	42920.939999999995
NA	1359757.3799999992	1821246.7799999984	671057.23

In the `https://github.com/fcorti/pentaho-8-reporting-for-java-developers` repository, more precisely, in the `Chapter 10 - Subreports and cross tabs/my_reports` path, you can find the `crosstab_mdx_datasource.prpt` report developing exactly the example described here. If you use this report, be aware that you will have to update the data source to point to the right path containing the `steelwheel.mondrian.xml` file.

As another example, let's develop a similar report using an SQL query instead of an MDX query. To begin with this second example, create an empty report (click on the blank report icon (◻) of the Report Designer) and setup a JDBC data source, created as described in Chapter 6, *Configuring JDBC and Other Data Sources*. The JDBC data source is supposed to be defined on the `SampleData (Local)` connection with the following query:

```
SELECT
  "PUBLIC"."QUADRANT_ACTUALS"."REGION",
  "PUBLIC"."QUADRANT_ACTUALS"."DEPARTMENT",
  SUM("PUBLIC"."QUADRANT_ACTUALS"."ACTUAL") AS "ACTUAL",
  SUM("PUBLIC"."QUADRANT_ACTUALS"."BUDGET") AS "BUDGET",
  SUM("PUBLIC"."QUADRANT_ACTUALS"."VARIANCE") AS "VARIANCE"
FROM
  "PUBLIC"."QUADRANT_ACTUALS"
```

```
GROUP BY
  "PUBLIC"."QUADRANT_ACTUALS"."REGION",
  "PUBLIC"."QUADRANT_ACTUALS"."DEPARTMENT"
```

Once done, point on the `Master Report` element in the **Structure** tab of report explorer. In particular, right click on the `Master Report` element and select the **Add Crosstab** item. After clicking the item, a cross tab wizard will be shown, as in the following screenshot. Fill in the fields, paying attention to change the **Aggregation** function to `Sum` for `ACTUAL`, `BUDGET`, and `VARIANCE`:

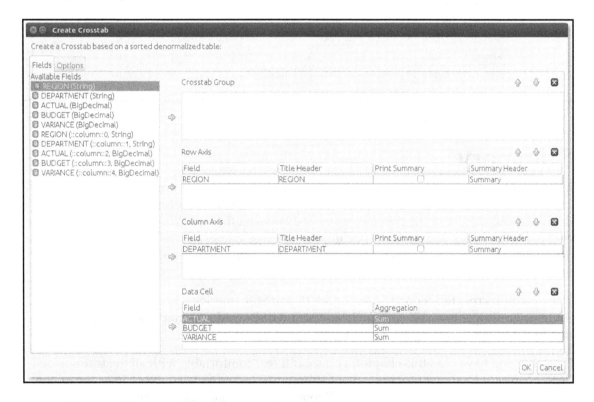

In the `https://github.com/fcorti/pentaho-8-reporting-for-java-developers` **repository**, more precisely, in the `Chapter 10 - Sub-reports and cross tabs/my_reports` path, you can find the `crosstab_sql_datasource.prpt` report developing exactly the example described here. Feel free to open it with Report Designer and play with settings and parameters.

The following screenshot shows the preview after clicking the eye icon (👁) in the report canvas:

| | DEPARTMENT Executive Management | | | DEPARTMENT Finance | | | DEPARTMENT Human |
REGIONAL	ACTUAL	BUDGET	VARIANCE	ACTUAL	BUDGET	VARIANCE	ACTUAL
Central	1776282.0 0	2043642.0 0	267360.00	3106680.0 0	3067361.0 0	-39319.00	3438863.0 0 0
Eastern	1507580.0 0	1483508.0 0	-24072.00	3039180.0 0	3010015.0 0	-29165.00	3212200.0 0 0
Southern	1507580.0 0	1523508.0 0	15928.00	3039180.0 0	3010015.0 0	-29165.00	3212200.0 0 0
Western	1507580.0 0	1443508.0 0	-64072.00	3039180.0 0	3000015.0 0	-39165.00	3212200.0 0 0

Summary

In this chapter, you built from scratch examples of subreports and cross tabs, exploring the capabilities offered by Pentaho Reporting. You built a master-detail subreport, which demonstrated the use of the parameters passed between the two. You also built a subreport containing the index of data (in our example, customer names). To have a reference for your future developments, you also read about a list of possible uses of subreports in advanced practical cases.

You also built cross tab reports based on MDX and SQL queries. These cross tab reports contained multiple row and column headers, and displayed summary data regarding sales numbers and actuals, budget, and variance.

Now that you have read this chapter, you should feel comfortable with all the features of Pentaho Report Designer (not only about subreports and cross tabs). From here ahead, the book will continue discovering Pentaho Reporting SDK from a development perspective. If you are a developer or an information technologist, now you are ready to start using Pentaho Report Designer and deal with complex reports and use cases.

As a developer, you should continue to read the rest of the book to learn more about how to develop and embed Pentaho Reporting Engine in your Java applications. If you are an information technologist, you can decide to stop here or try the adventure in the technical discovery of the Pentaho Reporting capabilities.

11

The PRPT Format and the Java API to Build It

This chapter is the first one entirely dedicated to the technical and advanced features of Pentaho Reporting. In the previous chapters of the book, you learnt everything about Pentaho Report Designer, and starting from here, you start to face the development using the Pentaho Reporting SDK.

In this chapter, you will learn about Pentaho Reporting's `.prpt` bundle file format, along with the details of Pentaho Reporting's Java API. You will be introduced to the schemas of the various XML files that persist the data source, parameters, expressions, layout, and style of a report.

With examples of Pentaho's Java API, you will learn how easy it is to build a report programmatically. You will walk through a complete example that demonstrates how to create different reporting bands, as well as different elements, within a report.

This chapter is highly technical and written as a tutorial for pure Java developers. At the end of this chapter, you will feel comfortable with the `.prpt` format, along with the basics around programmatically creating a Pentaho report. Later chapters will assume that you will be able to manage the content explained here, so read carefully and be sure you are confident with all the concepts explained.

Understanding the serialized report format

In the previous chapters, you have already seen the format of Pentaho reports, saved as `.prpt` bundle files. The `.prpt` format is a ZIP file format that includes all the necessary resources to render a report, also referred to as a bundle. The `.prpt` bundle file contains a set of XML files that are crucial to render a report, as well as additional resources, such as embedded images and subreports. This format is based on the OpenDocument format.

This section goes into detail about each of the primary files that make up a report, along with providing a simple example of a report written by hand. With the knowledge of the underlying file format, it is possible to generate reports outside of the Java environment.

Anatomy of a .prpt bundle file

To share the exact details of a `.prpt` bundle file, let's start with a concrete example. Feel free to choose a Pentaho report, randomly chosen from the ones that you already have in your development environment, or one downloaded from the `https://github.com/fcorti/pentaho-8-reporting-for-java-developers` repository.

Once the `.prpt` bundle file is chosen, unzip it as a regular compressed archive and you will see the following files and folders included (some files and folders are optional and really depend on the complexity of the report):

Name	Description
datasources	Folder containing `compound-ds.xml` and one file for each data source. For example, `sql-ds.xml` containing a JDBC data source, `mondrian-ds.xml` an Mondrian data source, and so on.
META-INF	Folder containing `manifest.xml`. The manifest file contains a reference to all the content files in the package.
resources	Folder containing the resources like images, and so on, included in the report definition.
subreport, ..., subreportN	Folders containing the defined subreports. One subfolder is created for each subreport, with the same content as the master report and a subset of files and folders included.
content.xml	This file remains intentionally empty. It can be used to inject global templates later.

Name	Description
`datadefinition.xml`	Contains the definitions of data sources (pointing to `compound-ds.xml` in the `datasources` folder), functions and expressions, and parameters.
`dataschema.xml`	May contain additional metadata used to increase the richness of a data source.
`layout.xml`	Defines the primary structure of report bands and elements.
`meta.xml`	This file is part of the OpenDocument standard, and contains information about the `.prpt` bundle file.
`mimetype`	It is a simple text file that contains the MIME type of the `.prpt` bundle file with value `application/vnd.pentaho.reporting.classic`.
`settings.xml`	Contains global configuration properties for a report, as well as a placeholder for future runtime information.
`styles.xml`	Defines what page format the report should be rendered as, style rules that dictate how a report should be rendered, global layout processors, a report watermark, and finally the page header and footer sections of a report.
`translation.properties,` ...	Localization files. See `Chapter 9`, *Internationalization and Localization* for further details. The content of the files is exactly the same as those you saw in the chapter dedicated to internationalization and localization.
`wizard-specification.xml`	Contains the data specified during the report definition, in case of use of the report wizard. The file is not defined if the report is not created using the report wizard.

In the following sections, you can read about the specific composition of each relevant file or folder. If a file (or a folder) is not covered or described enough, don't worry; take a look at an existing `.prpt` bundle file to understand its composition. The XML format is self-explanatory and the tags are verbose enough to be clear to the developers.

The description of the anatomy of a .prpt bundle file is relevant for two main reasons: firstly, so you can deeply understand the definition of the .prpt format, and secondly, so you can manually modify the .prpt bundle file without using Pentaho Report Designer. Of course, we are not saying that you should manually write a .prpt bundle file, but it's clear that by knowing the format in detail, you will have full control of your Pentaho reports.

The datadefintion.xml file and datasources folder

The datadefinition.xml file contains information about report input parameters and the report data source, as well as report functions and expressions. The root element in this XML file is data-definition, and uses the (http://reporting.pentaho.org/namespaces/engine/classic/bundle/data/1.0) namespace for XML validation.

Parameters

Parameters are defined as children of the data-definition/parameter-definition elements. There are two types of parameters: plain parameters and list parameters. Plain parameters are represented in XML as a plain-parameter element. Plain parameters define the following attributes:

Name	Description
default-value	The default value of the parameter
mandatory	If set to true, a value for this parameter is required before the report is rendered
name	The parameter name
type	The fully qualified Java type of the parameter

List parameters are represented in XML as a `list-parameter` element. In addition to sharing the same attributes as the plain parameter, list parameters also define the following attributes:

Name	Description
query	The query name providing the list of values to choose from.
allow-multi-selection	If set to true, this attribute allows multiple selections of parameter values from the query results, creating an array of objects versus a single object.
key-column	The key column is returned as the result within a row that was selected.
mandatory	If true, the parameter is mandatory.
strict-values	If set to true, validation is done on the parameter value to determine if it is part of the query results.
value-column	The value column is displayed as the selection when presenting data to the user. The `value-formula` attribute may be used in place of `value-column`.
value-formula	The value formula is displayed as the selection when presenting data to the user. The `value-column` attribute may be used in place of `value-formula`.

Subreports define a different XML element hierarchy for their parameters. In the context of a subreport, a parameter is passed in from the master report's context versus user or system input. Instead of using the `parameter-definition` element as a parent, subreports use a `parameter-mapping` element. Two subreport parameter types are defined: import and export. Their XML element tags are `import-parameter` and `export-parameter`. They both define the following two attributes:

Name	Description
alias	The alias of the parameter. For imported parameters, this is the name in the subreport. For exported parameters, this is the name in the master report.
name	The name of the parameter. For imported parameters, this is the name in the master report. For exported parameters, this is the name in the subreport.

Data source reference

A single reference to the report's data source is specified in the `datadefinition.xml` file, as a `data-definition/data-source` XML element. If multiple data sources are used in a single report, you must use a compound data source that combines different data sources. The `data-source` XML element defines the following attributes:

Name	Description
report-query	The named query used by the master report
limit	If specified, defines the limit of the number of rows returned by the primary query of the report
timeout	If specified, defines the query timeout for the primary query of the report
ref	A reference to the specified data source definition file

Functions and expressions

Every function and expression defined in a report is represented by an `expression` XML element. Expression elements have the following five attributes:

Name	Description
name	The name of the function or expression.
class	The class type of the function or expression. This is not required if specifying a formula.
deplevel	The dependency level of the function or expression, which determines the order of execution.
formula	If specified, defines a formula for execution.
initial	If specified, defines a formula for initial execution.

Expressions may also contain properties. These properties appear in the `properties` XML element as child property elements. Each `property` XML element contains the following attributes:

Name	Description
`name`	The name of the property
`class`	The class type of the property

Finally, each `property` XML element contains a text node with the value of the property.

Datasources folder

For each data source defined in a report, a data source file is created with the necessary information to connect to. Usually, these kind of files are stored in the `datasources` folder in the `.prpt` bundle file. Defining every data source file is out of scope for this chapter, but try to develop a sample report and then check the specific `.prpt` bundle file as an example.

As mentioned earlier, a compound data source is often used to refer to multiple data sources in a single report. For each data source type, there is an equivalent XML format. These formats are documented in their XML schema files, which are accessible when downloading the source distribution of the reporting engine and extensions.

layout.xml file

The `layout.xml` file defines the primary structure of report bands and elements. Each band is represented as an XML element, and each band's elements are contained in the band. Multiple XML namespaces are used in the context of the layout XML document. The primary namespaces include:

- `core`: This defines core elements and attributes
- `layout`: This defines the majority of the elements in this document
- `styles`: This define inline styles

The `styles` namespace will be discussed in more detail in the `styles.xml` section that will follow. The `core` namespace document is located at `http://reporting.pentaho.org/namespaces/engine/attributes/core`. The `layout` namespace, which is specified as the default namespace for this document, is located at `http://reporting.pentaho.org/namespaces/engine/classic/bundle/layout/1.0`.

The layout XML document contains a root layout XML element. This element contains root level band information. The `layout` element may contain attributes defining report level metadata, such as the title of the report. The following child XML elements may be specified in the layout element:

Name	Description
preprocessor	Any number of `preprocessor` elements may be defined in the report layout element. Preprocessors contain a `class` attribute that specifies the fully qualified `preprocessor` Java class and may contain the `property` elements for the preprocessor. Preprocessors may manipulate a report before it is rendered.
layout-processors	Certain functions that manipulate the layout of elements may appear in the `layout-processors` element of the layout document. For instance, `ItemHideFunction` is considered a layout processor, so if defined, it will be serialized in this portion of the document.
report-header	The `report-header` element specifies the layout of the report header. This element contains a child element titled `root-level-content`, which contains all references to child elements. Note that `report-header` is a report element. Therefore, it may contain general element attributes and child elements, defined later in the *Report elements* section of this chapter.
group	The `group` element defines the entire hierarchy of groups and detail bands defined in a report. This element hierarchy is defined in more detail in the *Group and detail band hierarchy* section of this chapter.

Name	Description
report-footer	The report-footer element specifies the layout of the report footer. This element contains a child element titled root-level-content, which contains all references to child elements. Note that report-footer is a report element. Therefore, it may contain general element attributes and child elements, defined later in the *Report elements* section of this chapter.

Also note that the report itself is represented as a report element. Therefore, in addition to the attributes and child elements defined previously, the report may also contain attributes and elements defined in report elements (these are covered later in the *Report elements* section of this chapter).

Group and detail band hierarchy

A group may contain either a group-body or data-body child XML element. A group-body contains the XML element group, used to represent a hierarchy of groupings. In addition to containing group-body or data-body, a group XML element may also contain the group-header and group-footer XML elements. The group-header and group-footer XML elements may contain a root-level-content XML element, which contains child layout elements.

The data-body XML element contains the bands relevant to row level data in your report. This XML element may contain detail-header, details, no-data, and details-footer child XML elements. Each of these elements may contain a root-level-content XML element, which contains child layout elements.

Report elements

Each report element defined in the previous chapters is represented in XML, defining its properties, as well as where it is located within a band. The most common elements are highlighted here.

All elements define the `style:element-style` child XML element, which contains styling information for the individual element. The most common style element is `style:spatial-styles`, which defines where in the band the element is located, as well as what size it should render as:

```
<style:element-style>
  <style:spatial-styles x="20" y="240" min-width="100" min-height="20"/>
</style:element-style>
```

The following is a list of some of the primary report elements, along with specific details on creating them:

Name	Description
label	The `label` XML element renders a label. This element contains a `core:value` child element, which uses XML text for the label value.
text-field	The `text-field` XML element renders a text field. This element contains a `core:field` attribute, which defines the field to render.
number-field	The `number-field` XML element renders a number field. This element contains a `core:field` attribute, which defines the field to render, as well as a `core:format-string` attribute, which defines the number format string to render.
date-field	The `date-field` XML element renders a date field. This element contains a `core:field` attribute, which defines the field to render, as well as a `core:format-string` attribute, which defines the date format string to render.
message	The `message` XML element renders a message. This element contains a `core:value` child element.
resource-label	The `resource-label` XML element renders a resource label. This element contains a `core:resource-identifier` attribute referencing the message bundle, as well as a `core:value` attribute, which specifies the key to use in the bundle.
resource-field	The `resource-field` XML element renders a resource field. This element contains a `core:resource-identifier` attribute referencing the message bundle, as well as a `core:field` attribute, which specifies the field that is used to determine the key to be resolved.

Name	Description
resource-message	The `resource-message` XML element renders a resource message. This element contains a `core:resource-identifier` attribute referencing the message bundle, as well as a `core:value` attribute, which specifies the message.
rectangle	The `rectangle` XML element renders a rectangle. The size of the rectangle is determined by the `style:spatial-sizes` element defined earlier. A `style:content-styles` XML element may be defined, which specifies attributes such as the Boolean attributes `draw-shape` and `fill-shape`, as well as color attributes such as `fill-color`. Colors are represented in RGB hexadecimal notation, for instance `#ff3333`.
horizontal-line	The `horizontal-line` XML element renders a horizontal line. The length of the line is determined by the `style:spatial-sizes` XML element defined earlier. A `style:content-styles` XML element is defined to specify the line style and color.
vertical-line	The `vertical-line` XML element renders a vertical line. The length of the line is determined by the `style:spatial-sizes` XML element defined earlier. A `style:content-styles` XML element is defined to specify the line style and color.
sub-report	A `sub-report` XML element renders a subreport. The attribute `href` specifies where the subreport is located in the `.prpt` bundle. This XML element may also contain information about its location and style via the `style:element-style` child XML element, as well as input and output parameter mappings via the `input-parameter` and `output-parameter` XML elements. These mappings are configured with the `master-fieldname` and `detail-fieldname` attributes.
content	A `content` XML element renders an image. The location of the image binary is determined by the `core:value` XML element. The scale and aspect ratio properties for a `content` element may be customized by specifying a `style:content-styles` element, with the attributes `scale` and `keep-aspect-ratio`.

Name	Description
content-field	A content-field XML element renders a dynamic image-based on a field. The location of the dynamic content to render is determined by the core:field XML element. The scale and aspect ratio properties for a content-field element may be customized by specifying a style:content-styles element, with the attributes scale and keep-aspect-ratio.

Additional report element types are defined in Pentaho Reporting. Those listed in the table are the most common elements, along with some of their primary properties and styles.

settings.xml file

The settings.xml file contains global configuration properties for a report, as well as a placeholder for future runtime information.

One example of a configuration setting is related to the execution of formula expressions. If you set the property org.pentaho.reporting.engine.classic.core.function.LogFormulaFailureCause to true, and you have your Log4j logging set to debug, you will receive a stack trace, in addition to an error message, when the formula fails.

Additional configuration properties are available, primarily for use in design tools such as Pentaho Report Designer. Rarely would you need to define a configuration property while generating a report.

styles.xml file

The styles.xml file defines what page format the report should be rendered as, style rules that dictate how a report should be rendered, global layout processors, a report watermark, and finally the page header and footer sections of a report.

The `styles.xml` file contains the `style` root XML element, and includes namespaces relevant to rendering styles, including the `core` and `layout` namespaces defined earlier, as well as the `style` namespace as the default namespace, which is located at `http://reporting.pentaho.org/namespaces/engine/classic/bundle/style/1.0`. The following child elements may be specified in the `style` XML element:

Name	Description
`page-definition`	The `page-definition` XML element contains attributes defining the report's page properties. The attribute `pageformat` specifies the page format type. The attributes `horizontal-span` and `vertical-span` define how many pages a report should span across. The `width` and `height` attributes define the width and height of the paper. The `orientation` attribute defines whether the page should be laid out as portrait, landscape, or reverse-landscape. The attributes `margin-top`, `margin-left`, `margin-bottom`, and `margin-right` define the margin values for the report.
`style-rule`	Multiple `style-rules` may be defined in the report. A style rule has the `name` and `parent` attributes, which define the inheritance tree of a group of styles. Within the `style-rule`, style elements such as `text-styles` and `spatial-styles` are defined, which contain specific styling information.
`layout:layout-processors`	Certain functions that manipulate the layout of the entire report may appear in the `layout-processors` section of the styles document.
`layout:watermark`	The `watermark` XML element is rendered in the background, behind other bands in a report. This element contains a child element titled `root- level-content`, which contains all references to child elements. Note that `watermark` is a report element, so it may contain general element attributes and child elements as defined earlier.
`layout:page-header`	The `page-header` XML element defines the contents of the header for each page. This element contains a child element titled `root-level-content`, which contains all references to child elements. Note that `page-header` is a report element, so it may contain general element attributes and child elements, defined earlier.

Name	Description
layout:page-footer	The page-footer XML element defines the contents of the footer for each page. This element contains a child element titled root-level-content, which contains all references to child elements. Note that page-footer is a report element, so it may contain general element attributes and child elements, defined earlier.

Manual creation of a .prpt bundle file

Now that you have learned about all the different files that make up a .prpt bundle file, let's see how to create it manually. Instead of putting here all the content of the mandatory files require to compose a .prpt bundle file, let's use the https://github.com/fcorti/pentaho-8-reporting-for-java-developers repository; specifically, let's use the folder stored in Chapter 11 - The PRPT format and the Java API to build it/my_reports/uncompressed_prpt.

Take your time to examine the folder structure and each file contained in it. All together, they define a very simple report with a JDBC data source and few elements.

Once the folder structure is identified, select all the files included in it and compress them according to your operating system (using the .zip format). Save the resulting file with the name example_xml.prpt. Now, open the example_xml.prpt file in Pentaho Report Designer and click the eye icon ( ) to preview it. You should see a report that looks like the following:

10,100	Mon Jan 06 00:00:00 CET 2003	Shipped
10,101	Thu Jan 09 00:00:00 CET 2003	Shipped
10,102	Fri Jan 10 00:00:00 CET 2003	Shipped
10,103	Wed Jan 29 00:00:00 CET 2003	Shipped
10,104	Fri Jan 31 00:00:00 CET 2003	Shipped
10,105	Tue Feb 11 00:00:00 CET 2003	Shipped
10,106	Mon Feb 17 00:00:00 CET 2003	Shipped
10,107	Mon Feb 24 00:00:00 CET 2003	Shipped
10,108	Mon Mar 03 00:00:00 CET 2003	Shipped
10,109	Mon Mar 10 00:00:00 CET 2003	Shipped
10,110	Tue Mar 18 00:00:00 CET 2003	Shipped
10,111	Tue Mar 25 00:00:00 CET 2003	Shipped
10,112	Mon Mar 24 00:00:00 CET 2003	Shipped

In the `https://github.com/fcorti/pentaho-8-reporting-for-java-developers` **repository, in the path** `Chapter 11 - The PRPT format and the Java API to build it/my_reports,` **you** can find `example_xml.prpt`, developing exactly the example described here.

Building a report using Pentaho Reporting Java API

Now that you have built a report using the Pentaho Reporting XML format, it's time to learn how to do a similar exercise, by building a report using Pentaho Reporting Java API. To avoid going over the entire Javadoc of Pentaho Reporting, this chapter covers only the essentials. This includes references to important packages, making it easier to find the classes, factories, and interfaces that you need to build your report. Pentaho Reporting's Javadoc is available at `http://javadoc.pentaho.com/reporting/`.

The first step in working with Pentaho Reporting's API is to initialize the reporting engine and create an empty `MasterReport` object:

```
// Initialize the reporting engine
ClassicEngineBoot.getInstance().start();

// Create a report object
MasterReport report = new MasterReport();
```

The `ClassicEngineBoot` and `MasterReport` classes are located in the `org.pentaho.reporting.engine.classic.core` Java package.

Once you have created a report object, you are ready to step through the various components that make up an entire report. The following sections demonstrate setting up a data source, adding parameters to a report, including a function, adding layout bands to the report, adding elements to a report (you will learn how to add labels and charts as an example), and customizing the report page definition.

Adding a data source

In Chapter 6, *Configuring JDBC and Other Data Sources*, you saw many different types of data sources, all of them managed programmatically by `DataFactory`, which will be detailed in the next chapter. Here is a simple example of a `DataFactory` definition, along with code to bind it to the report:

```
// Define a simple TableModel.
DefaultTableModel tableModel = new DefaultTableModel (
  new Object[][]
  {
    {"Line One", "Product One", 10, 100},
    {"Line Two", "Product Two", 20, 200},
    ...
  },
  new String[] {"Line", "Product", "Cost", "Quantity"}
);

// Create a TableDataFactory.
final TableDataFactory dataFactory = new TableDataFactory();
dataFactory.addTable("default", tableModel);

// Add the factory to the report.
report.setDataFactory(dataFactory);
```

Defining parameters

By defining parameter types and validation information about parameters, the reporting engine can validate incoming parameters. This information is also available to the system executing the report, allowing for user prompting. Parameters are managed using the `ReportParameterDefinition` API. This API is defined in the package `org.pentaho.reporting.engine.classic.core.parameters`, along with all the other classes and interfaces discussed in this section.

The ReportParameterDefinition API defines individual parameter definitions, as well as the ReportParameterValidator class, which verifies that the entries are valid. The following example demonstrates the use of Pentaho Reporting's default implementation, the DefaultParameterDefinition class. Individual parameters use the ParameterDefinitionEntry API. Available implementations of entries include PlainParameter, DefaultListParameter, and DefaultFormulaListParameter. The following code demonstrates the configuration of a PlainParameter called Product:

```
// Define a plain parameter.
PlainParameter entry = new PlainParameter("Product", String. class);

// Make the parameter Mandatory.
entry.setMandatory(true);

// Add the parameter to our parameter definition.
paramDef.addParameterDefinition(entry);
```

Including functions and expressions

To add a function or expression to a Pentaho Report, simply create the function or expression instance and call report.addExpression(Expression expression). All expressions that get added to a report must implement the Expression interface. All functions added to a report must implement the Function interface, which extends the Expression interface. Most of the functions discussed earlier in this book, along with the Expression and Function interfaces, are defined within the package org.pentaho.reporting.engine.classic.core.function or a subpackage. Expression implementations use the Java bean standard getters and setters for configuring their properties. The following code demonstrates creating a FormulaExpression instance and adding it to a report:

```
// Create a formula expression.
FormulaExpression formula = new FormulaExpression();

// Configure the formulas properties.
formula.setName("totalCost");
formula.setFormula("=[Cost]*[Quantity]");

// Add the expression to the report.
report.addExpression(formula);
```

Defining the report layout

Similar to the `layout.xml` document described earlier in this chapter, defining the Java beans that make up the report layout includes the common report bands such as the report header and footer, as well as the group band hierarchy that also includes the details band.

Common report bands

For each band defined in a report, such as report header, report footer, page header, and page footer, there are equivalent Java classes that are available, all extending from the common abstract class `Band`, located in the `org.pentaho.reporting.engine.classic.core` package. These bands are all located in the same package.

Each band defines a set of Java bean properties, but most simply use those defined in the `Band` abstract class. One of the primary methods defined in this class is `addElement(Element element)`, which you will use later when creating elements and adding them to their parent bands. A subset of `Band` implementations also implement the `RootLevelBand` interface, which allows the addition of subreports to the band via the `addSubReport(SubReport subreport)` method. Bands such as page header, page footer, and watermark do not allow rendering of subreports. The following is an example of setting the report header and report footer in a report:

```
// Creating report header and footer objects.
ReportHeader reportHeader = new ReportHeader();
ReportFooter reportFooter = new ReportFooter();

// Adding the report header and footer to the report.
report.setReportHeader(reportHeader);
report.setReportFooter(reportFooter);
```

It can't get any easier than that!

Group band hierarchy

Group bands also follow this simple Java bean paradigm. Because it is possible to nest groups, the API is a little bit more advanced. The `RelationalGroup` class is used for regular relational groupings. `CrosstabGroup` is used for defining cross tabs within a report. The `CrosstabGroup` API is out of the scope of this chapter, but is well documented in Javadoc.

The RelationalGroup class may contain a group header and group footer, as well as a GroupBody implementation. GroupBody is an abstract class that SubGroupBody and GroupDataBody extend. SubGroupBody allows for nested groups, and GroupDataBody contains ItemBand, as well as three other less used bands, DetailHeader, DetailsFooter, and NoDataBand.

To configure the RelationalGroup class, you must provide a set of data row fields that define the grouping. This may be done via the addField(String field), setFields(List fields), or setFieldsArray(String[] fieldsArray) method calls. In this example, you will define RelationalGroup and ItemBand, and group by the Name field. Note that the ItemBand class represents a details band in a report.

```
// Creating the root relational group.
RelationalGroup group = new RelationalGroup();

// Using "Line" as the root grouping.
group.addField("Line");

// Creating a group data body.
GroupDataBody groupData = new GroupDataBody();

// Creating an item band.
ItemBand itemBand = new ItemBand();

// Place the item band within the group data body.
groupData.setItemBand(itemBand);

// Place the group data body within the root group:
group.setBody(groupData);

// Setting the root group within the report.
report.setRootGroup(group);
```

Adding elements to the report

Now that you have set up all the bands for your report, you are ready to start adding elements. Unlike the previous classes and interfaces introduced for bands, all elements share a single class implementation, Element, and are created by element factories. The Element class is located in the org.pentaho.reporting.engine.classic.core package. The primary set of element factories is located in the org.pentaho.reporting.engine.classic.core.elementfactory package.

To use a factory, first instantiate the factory object and then configure the Java bean setters of the factory. Once you have built your element within the factory object, call `createElement()` to retrieve the `Element` instance, which you will then add to your report.

Adding a label element

As a demonstration of how to use a factory, the following code instantiates an `Element` using the `LabelElementFactory` class:

```
// Creating a label element factory instance.
LabelElementFactory factory = new LabelElementFactory();

// Configuring the label's text.
factory.setText("Product");

// Configure the label's location and size.
factory.setX(1f);
factory.setY(1f);
factory.setMinimumWidth(100f);
factory.setMinimumHeight(20f);

// instantiate the label element
Element label = factory.createElement();
```

In this example, you instantiated the factory, set a value for the label, and then generated the label `Element` instance. Factories also expose style attributes as Java bean setters, so it's possible to configure the location, size, and font style of this element.

Now, add the label to your `ReportHeader` instance defined earlier:

```
// Adding the label to the report header.
reportHeader.addElement(label);
```

It is important to note that for the Java bean properties not set, elements inherit their default values from their parent band. For instance, you can specify the bold attribute on the `ReportHeader` instance, and all text elements will default to that value:

```
// Setting the bold property to true, inherited by all child text elements.
reportHeader.getStyle().setStyleProperty(TextStyleKeys.BOLD, true);
```

Adding a chart element

As the last and most meaningful example, let's show how to programmatically add a chart to the report. In this example, you will learn how to include a bar chart, based on the `Cost` field per `Product` field. As you learnt in `Chapter 7`, *Including Graphics and Charts in Reports*, a chart element requires a data collector; in case of bar charts, the collector is `CategorySetDataCollector`. The following is the definition of the `collector` object:

```
// Defining a data collector for the chart.
CategorySetDataCollector collector = new CategorySetDataCollector();
collector.setName("CategorySetCollectorFunction");
collector.setSeriesColumn(0, "Cost");
collector.setSeriesName(0, "");
collector.setValueColumn(0, "Cost");
collector.setCategoryColumn("Product");
collector.setAutoGenerateMissingSeriesNames(false);
```

All the possible chart types are available in the `org.pentaho.reporting.engine.classic.extensions.legacy.charts` package. In case of bar charts, the `BarChartExpression` object must be used as described in the following source code:

```
// Chart layout.
BarChartExpression chartExpression = new BarChartExpression();
chartExpression.setShowLegend(false);
chartExpression.setSeriesColor(
  new String[] {"#abcd37","#0392ce","#f9bc02","#66b033","#cc0099"}
);
```

As you saw previously for the label, an `Element` object is used to add the bar chat to the report:

```
// Declaring an element for the chart.
Element chartElement = new Element();
chartElement.setElementType(new LegacyChartType());
chartElement.setName("MySuperCoolChartFromApi");
chartElement.setAttributeExpression(
  AttributeNames.Core.NAMESPACE,
  AttributeNames.Core.VALUE,
  chartExpression);
chartElement.setAttribute(
  LegacyChartElementModule.NAMESPACE,
  LegacyChartElementModule.PRIMARY_DATA_COLLECTOR_FUNCTION_ATTRIBUTE,
  collector);
chartElement.getStyle().setStyleProperty(
  ElementStyleKeys.MIN_HEIGHT,
  200F);
```

```
chartElement.getStyle().setStyleProperty(
  ElementStyleKeys.MIN_WIDTH,
  500F);

// Adding the chart to the report header.
reportHeader.addElement(chartElement);
```

Developing an example of Pentaho report

In this example, you will take what you have learnt earlier and incorporate it into a simple Java application. Starting from the basic example shared in Chapter 3, *Getting Started with Reporting SDK*, you change the PentahoServlet1 class to programmatically build the report (the class is renamed as PentahoServlet). The idea is to manually build the report, in a manner similar to what you saw in the previous sections.

In particular, the report will contain:

- A table data source listing some dummy products with cost and quantity as measures
- A formula named totalCostPerProduct calculating [Cost]*[Quantity]
- The report header and footer
- A bar chart showing the cost per product in the report header
- A couple of labels (Product and TotalCost) in the report header
- Two fields in the report details, for the product (a text field) and the total cost (a number field)

Instead of explaining here what to add/remove to/from the Maven project, it is more interesting to share the final version of the source code and describe how to run it. The complete version of the source code developing the report can be found in the https://github.com/fcorti/pentaho-8-reporting-for-java-developers repository, in the Chapter 11 - The PRPT format and the Java API to build it/pentaho-reporting-manual-build folder.

Download the `pentaho-reporting-manual-build` folder to your local machine, open a Terminal, move into this folder, and execute the following command:

```
mvn clean package
```

Once done, it's time to to run the project, by executing the following command:

```
java -jar target/dependency/jetty-runner.jar target/*.war
```

Open a browser at `http://localhost:8080` and you should see a report in PDF format, like the following screenshot:

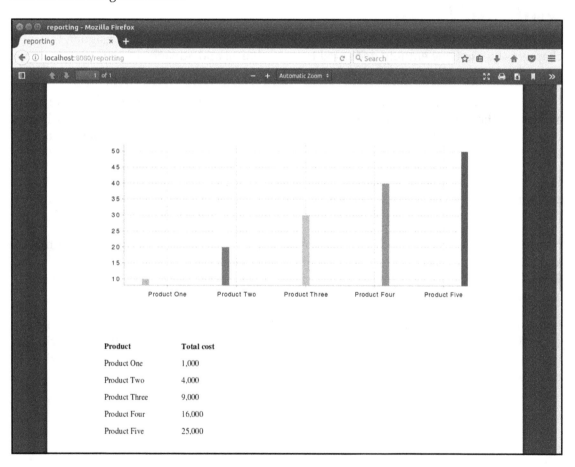

Take your time to dive deep into the details of the project and run it in your development environment. It would be great if you could try to modify the source code to use a JDBC data source instead of the table data source (the SampleData schema is included in the Maven project in the resources folder), if you could make the report more appealing by changing the layout, or if you could add one parameter to make it work from Java.

Summary

After the discovery of the basic and advanced features of Pentaho Report Designer, this chapter is the first one entirely dedicated to the technical and advanced features of Pentaho Reporting SDK.

In this chapter, you learnt everything about Pentaho Reporting's .prpt bundle file format, along with the details of Pentaho Reporting's Java API. You were introduced to the schemas of the various XML files that persist the data source, parameters, expressions, layout, and style of a report.

With examples of Pentaho's Java API, you learned how easy it is to build a report programmatically. You walked through a complete example that demonstrated creating different reporting bands, as well as different elements, within a report.

Now that you have read this chapter, you should feel comfortable with the .prpt format and all the technical details around developing a Pentaho Report using the Pentaho Reporting API. This is an advanced task for developers, creating complex Pentaho reports, embedded in your custom projects using Java.

In the next chapter, you will see how to work with data sources (already covered in Chapter 6, *Configuring JDBC and Other Data Sources*) from the development perspective. You will see how to develop a Pentaho report programmatically, using Pentaho reporting SDK and dealing with all the possible types of data sources.

12
Developing Using Data Sources

In this chapter, you will work with various methods for loading data in the Pentaho Reporting Engine, and dig deep into how the Pentaho Reporting Engine interacts with these data sources to render a report. In Chapter 6, *Configuring JDBC and other data sources*, you learned how to create and use all the available types of data sources, right within Pentaho Report Designer. In this chapter, you will see, with the help of examples, how to embed the included DataFactory implementations in your environment. You will also learn the details of the Pentaho Reporting Engine Data API specification, allowing you to implement your own DataFactory, if necessary.

This chapter is highly technical and written as a tutorial for pure Java developers. At the end of this chapter, you will feel comfortable with all types of data sources, from a developer's perspective, for creating all the possible Pentaho reports. The content explained in this chapter is relevant if you want to control all the possible data presented in a report, as a developer creating your own Java application as embedding Pentaho Reporting Engine.

Pentaho Reporting Engine Data API

The **Pentaho Reporting Engine Data API** is a simple API that describes how Pentaho Reporting accesses data to populate reports. In this section, you will learn about the core interfaces of the API. All the individual implementations discussed later in this chapter implement this API.

There are two main Java interfaces related to the Pentaho Reporting Engine Data API. The first interface you will learn about is `org.pentaho.reporting.engine.classic.core.DataFactory`. The primary purpose of the `DataFactory` interface is to generate an object that implements the `javax.swing.table.TableModel` interface. The `TableModel` interface is a very simple API for accessing two-dimensional cell data. These two simple APIs are combined to manage all data input into Pentaho Reporting.

To implement your own Java data source for the Pentaho Reporting Engine, all you need to do is implement the `DataFactory` and `TableModel` interfaces. But most likely, you will be able to take advantage of one of the many existing `DataFactory` implementations to load your data.

The DataFactory interface

The `DataFactory` interface defines a couple of fields and some methods, discussed in this section. Any parameter specified in the report definition file is available as part of the `DataRow` parameter's object. If the query is used as part of a sub-report, parameters passed into the sub-report from the master report are made available as well. If there is a problem executing the query, the implementer may throw `ReportDataFactoryException`, which will be properly handled by the Reporting Engine.

Following are the fields, defined with brief descriptions of their uses and meanings:

Field	Description
QUERY_LIMIT	The maximum number of resulting rows to be returned. If set to zero, returns all rows.
QUERY_TIMEOUT	The maximum time to wait for a query to return. If set to zero, no timeout should be used.

Following are the methods, defined with brief descriptions of their uses and meanings:

Method	Description
void cancelRunningQuery()	If supported by the implementing DataFactory, the cancelRunningQuery method call will cancel the currently executing query of DataFactory.
Object clone()	Cloning the current DataFactory object.
void close()	The close method is called once processing of all the TableModel interfaces generated by this DataFactory is complete.
DataFactory derive()	The derive method creates a new DataFactory that should be independent of the parent DataFactory. Often, this is simply making a call to the clone() method of the DataFactory implementation.
String[] getQueryNames()	The getQueryNames method returns a list of available query names the DataFactory interface is currently aware of.

void initialize(
  Configuration configuration,
  ResourceManager resourceManager,
  ResourceKey contextKey,
  ResourceBundleFactory resourceBundleFactory)
	The initialize method provides DataFactory with access to the reporting engine's ResourceManager, allowing DataFactory to access resources it may need to load properly. The ResourceManager class is the same class that is used to load a report from the file system.

boolean isQueryExecutable(
  String query,
  DataRow parameters)
	Checks whether the query would be executable by this DataFactory.

void open()	The open method is called during the initialization process, allowing DataFactory to initialize if necessary.

TableModel queryData(
  String query,
  DataRow parameters)
	The queryData method is called by the reporting engine to load a TableModel object. This is the main factory method. Both a query name and a set of parameters are passed to DataFactory.

The TableModel interface

The `javax.swing.table.TableModel` interface is part of the Java Platform API. Pentaho Reporting uses the `TableModel` interface to access the two-dimensional data necessary to render a report. Portions of the `TableModel` interface are not used in the Pentaho Reporting Engine. Specifically, the following four methods are not used: `isCellEditable`, `setValueAt`, `addTableModelListener`, and `removeTableModelListener`. All the unused methods are related to updating `TableModel`. The Pentaho Reporting Engine uses the `TableModel` interface in a read-only fashion, so these methods are not applicable. The following four methods are utilized by the reporting engine:

Method	Description
`Class<?> getColumnClass(int columnIndex)`	Returns the most specific super class for all the cell values in the column.
`int getColumnCount()`	Returns the number of columns `TableModel` contains.
`String getColumnName(int columnIndex)`	Returns the column name of the specified column index.
`int getRowCount()`	Returns the number of rows `TableModel` contains.
`Object getValueAt(int rowIndex, int columnIndex)`	Returns a particular cell of data based on the specified row and column index. This is the main method for retrieving information from the `TableModel` instance.

DataFactory serialization

In addition to these core interfaces, the Data API also defines interfaces and base implementations for serializing and de-serializing `DataFactory` implementations. This makes it possible for a user to define a data source in a client tool, and have that information available to the reporting engine during execution of the report on the server. The related interfaces for this portion of the API are `DataFactoryReadHandler` and `DataFactoryWriteHandler`.

Additional data source metadata

As an extension to `TableModel`, the Pentaho Reporting Engine provides the `MetaTableModel` interface. `MetaTableModel` defines an API to access additional metadata that might be available as part of the data source. Examples of additional metadata can be font or style information.

Accessing data throughout a report

Once you have configured your `DataFactory` implementation, it is important to know how to access this data within a report. As mentioned in `Chapter 11`, *The PRPT format and the Java API to build it*, elements that contain the field name property access row data via the column headers provided by the data source. In addition to accessing the fields directly, you may also access this data in functions and formulas.

Functions in Pentaho Reporting contain a property named `Field` or `Fields` that allow you to select a list of fields from the defined data source. To reference a field in a formula, you need to place brackets around the field name. An example reference to a field name in a formula can be `[Product]`.

When using `DataFactory` that isn't supported directly in the Report Designer, such as the `hibernate.HQLDataFactory`, you need to manually type the name of the fields into the Report Designer. Another issue with using non-supported `DataFactory` classes in the Report Designer is that the report preview won't be available for use. One strategy to avoid these issues is to build a sample dataset, which contains the identical column headers in a Report Designer supported `DataFactory` implementation, in order to verify that reports look as expected.

Existing DataFactory implementations

Now that you have learnt the Pentaho Reporting Engine Data API basics, in this section, you will dive deep into the `DataFactory` implementations available as part of the Pentaho Reporting Engine. For better understanding, you will learn about the commonly used `DataFactory` implementations, including working examples for the most common and used factories. As you saw many times in the previous chapters of the book, all the examples are available in the `https://github.com/fcorti/pentaho-8-reporting-for-java-developers` repository; specifically, in the `Chapter 12 - Developing using data sources` folder.

In all the following examples, you will not find the preview of the final reports. This is not because the layout is not relevant, but, this chapter is focused more on the data source configuration. The suggestion is always the same as we shared in the past chapters: considering that you have the full source code available and your goal is to learn Pentaho Reporting, try to run the examples in your development environment as an exercise.

TableDataFactory

The `org.pentaho.reporting.engine.classic.core.TableDataFactory` class is the simplest form of `DataFactory` for loading data into the Pentaho Reporting Engine. `TableDataFactory` manages a set of existing `TableModel` instances and makes them available to the reporting engine.

To construct `TableDataFactory`, you can either use the default constructor or the following convenience constructor:

```
public TableDataFactory(final String name, final TableModel tableModel);
```

This convenience constructor adds a `TableModel` instance with a particular name to the list of `TableModel` instances that `TableDataFactory` is aware of. The other method for adding the `TableModel` instances to `TableDataFactory` is via the following API call:

```
public void addTable(final String name, final TableModel tableModel);
```

The `addTable` method adds an additional table to the list of named `TableModel` instances, which are maintained by `TableDataFactory`:

While there is no `DataFactory` CSV defined, a helper class named `CSVTableModelProducer` is available, which is located in the `org.pentaho.reporting.engine.classic.core.modules.misc.tablemodel` package. This `CSVTableModelProducer` class will generate another class, `CSVTableModel`, which you could then add to `TableDataFactory`.

TableDataFactory example

An example of Pentaho Report's development using the `TableDataFactory` class can be found in the `https://github.com/fcorti/pentaho-8-reporting-for-java-developers` repository; specifically, in the `Chapter 12 - Developing using data sources` folder. Inside the folder, you will find the `pentaho-reporting-data-table` project, using the `PentahoServlet` class with the following source code:

```
// Loading the Table DataFactory.
DefaultTableModel tableModel = new DefaultTableModel(
  new Object[][] {
    {"Product A", 123},
    {"Product B", 234},
    {"Product C", 345},
    {"Product D", 456}
  },
  new String[] {"Product", "Cost"});
TableDataFactory dataFactory = new TableDataFactory();
dataFactory.addTable("default", tableModel);
report.setDataFactory(dataFactory);
```

To run the project, download the `pentaho-reporting-data-source-table` folder in your local machine, open a terminal, move into this folder, and execute the following commands in the given sequence:

```
mvn clean install
mvn package
java -jar target/dependency/jetty-runner.jar target/*.war
```

Open a browser at `http://localhost:8080`, and you should see the Pentaho report in PDF format as a result.

SQLReportDataFactory

The `org.pentaho.reporting.engine.classic.core.modules.misc.datafactory.sql.SQLReportDataFactory` class allows you to easily use JDBC and SQL to populate your reports.

To set up `SQLReportDataFactory` correctly in your environment, you first need to create an instance of `ConnectionProvider`. Three `ConnectionProvider` implementations are available for use (`StaticConnectionProvider`, `DriverConnectionProvider`, and `JndiConnectionProvider`). The `ConnectionProvider` interface and three implementations are available in the same package as `SQLReportDataFactory`.

The `ConnectionProvider` interface defines a single `createConnection` method, which should return a JDBC connection for `SQLReportDataFactory` to use when generating a result set to populate a report.

StaticConnectionProvider

The first implementation of `ConnectionProvider` is the `StaticConnectionProvider` class, which takes in an existing `java.sql.Connection` object as part of its constructor:

```
ConnectionProvider conn = new StaticConnectionProvider(sqlConn);
```

DriverConnectionProvider

The second implementation of `ConnectionProvider` is the `DriverConnectionProvider` class, which allows you to easily configure a connection. `DriverConnectionProvider` has a default constructor, and must be configured via setter methods. In the following table, some of the most relevant methods are introduced:

Method	Description
`void setDriver( String driver)`	The `setDriver` method's driver value should be set to the fully qualified name of the driver class used in JDBC.
`void setUrl( String url);`	The `setUrl` method's URL value should be set to the JDBC URL for connecting to a database.
`void setProperty( String name, String value);`	The `setProperty` method adds an additional property to the JDBC configuration properties. Properties such as `user` and `password` are often passed in through the properties list for a new connection to be generated via `java.sql.DriverManager`.

Be aware that by using `DriverConnectionProvider`, you will create a new connection to the underlying database every time the `createConnection` method is called on the API. This is not good or bad, but it's something you should be aware of during your development.

JndiConnectionProvider

The third available `ConnectionProvider` is `JndiConnectionProvider`. `JndiConnectionProvider` uses **Java's Naming and Directory Interface (JNDI)** to obtain a connection to a database. It has a default constructor, along with the following setter methods, that may be configured to connect to a JNDI data source. Only the connection path property is mandatory.

In the following table, some of the most relevant methods are introduced:

Method	Description
`void setConnectionPath( String connectionPath)`	The `setConnectionPath` method should be set to the full JNDI path of your JDBC data source
`void setUsername( String username)`	The `setUsername` method is an optional field, which may be required when connecting to your data source
`void setPassword( String password)`	The `setPassword` method is an optional field, which may be required when connecting to your data source

JNDI is available in many application servers. It may also be used in a regular Java application with the help of simple JNDI, available at `http://www.osjava.org/simple-jndi`. The following list shows the examples of JNDI connection strings in different environments, assuming that you've already configured the JNDI data sources in that environment:

- **Tomcat java**: `comp/env/jdbc/<DataSourceName>`
- **JBoss java**: `<DataSourceName>`

Using SQLReportDataFactory

Once `ConnectionProvider` has been created, it's now time to set up the `SQLReportDataFactory` instance. `SQLReportDataFactory` contains two constructors: the first constructor takes `ConnectionProvider`, and the second constructor takes an existing `Connection`, which uses `StaticConnectionProvider` under the hood to provide the connection.

In addition to configuring `ConnectionProvider`, you also must provide `SQLReportDataFactory` with queries to execute. Use the `setQuery` method to configure named queries:

```
void setQuery(final String name, final String queryString)
```

The `setQuery` method takes in the name of the query and the SQL query itself. As mentioned earlier, the master reports in the examples in this chapter use the name `default` to reference the main query.

To incorporate report parameters in the query, you may specify variables with the following format in your SQL: `${<PARAMETER NAME>}`. A `PreparedStatement` is generated, and these variables are parameterized appropriately via the JDBC specification, in order to avoid potential SQL injection attacks. In addition to traditional SQL statements, you may also make a call to a SQL stored procedure. These calls begin with the string `call`, and are recognized by `SQLReportDataFactory`, ensuring that the correct JDBC API method is executed.

As mentioned earlier, the `QUERY_LIMIT` and `QUERY_TIMEOUT` parameters, made available to all `DataFactory` instances, also apply to `SQLReportDataFactory`. These values are passed on to the `Connection` object. Therefore, the underlying JDBC driver must also support these properties to have an effect.

SQLReportDataFactory example

In this section, you will see two complete Maven projects, both using `SQLReportDataFactory` to populate a Pentaho report. Both the examples are very basic and are focused on the data source definition instead of the report's layout. The two Maven projects develop the same Pentaho report using two different providers: `StaticConnectionProvider` and `DriverConnectionProvider`.

The complete source code for developing the report can be found in the `https://github.com/fcorti/pentaho-8-reporting-for-java-developers` repository; specifically, in the `Chapter 12 - Developing using data sources` folder. Inside the folder, you will find the `pentaho-reporting-data-source-static-jdbc` project, using the `PentahoServlet` class with the following source code:

```
...

// Defining the connection provider.
Connection connection = DriverManager.getConnection(
  "jdbc:hsqldb:./resources/sampledata/sampledata",
  "pentaho_user",
  "password");
StaticConnectionProvider provider = new
StaticConnectionProvider(connection);

// Defining the query.
SQLReportDataFactory dataFactory = new SQLReportDataFactory(provider);
String sqlQuery = "SELECT PRODUCTNAME, QUANTITYINSTOCK FROM PRODUCTS";
dataFactory.setQuery("default", sqlQuery);
report.setDataFactory(dataFactory);

...
```

To run the project, download the `pentaho-reporting-data-source-static-jdbc` folder to your local machine, open a terminal, move into this folder, and execute the following commands in the given sequence:

```
mvn clean install
mvn package
java -jar target/dependency/jetty-runner.jar target/*.war
```

Then open a browser at `http://localhost:8080`, and you should see the Pentaho report in PDF format as a result.

In the same `Chapter 12 - Developing using data sources` folder, inside the `pentaho-reporting-data-source-jdbc` subfolder, you will find the other project, using the `DriverConnectionProvider` class, with the following source code:

```
...

// Defining the connection provider.
DriverConnectionProvider provider = new DriverConnectionProvider();
provider.setDriver("org.hsqldb.jdbcDriver");
provider.setProperty("user", "pentaho_user");
provider.setProperty("password", "password");
```

```
provider.setUrl("jdbc:hsqldb:./resources/sampledata/sampledata");

// Defining the query.
SQLReportDataFactory dataFactory = new SQLReportDataFactory(provider);
String sqlQuery = "SELECT PRODUCTNAME, QUANTITYINSTOCK FROM PRODUCTS";
dataFactory.setQuery("default", sqlQuery);
report.setDataFactory(dataFactory);

...
```

To run the project, execute exactly the same tasks as described previously; download the `pentaho-reporting-data-source-jdbc` folder to your local machine, open a terminal, move into this folder, and execute the following commands in the given sequence:

```
mvn clean install
mvn package
java -jar target/dependency/jetty-runner.jar target/*.war
```

Then open a browser at `http://localhost:8080`, and you should see the Pentaho report in PDF format as a result.

As you can see, inside the source code of both the projects, `SQLReportDataFactory` is used in exactly the same way and the resulting report is the same in terms of layout.

XPathDataFactory

The `org.pentaho.reporting.engine.classic.extensions.datasources.xpath.XPath DataFactory` class allows you to populate your report based on XML data, provided that it is formatted in a specific way. This `DataFactory` accepts XML formatted as rows and columns, where the **XPath** expression returns a list of row elements that contain column elements. Each column element's node name represents the column name, and each column's text data represents the column's value. An example of a row supported by `XPathDataFactory` is:

```
<Row>
 <Column1>Row 1 Data In Column 1</Column1>
 <Column2>Row 1 Data In Column 2</Column2>
</Row>
```

By default, the column values are typed as Java strings. `XPathDataFactory` provides a mechanism to specify certain Java data types, including the following:

- `java.lang.String`
- `java.sql.Date`
- `java.math.BigDecimal`
- `java.sql.Timestamp`
- `java.lang.Integer`
- `java.lang.Double`
- `java.lang.Long`

These types can be specified in the XML as either a preprocessor step or a comment:

- **Preprocessor step**: `<?pentaho-dataset java.lang.Integer, java.lang.String?>`
- **Root document comment**: `<!-- java.lang.Integer, java.lang.String -->`
- **Root result set comment:** `<!-- java.lang.Integer, java.lang.String -->`

The column types should appear in the same order as the elements in the first row. Beyond the first row, the order of columns is not relevant. The names of the columns will be used to place them in the correct position of the generated `TableModel`. Both the `java.sql.Date` and `java.sql.Timestamp` classes require a long numeric value corresponding to milliseconds since January 1, 1970, 00:00:00 GMT.

To create `XPathDataFactory`, use the default constructor. To configure `XPathDataFactory`, you must specify an XML file, along with a set of XPath queries. For a good introduction to XPath, see `http://www.w3.org/TR/xpath`.

In the following table, some of the most relevant methods are introduced:

Method	Description
`void setXqueryDataFile( String filename)`	`XPathDataFactory` uses Pentaho Reporting Engine's `ResourceManager` for loading the XPath file. To set the location of the XML file, use this method.
`void setQuery( String name, String xpath)`	Named queries may be added with this method.

There is no standard way to easily sort row data via XPath, so be sure to have your data in the correct order before loading it with XPathDataFactory. The inability to sort limits the capabilities of this DataFactory.

XPathDataFactory example

An example of Pentaho Report's development using the XPathDataFactory class can be found in the https://github.com/fcorti/pentaho-8-reporting-for-java-developers repository; specifically, in the Chapter 12 - Developing using data sources folder. Inside the folder, you will find the pentaho-reporting-data-source-xpath project, using the PentahoServlet class with the following source code:

```
// Load report xpath data.
XPathDataFactory factory = new XPathDataFactory();
factory.setXqueryDataFile("file:./resources/xpathexample.xml");
factory.setQuery("default", "/ExampleResultSet/Row", false);
report.setDataFactory(factory);
```

Following is the content of the xpathexample.xml file:

```
<?xml version="1.0" encoding="UTF-8"?>
<?pentaho-dataset java.lang.String,java.lang.String,java.lang.Integer?>
<ExampleResultSet>
  <Row>
    <NAME>LibBase</NAME>
    <DESCRIPTION>Base library containing common functions </DESCRIPTION>
    <SIZE>113210</SIZE>
  </Row>
  <Row>
    <NAME>LibLoader</NAME>
    <DESCRIPTION>Loading and caching library</DESCRIPTION>
    <SIZE>53552</SIZE>
  </Row>
</ExampleResultSet>
```

Note that the Maven pom.xml file should also include the following dependency to download the correct libraries:

```
<dependency>
  <groupId>pentaho-reporting-engine</groupId>
  <artifactId>pentaho-reporting-engine-classic-extensions-
xpath</artifactId>
  <version>8.0-SNAPSHOT</version>
</dependency>
```

To run the project, download the `pentaho-reporting-data-source-xpath` folder to your local machine, open a terminal, move into this folder, and execute the following commands in the given sequence:

```
mvn clean install
mvn package
java -jar target/dependency/jetty-runner.jar target/*.war
```

Then open a browser at `http://localhost:8080`, and you should see the Pentaho report in PDF format as a result.

HQLDataFactory

The `org.pentaho.reporting.engine.classic.extensions.datasources.hibernate.HQLDataFactory` class allows you to populate your report based on a Hibernate query. **Hibernate** is an open source relational persistence engine. It allows you to easily persist your Java objects to a database.

Much like many of the other `DataFactory` implementations, `HQLDataFactory` is configured with information to connect to Hibernate, along with the ability to specify named queries. The `HQLDataFactory` API defines an interface called `SessionProvider`, which it uses to gain access to the current hibernate `Session` object. `SessionProvider` contains a single API method, `getSession()`, which returns an instance of `org.hibernate.Session`. There are two implemented versions of this session provider: `StaticSessionProvider` and `DefaultSessionProvider`.

At this time, `HQLDataFactory` is not available as a data source within Pentaho Report Designer, so code is required to utilize Hibernate as a data source.

 `HSQLDataFactory` is documented here because it is quoted in the official Javadoc website (`http://javadoc.pentaho.com/reporting/`). As you can see from Pentaho's artifact repository regarding the hibernate extension, found at this link:`http://repository.pentaho.org/artifactory/repo/pentaho-reporting-engine/pentaho-reporting-engine-classic-extensions-hibernate/`, the library is not supported anymore and the latest update is on the 3.9.2-GA release.

StaticSessionProvider

`StaticSessionProvider` simply takes in the `org.hibernate.Session` object as a constructor parameter, making the already existing `Session` object available to `HQLDataFactory`. This would be used if your system already has an initialized Hibernate session.

DefaultSessionProvider

`DefaultSessionProvider` requires no constructor parameters, and uses the following API call to generate `SessionFactory` from Hibernate:

```
sessionFactory = new Configuration().configure(). buildSessionFactory();
```

The created `sessionFactory` instance is used to create new sessions, which `HQLDataFactory` uses to query Hibernate.

`HQLDataFactory` provides two constructors. The first constructor takes in `SessionProvider`, as described earlier. The second constructor simply takes in a Hibernate `Session` instance, which it uses to query Hibernate. This constructor uses `StaticSessionProvider`, under the covers, to pass the `Session` into the `HQLDataFactory`.

Once you've instantiated your factory, you may add named queries to the factory by making the following API call:

```
void setQuery(String name, String queryString);
```

The `setQuery` method takes in the name of the query, and the Hibernate query, in order to execute.

`HQLDataFactory` uses Hibernate's query language, which is well-documented at http:// www.hibernate.org/hib_docs/reference/en/html/queryhql.html. You may include report parameters in your query by using the HQL syntax `:ParameterName`. The max results and query timeout parameters are supported by `HQLDataFactory`.

PmdDataFactory

The
`org.pentaho.reporting.engine.classic.extensions.datasources.pmd.PmdData Factory` class allows you to populate your report using a Pentaho Metadata Query. Pentaho Metadata allows a database administrator to define a business layer of their relational data for end users, simplifying the ability to query the data, as well as protecting users from the complexities that may exist in a database schema. Pentaho's **Metadata Query Language** (**MQL**) is an XML-based query model that simplifies querying databases, and is currently used in the Pentaho Report Designer and **Pentaho Web Ad Hoc Report** client tools. In order for `PmdDataFactory` to initialize properly, it must have access to certain Pentaho Metadata configuration properties that can be configured at runtime, or be passed in by a configuration file.

XMI file

As introduced in `Chapter 6`, Configuring JDBC and other data sources, the **XMI** file contains a serialized version of the defined metadata model, and is required in order to execute MQL queries. The XMI file contains information regarding how to connect to the relational data source, as well as the business model mapping of the relational data. This file is loaded at runtime into the configured repository of Pentaho Metadata. The XMI file may be configured by calling the `setXmiFile` method. This file is loaded with Pentaho Reporting Engine's `ResourceManager`.

Domain Id

The metadata domain id is used to map a name to the XMI file in the metadata repository. This name is also referenced in the MQL query file. Therefore, it is important to use the same name in the MQL query and `PmdDataFactory`. The domain may be set by the `setDomainId` method.

IPmdConnectionProvider

PmdDataFactory uses the IPmdConnectionProvider interface to obtain the metadata domain objects, as well as the database connection for the query. IPmdConnectionProvider must be specified via the setConnectionProvider method. A default implementation, PmdConnectionProvider, manages loading the XMI file as well as determining the database connection to be used, based on metadata information provided in the XMI file.

The following table shows the most relevant method of the IPmdConnectionProvider class:

Method	Description
IMetadataDomainRepository getMetadataDomainRepository(String domain, ResourceManager resourceManager, ResourceKey contextKey, String xmiFile)	Returns a metadata repository based on the domain id and XMI file

PmdDataFactory example

An example of Pentaho report's development using the PmdDataFactory class can be found in the https://github.com/fcorti/pentaho-8-reporting-for-java-developers repository; specifically, in the Chapter 12 - Developing using data sources folder. Inside the folder, you will find the pentaho-reporting-data-source-pmd project, using the PentahoServlet class with the following source code:

```
// Loading MQL data source.
PmdDataFactory factory = new PmdDataFactory();
factory.setConnectionProvider(new PmdConnectionProvider());
factory.setXmiFile("resources/metadata.xmi");
factory.setDomainId("test");
factory.setQuery(
  "default",
  "<?xml version='1.0' encoding='UTF-8'?>" +
  "<mql>" +
    "<domain_id>test</domain_id>" +
    "<model_id>BV_ORDERS</model_id>" +
    "<options>" +
      "<disable_distinct>false</disable_distinct>" +
      "<limit>-1</limit>" +
    "</options>" +
```

```
  "<selections>" +
    "<selection>" +
      "<view>CAT_PRODUCTS</view>" +
      "<column>BC_PRODUCTS_PRODUCTNAME</column>" +
      "<aggregation>NONE</aggregation>" +
    "</selection>" +
    "<selection>" +
      "<view>CAT_PRODUCTS</view>" +
      "<column>BC_PRODUCTS_MSRP</column>" +
      "<aggregation>AVERAGE</aggregation>" +
    "</selection>" +
  "</selections>" +
  "<constraints/>" +
  "<orders/>" +
"</mql>",
null,
null);
report.setDataFactory(factory);
```

Note that the project uses the `resources/metadata.xmi` file and the `resources/sampledata` HyperDB (linked from the `metadata.xmi` file).

Also note that the Maven `pom.xml` file should also include the following dependency to download the correct libraries:

```
<dependency>
  <groupId>pentaho-reporting-engine</groupId>
  <artifactId>pentaho-reporting-engine-classic-extensions-pmd</artifactId>
  <version>8.0-SNAPSHOT</version>
</dependency>
<dependency>
  <groupId>pentaho</groupId>
  <artifactId>pentaho-metadata</artifactId>
  <version>8.0-SNAPSHOT</version>
</dependency>
```

To run the project, download the `pentaho-reporting-data-source-pmd` folder to your local machine, open a terminal, move into this folder, and execute the following commands in the given sequence:

```
mvn clean install
mvn package
java -jar target/dependency/jetty-runner.jar target/*.war
```

Then open a browser at `http://localhost:8080`, and you should see the Pentaho report in PDF format as a result.

KettleDataFactory

The
`org.pentaho.reporting.engine.classic.extensions.datasources.kettle.KettleDataFactory` class allows you to populate your report from a Kettle transformation. **Kettle** is a data integration tool, also known as an **Extract Transform and Load** (ETL) tool. Kettle transformations support a multitude of data source inputs and transformation capabilities. Kettle, also known as **Pentaho Data Integration**, provides mechanisms to incorporate data from Excel, SQL, XML, Text, and many other data sources. It also provides the ability to combine the results into a single result set, which Pentaho Reporting can use to render a report.

To initialize `KettleDataFactory`, you must provide the location for the Kettle transformation to execute, along with the step within the transformation to use the data from. This is done via the `KettleTransformationProducer` interface. There are two implementations of `KettleTransformationProducer` that are provided. The first is `KettleTransFromFileProducer`, which loads a Kettle transformation from the file system. The `KettleTransFromFileProducer` class must be instantiated with the following parameters:

```
final String transformationFile, // the path of the transformation file to
execute.
final String stepName, // the step name to collect data from.
final FormulaArgument[] argumentNames, // the names of reporting properties
to be passed into Kettle via Transformation Arguments.
final FormulaParameter[] variableNames // the names of reporting properties
to be passed into Kettle via Transformation Parameters.
```

The second implementation of `KettleTransformationProducer` is `KettleTransFromRepositoryProducer`. This loads the transformation from an existing Kettle repository. The `KettleTransFromRepositoryProducer` class must be instantiated with the following parameters:

```
final String repositoryName, // the repository name.
final String directoryName, // the repository directory.
final String transformationName, // the transformation name in the
repository.
final String stepName, // the step name to collect data from.
final String username, // the repository user name.
final String password, // the repository password.
final FormulaArgument[] argumentNames, // the names of reporting properties
to be passed into Kettle via Transformation Arguments.
final FormulaParameter[] variableNames // the names of reporting properties
to be passed into Kettle via Transformation Parameters.
```

`KettleDataFactory` has a default constructor. To add Kettle transformation queries to `KettleDataFactory`, call the `setQuery(String,` `KettleTransformationProducer)` method.

KettleDataFactory example

An example of Pentaho report's development using the `KettleDataFactory` class can be found in the `https://github.com/fcorti/pentaho-8-reporting-for-java-developers` repository; specifically, in the `Chapter 12 - Developing using data sources` folder. Inside the folder, you will find the `pentaho-reporting-data-source-kettle` project, using the `PentahoServlet` class with the following source code:

```
// Loading Kettle data source.
KettleTransFromFileProducer producer = new KettleTransFromFileProducer (
  "resources/CSV Input - Reading customer data.ktr",
  "Dummy (do nothing)",
  new FormulaArgument[0],
  new FormulaParameter[0]);
KettleDataFactory factory = new KettleDataFactory();
factory.setQuery("default", producer);
report.setDataFactory(factory);
```

Note the the project uses the `resources/CSV Input - Reading customer data.ktr` file, which contains a transformation for Pentaho Data Integration and `resources/file/customer-100.txt`, used for the transformation.

Also note that the Maven `pom.xml` file should also include the following dependency to download the correct libraries:

```
<dependency>
  <groupId>pentaho-reporting-engine</groupId>
  <artifactId>pentaho-reporting-engine-classic-extensions-
kettle</artifactId>
  <version>8.0-SNAPSHOT</version>
</dependency>
<dependency>
  <groupId>pentaho-kettle</groupId>
  <artifactId>kettle-core</artifactId>
  <version>8.0-SNAPSHOT</version>
</dependency>
<dependency>
  <groupId>pentaho-kettle</groupId>
  <artifactId>kettle-engine</artifactId>
  <version>8.0-SNAPSHOT</version>
</dependency>
```

To run the project, download the `pentaho-reporting-data-source-kettle` folder to your local machine, open a terminal, move into this folder, and execute the following commands in the given sequence:

```
mvn clean install
mvn package
java -jar target/dependency/jetty-runner.jar target/*.war
```

Then open a browser at `http://localhost:8080`, and you should see the Pentaho report in PDF format as a result.

BandedMDXDataFactory and DenormalizedMDXDataFactory

Accessing an **Online Analytical Processing** (**OLAP**) data source, in case a multi-dimensional engine is involved, has been described in `chapter 6`, *Configuring JDBC and other data sources*. To cover all the possible use cases, Pentaho Reporting Engine Data API defines two different packages:
`org.pentaho.reporting.engine.classic.extensions.datasources.mondrian` and `org.pentaho.reporting.engine.classic.extensions.datasources.olap4j`.

The first one, `org.pentaho.reporting.engine.classic.extensions.datasources.mondrian`, clearly manages the **Mondrian** (`http://community.pentaho.com/projects/mondrian`) data source, and the second one, `org.pentaho.reporting.engine.classic.extensions.datasources.olap4j`, manages the **OLAP4J** (`http://www.olap4j.org`) data source types.

In both packages, two classes allow you to populate your report: the `BandedMDXDataFactory` class, to manage normalized **multi-dimensional expression** (**MDX**) queries, and the `DenormalizedMDXDataFactory` class, to manage denormalized **multi-dimensional expression** (**MDX**) queries.

 For definitions and examples of normalized and denormalized MDX queries, take a look at `Chapter 6`, *Configuring JDBC and other data sources*; in particular, the *OLAP data source* section.

Natively, OLAP data sources support result sets with more than two axes. In a traditional result set used by Pentaho Reporting, there are column headers along with rows of data. When using OLAP data, the data source needs to determine how to map the richer OLAP data into a standard `TableModel` data source.

BandedMDXDataFactory

With `BandedMDXDataFactory`, the factory maps the row and column axes of the OLAP result set to `TableModel`. The column headers display the dimensions selected in the column axis. The rows show the selected row axis information. For instance, if a year was selected from the time dimension on the column axis, in the column header you would see the member name `[Time].[2017]`.

The configuration of the `BandedMDXDataFactory` object for Mondrian and OLAP4J is developed differently, even if they use the same classes and principles. In case of Mondrian, the configuration is done using the `setDataSourceProvider(DataSourceProvider dataSourceProvider)` method to setup the connection to the RBDMS schema, and the `setCubeFileProvider(CubeFileProvider cubeFileProvider)` method to setup the connection to the Mondrian schema. As you can see in the Javadoc website (`http://javadoc.pentaho.com/reporting`), `DataSourceProvider` is implemented by `DriverDataSourceProvider` and `JndiDataSourceProvider`, and `CubeFileProvider` is implemented by `DefaultCubeFileProvider`.

In case of OLAP4J, you must first create an object that implements the `OlapConnectionProvider` interface, which will be used directly in the `BandedMDXDataFactory`'s constructor. `DriverConnectionProvider` and `JndiConnectionProvider` provide an implementation.

Once you have created the factory, in the cases of Mondrian and OLAP4J, you may add **multi-dimensional expression (MDX)** queries by calling the `setQuery (String name, String mdxQuery)` method.

DenormalizedMDXDataFactory

DenormalizedMDXDataFactory maps all the axes of the OLAP result set to TableModel, in a denormalized or flattened fashion. The column headers display the dimensional metadata selected in the axes, as well as the selected measure metadata. For instance, if a year was selected from the time dimension, in the column header you would see the level name [Time].[Year]. DenormalizedMDXDataFactory is often used with crosstabs and will be used again in Chapter 13, *Internationalization, sub-reports and cross-tabs using Java*.

BandedMDXDataFactory example

In this section, you will see two complete Maven projects developing exactly the same Pentaho report: one using the Mondrian native provider and the other using the OLAP4J provider to access the same Mondrian schema. As introduced earlier in the chapter, in both cases, BandedMDXDataFactory will be used, even if two different implementations will be used.

The first example is about using the Mondrian native provider. The complete source code developing the Pentaho report can be found in the https://github.com/fcorti/pentaho-8-reporting-for-java-developers repository; specifically, in the Chapter 12 - Developing using data sources folder. Inside the folder, you will find the pentaho-reporting-data-source-mondrian project, using the PentahoServlet class with the following source code:

```
...

// Data source provider.
DriverDataSourceProvider dsProvider = new DriverDataSourceProvider();
dsProvider.setDriver("org.hsqldb.jdbcDriver");
dsProvider.setProperty("user", "pentaho_user");
dsProvider.setProperty("password", "password");
dsProvider.setUrl("jdbc:hsqldb:./resources/sampledata/sampledata");

// Mondrian cube provider.
DefaultCubeFileProvider cubeProvider = new DefaultCubeFileProvider();
cubeProvider.setMondrianCubeFile("./resources/steelwheels.mondrian.xml");

// Loading Mondrian data source.
BandedMDXDataFactory factory = new BandedMDXDataFactory();
factory.setDataSourceProvider(dsProvider);
factory.setCubeFileProvider(cubeProvider);
factory.setQuery(
  "default",
  "SELECT " +
```

```
    "{[Measures].[Sales]} ON COLUMNS," +
      "{Descendants([Time].Children, [Time].[Months])} ON ROWS" +
    "FROM" +
      "[SteelWheelsSales]");
  report.setDataFactory(factory);
```

...

To run the project, download the `pentaho-reporting-data-source-mondrian` folder to your local machine, open a terminal, move into this folder, and execute the following commands in this sequence:

```
mvn clean install
mvn package
java -jar target/dependency/jetty-runner.jar target/*.war
```

Then open a browser at `http://localhost:8080`, and you should see the Pentaho report in PDF format as a result.

In the same `Chapter 12 - Developing using data sources` folder, inside the `pentaho-reporting-data-source-olap4j` subfolder, you will find the other project, using the OLAP4J provider and containing the `PentahoServlet` class with the following source code:

...

```
// Loading OLAP data.
DriverConnectionProvider provider = new DriverConnectionProvider();
provider.setDriver("mondrian.olap4j.MondrianOlap4jDriver");
provider.setUrl("jdbc:mondrian: ");
provider.setProperty("Catalog", "./resources/steelwheels.mondrian.xml");
provider.setProperty("JdbcUser", "pentaho_user");
provider.setProperty("JdbcPassword", "password");
provider.setProperty("Jdbc",
"jdbc:hsqldb:./resources/sampledata/sampledata");
provider.setProperty("JdbcDrivers", "org.hsqldb.jdbcDriver");

// Creating the factory.
BandedMDXDataFactory factory = new BandedMDXDataFactory(provider);
factory.setQuery(
 "default",
 "SELECT " +
 "{[Measures].[Sales]} ON COLUMNS," +
  "{Descendants([Time].Children, [Time].[Months])} ON ROWS" +
  "FROM" +
  "[SteelWheelsSales]");
report.setDataFactory(factory);
```

. . .

To run the project, execute exactly the same tasks as described previously; download the `pentaho-reporting-data-source-olap4j` folder to your local machine, open a terminal, move into this folder, and execute the following commands in this sequence:

```
mvn clean install
mvn package
java -jar target/dependency/jetty-runner.jar target/*.war
```

Then open a browser at `http://localhost:8080`, and you should see the Pentaho report in PDF format as a result.

As you can see running both the projects, the Pentaho report is exactly the same in terms of layout and content, and this is logical as they are two different ways (one using the native Mondrian provider and the other using the OLAP4J provider) of accessing the same Mondrian schema with the same MDX query.

CompoundDataFactory

The `org.pentaho.reporting.engine.classic.core.CompoundDataFactory` class is a useful factory when working with sub-reports that contain different data sources than the primary report. For instance, with `CompoundDataFactory`, you may use `SQLReportDataFactory` for your master report query and `XPathDataFactory` for a sub-report query. `CompoundDataFactory` has a default constructor, and you may add child data factories by calling the `add(DataFactory)` or `add(index, DataFactory)` methods. The `DataFactory` instances are queried in the order of their index.

All reports generated by the Report Designer use `CompoundDataFactory`, making it possible for the users to add different types of data sources to their reports in the user interface.

ScriptableDataFactory

The
`org.pentaho.reporting.engine.classic.extensions.datasources.scriptable.`
`ScriptableDataFactory` class allows you to populate your report from a script compliant
with the Bean Scripting Framework. The **Bean Scripting Framework (BSF)** is a set of Java
classes which provides scripting language support in Java applications, and access to Java
objects and methods from scripting languages.

`ScriptableDataFactory`, using the Bean Scripting Framework to execute query scripts in
different scripting languages, returns `TableModel`, which can be used as data source in
your Pentaho report. The mechanism is always the same as in the previous (and most
common) examples.

Summary

In this chapter, you worked again with various methods for loading data into the Pentaho
Reporting Engine, after the introduction done in `Chapter 6`, *Configuring JDBC and other data
sources*. At the beginning of this chapter, you were introduced to the Pentaho Reporting
Engine Data API, discovering the `DataFactory` interface together with the `TableModel`
interface and their relation and use.

After you saw all the available `DataFactory` implementations, with descriptions of the
technical details for the best use, as well as some concrete examples to show how to use
them during the development, you learnt how to access the data to build your Pentaho
report.

Now that you have read this chapter, you should feel comfortable with the Pentaho
Reporting Engine Data API and all the technical details around developing a Pentaho
Report programmatically. This is an advanced task for developers: creating complex
Pentaho reports, embedded in your custom projects using Java.

In the next chapter, you will see some other advanced features, already covered in `Chapter
9`, *Internationalization and localization* and `Chapter 10`, *Subreports and cross tabs*. During the
read, you will continue to deal with the development of a Pentaho report programmatically
using the Pentaho Reporting SDK.

13

Internationalization, Subreports, and Cross Tabs Using Java

After Chapter 12, *Developing Using Data Sources*, in this chapter you will continue to discover the advanced features already covered in Chapter 9, *Internationalization and Localization* and Chapter 10, *Subreports and Cross Tabs*, but from a development perspective. As usual, the description will be using the *learning by example* approach, with the help of concrete and working projects.

You will start by learning all about the development of Pentaho reports localized in all the languages you may want. Then you will see how to develop a subreport programmatically using Java, and, last but not least, you will see how to develop cross tabs using Java.

This chapter is highly technical and written as a tutorial for Java developers. At the end of this chapter, you will feel comfortable with all the advanced features of Pentaho Reporting, from a developer's perspective. This chapter is the last one covering the existing features for building your own Java application and embedding the Pentaho Reporting Engine.

Internationalization and localization using Java

As you learnt in Chapter 9, *Internationalization and Localization*, as with all modern software, Pentaho Reporting is developed following all the best practices and patterns to support internationalization, so that it can be adapted to various languages and regions without engineering changes. In this section in particular, you will reach the same level of expertise, but from a Java perspective. In the following sections, you will go through the basics of Pentaho report localization from a Java perspective; then you will move on to understand how to test localization, and finally, you will see a fully working example of some source code, available in the well known GitHub repository.

Resources for localization using Java

To internationalize a report, you must use the resource elements available within Pentaho Reporting when creating your report. Each resource element defines a resource base and a resource key reference. Normally, the resource base refers to the name of the message properties file in which localized names are kept. For default handling of resource bundles in Java, see Java's *i18n* tutorial on resource bundles at http://java.sun.com/docs/books/tutorial/i18n/resbundle/concept.html.

Once you have built your report, you will want to configure your application to access the resource bundle files. Pentaho Reporting defines the ResourceBundleFactory API, which allows you to customize how these files are loaded. By default, a report is configured to use the DefaultResourceBundleFactory implementation, which uses Java's ResourceBundle implementation. This implementation resolves the provided resource base value on the Java classpath.

The ResourceBundleFactory is also responsible for determining the specific locale to use when rendering the report. The DefaultResourceBundleFactory uses the default system locale, but also contains the setLocale() method for configuring the locale if necessary. This behavior will be used in our examples to control the final version of the report by setting the default locale.

Using the resource elements in your report allows you to localize labels, fields, and messages, as you learnt in Chapter 9, *Internationalization and Localization*. In particular, resource-label has a corresponding class in ResourceLabelElementFactory, resource-field has a corresponding class in ResourceFieldElementFactory, and resource-message has a corresponding class in ResourceMessageElementFactory. In the following example, you will see how to use ResourceLabelElementFactory only, but the use of the other resource factories follows the same principles.

Testing the localization using Java

As you read in the previous section, the control of ResourceBundle is done using the locale. By default, the system locale is used and can be made explicit with the following source code:

```
Locale locale = new Locale();
```

If you want to control (and change) the default locale, you can setup its value with the following source code (the example shows how to set the Spanish language):

```
Locale locale = new Locale("es");
Locale.setDefault(locale);
```

This small piece of code is extremely useful during the tests, if you want to programmatically control the locale of your Pentaho report. In the following example, you will see how to switch from the default locale to a custom locale to test the final version.

An example of report localization using Java

To show in practice an example of report localization using Java, let's use the https://github.com/fcorti/pentaho-8-reporting-for-java-developers repository; specifically, the project pentaho-reporting-localization, stored in the Chapter 13 – Internationalization, sub-reports and cross-tabs using Java folder.

Before checking the source code, let's examine the content of the resources folder, where you can find two property files:

- my-first-reporting-project_en.properties: This contains the resource keys for the English language
- my-first-reporting-project_es.properties: This contains the resource keys for the Spanish language

You have already learnt the basics of the *i18n* representation and you have already used these properties in the examples of Chapter 9, *Internationalization and Localization*. To include the property files in the distribution package of the project, add the following resources tag to the pom.xml file:

```
...
<build>
  <finalName>pentaho-reporting-web-app</finalName>
  <resources>
    <resource>
      <directory>resources</directory>
    </resource>
  </resources>
  <plugins>
    ...
  </plugins>
</build>
```

Let's move now to look inside the well-known PentahoServlet class, where you can find the following source code:

```
...

// Defining the default locale.
Locale locale = new Locale("es");
Locale.setDefault(locale);

// Adding a resource label to the report header band.
ResourceLabelElementFactory labelFactory = new
ResourceLabelElementFactory();
labelFactory.setResourceKey("ORDERNUMBER");
labelFactory.setResourceBase("my-first-reporting-project");
...
Element labelField = labelFactory.createElement();
reportHeader.addElement(labelField);

...
```

As you can see, the first task is to set up the Spanish language as default locale. This is done using `Locale locale = new Locale("es")` and then using the `locale` variable as the default. Once done, the `ResourceLabelElementFactory` class is declared to create the `resource-label` element. The `setResourceKey` method enables you to point to the correct description in the properties file and the `setResourceBase` method enables you to point to the correct properties file. All the rest of the methods are similar to the one used in the previous examples.

To run the project, open a Terminal, move into the project's folder, and execute the following commands in this sequence:

```
mvn clean install
mvn package
java -jar target/dependency/jetty-runner.jar target/*.war
```

Opening a browser at `http://localhost:8080`, you should see the Pentaho report as in the following screenshot:

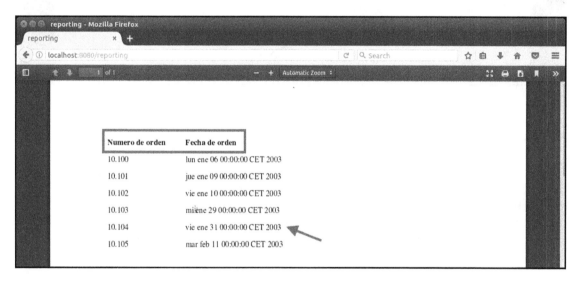

To change the default language, as described previously in the chapter, change the locale to `Locale locale = new Locale("en")`. In this way, you will ask the project to use the English locale as default. By compiling the project again and repeating the preceding commands, you will get the following preview, with the labels that were changed simply changing the locale:

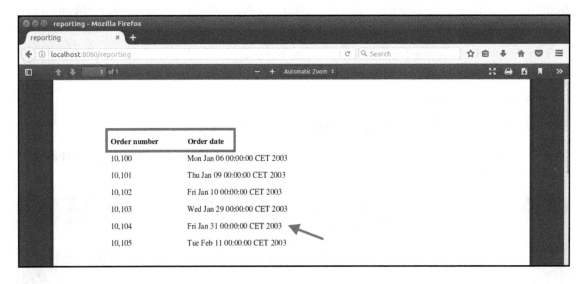

Subreports using Java

As you learnt in `Chapter 10`, *Subreports and Cross Tabs*, subreports in Pentaho Reporting allow you to include fully featured reports inside a master report. In this section in particular, you will reach the same level of expertise from a Java perspective. In the following sections, you will go through the basics of Pentaho subreports, then you will move on to understand a fully working example of source code, available in the GitHub repository.

Subreports using Java

To understand the development of subreports using Java, let's describe the various components used for its definition. First is the `SubReport` class, used to declare and manage subreport instances in `MasterReport`. Differently from a regular element, a subreport is added to a report's band using the `addSubReport(SubReport subReport)` method.

As you saw in `Chapter 10`, *Subreports and Cross Tabs*, subreports always use a different data source for the content definition. Using Java, all the declared queries in `MasterReport` are inherited by default from the subreports, but it is required to specify the query for `MasterReport` and `SubReport`, by using the `setQuery` method.

As often happens, a subreport may use one or more parameters coming from `MasterReport` to guide the correct rendering. To specify the input parameters, the `SubReport` class provides the `addInputParameter(String outerName, String sourceColumn)` method.

Apart from the topics discussed previously, the use of `SubReport` is similar to a regular `MasterReport` where you can add elements, customize the layout, and so on.

An example of subreport using Java

To show in practice an example of subreport using Java, let's use the `https://github.com/fcorti/pentaho-8-reporting-for-java-developers` repository; specifically, the project `pentaho-reporting-subreport`, stored in the `Chapter 13 - Internationalization, sub-reports and cross-tabs using Java` folder.

As you can see from the `PentahoServlet` class, `DataFactory` declares the `default` query and the `default2` query using the following piece of code:

```
// Defining the queries.
SQLReportDataFactory dataFactory = new SQLReportDataFactory(provider);
dataFactory.setQuery(
 "default",
 "SELECT ORDERNUMBER, ORDERDATE FROM ORDERS");
dataFactory.setQuery(
 "default2",
 "SELECT PRODUCTCODE, QUANTITYORDERED, PRICEEACH FROM ORDERDETAILS " +
 "WHERE ORDERNUMBER=${ORDERNUMBER} ORDER BY ORDERLINENUMBER ASC LIMIT 5");
report.setDataFactory(dataFactory);
```

Pay a lot of attention to giving the queries declared in `DataFactory` unique names. If you don't do that, the behavior of your application will be unpredictable, and you will experience a painful waste of time understanding where exactly the problem is.

As described previously in the chapter, `MasterReport` and `SubReport` declare the query they are going to use with the following code:

```
. . .
report.setQuery("default");
. . .
subReport.setQuery("default2");
. . .
```

In the following piece of Java code, you can find the declaration of the `SubReport` object, an example of addition of elements to the subreport's band, and the inclusion of the subreport in the main report:

```
. . .

// Creating the subreport.
SubReport subReport = new SubReport();
subReport.setQuery("default2");
subReport.addInputParameter("ORDERNUMBER", "ORDERNUMBER");

. . .

// Adding a field to the subreport's details band.
TextFieldElementFactory textFactory2 = new TextFieldElementFactory();
. . .
Element textField2 = textFactory2.createElement();
subReport.getItemBand().addElement(textField2);

. . .

// Adding the subreport to the report's details band.
itemBand.addSubReport(subReport);

. . .
```

To run the project, open a Terminal, move into the project's folder, and execute the following commands in this sequence:

```
mvn clean install
mvn package
java -jar target/dependency/jetty-runner.jar target/*.war
```

Opening a browser at `http://localhost:8080`, you should see the Pentaho report as in the following screenshot:

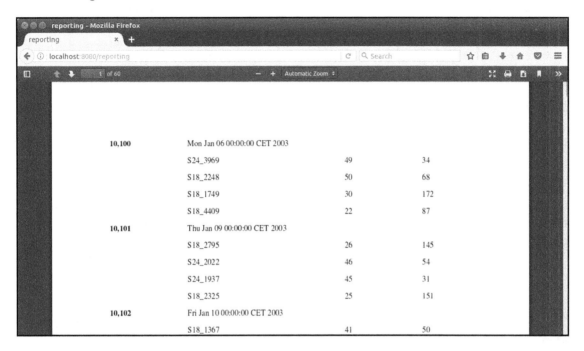

> As you can see, the resulting Pentaho report is exactly the same as the one we developed in `Chapter 10`, *Subreports and Cross Tabs*, using Pentaho Report Designer. In other words, here you reach the same expertise on Pentaho Report Designer, but using your Java skills in development.

Cross tab using Java

In `Chapter 10`, *Subreports and Cross Tabs*, you learnt all about cross tabulation (or cross tab), allowing you to view dimensional data in a Pentaho report. In this section in particular, you will reach the same level of expertise from a Java perspective. In the following sections, you will go through the basics of Pentaho cross tab and then you will move on to understand a fully working example of source code, available in the GitHub repository.

Cross tabs using Java

To understand the development of cross tab using Java, let's introduce the various components used for its definition. First is the `CrosstabGroup` class, used to declare and manage cross tab instances in `MasterReport`. Differently from a regular element, a cross tab is added to a report using the `addRootGroup(CrosstabGroup crosstabGroup)` method.

As you saw in `Chapter 10`, *Subreports and Cross Tabs*, cross tabs can use an MDX query or a more traditional SQL query with an MDX-like structure. In every case, the composition of the cross tab is done in steps: first defining the cross tab rows, then defining the cross tab columns, and only at the end defining the cross tab details.

The definition of the cross tab rows starts from the `CrosstabRowGroupBody` object, identified from the `getBody()` method of the `CrosstabGroup` instance. Once identified, the `getGroup()` method defines the `CrosstabRowGroup` instance to be used to setup the query field (using the `setField(String field)` method), the element presenting the title (using the `getTitleHeader().addElement(Element element)` method), and the element representing the row values (using the `getHeader().addElement(Element element)` method).

The definition of the cross tab columns starts from the `CrosstabColumnGroupBody` object, identified from the `getBody()` method of the `CrosstabRowGroup` instance used previously. Once identified, the `getGroup()` method defines the `CrosstabColumnGroup` instance to be used to setup the query field (using the `setField(String field)` method), the element presenting the title (using the `getTitleHeader().addElement(Element element)` method), and the element representing the column values (using the `getHeader().addElement(Element element)` method).

The definition of the cross tab details is done by adding a new instance of the `CrosstabCell` element to the `CrosstabCellBody` instance, identified using the `getBody()` method of the `CrosstabColumnGroup` instance used previously. The `CrosstabCell` element is defined using the `addElement(Element element)` method where `Element` added is the query field containing the measure to be aggregated.

An example of cross tab using Java

To show in practice an example of cross tab using Java, let's use the `https://github.com/fcorti/pentaho-8-reporting-for-java-developers` repository; specifically, the project `pentaho-reporting-crosstab`, stored in the `Chapter 13 - Internationalization, sub-reports and cross-tabs using Java` folder.

As you can see from the `PentahoServlet` class, `DataFactory` declares an MDX query in a Mondrian cube provider. The Mondrian schema used in this example is the one you have already seen in `Chapter 6`, *Configuring JDBC and Other Data Sources*. Following is the source code defining the MDX query:

```
factory.setQuery(
 "default",
 "SELECT " +
 " CrossJoin([Markets].Children, [Time].Children) ON ROWS," +
 " [Measures].[Sales] ON COLUMNS " +
 "FROM [SteelWheelsSales]");
```

In the following piece of source code, we see the complete setup of the `CrosstabGroup` instance:

```
...

// Defining the cross tab.
CrosstabGroup crosstabGroup = new CrosstabGroup();

// Defining the cross tab rows.
CrosstabRowGroupBody rowBody = (CrosstabRowGroupBody)
crosstabGroup.getBody();
CrosstabRowGroup rowGroup = rowBody.getGroup();
rowGroup.setField("[Markets].[Territory]");
rowGroup.getTitleHeader().addElement(createDataItem("[Markets].[Territory]"
));
rowGroup.getHeader().addElement(createFieldItem("[Markets].[Territory]"));

// Defining the cross tab columns.
CrosstabColumnGroupBody columnGroupBody = (CrosstabColumnGroupBody)
rowGroup.getBody();
CrosstabColumnGroup columnGroup = columnGroupBody.getGroup();
columnGroup.setField("[Time].[Years]");
columnGroup.getTitleHeader().addElement(createDataItem("[Time].[Years]"));
columnGroup.getHeader().addElement(createFieldItem("[Time].[Years]"));

// Defining the cross tab details.
CrosstabCellBody body = (CrosstabCellBody) columnGroup.getBody();
```

```
CrosstabCell cell = new CrosstabCell();
cell.addElement( createFieldItem("[Measures].[Sales]" ));
body.addElement(cell);

report.setRootGroup(crosstabGroup);

...
```

To run the project, open a Terminal, move into the project's folder, and execute the following commands in this sequence:

```
mvn clean install
mvn package
java -jar target/dependency/jetty-runner.jar target/*.war
```

Opening a browser at `http://localhost:8080`, you should see the Pentaho report as in the following screenshot:

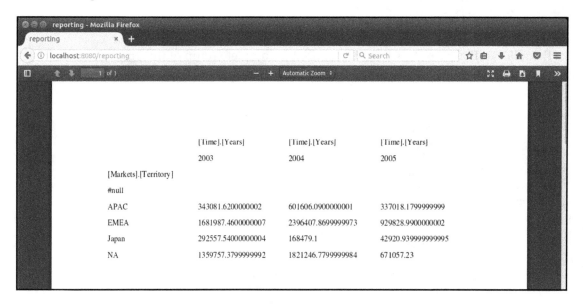

 As you can see, the resulting Pentaho report is exactly the same as the one we developed in `Chapter 10`, *Subreports and Cross Tabs*, using Pentaho Report Designer. In other words, here you reach the same expertise on Pentaho Report Designer, but using your Java skills in development.

Summary

In this chapter, you completed the journey into the advanced features of Pentaho Reporting from a development perspective. With the help of practical and useful examples, you started by learning how to develop a Pentaho report in different languages with the support of the Java *i18N*. Then you saw how to develop a subreport programmatically using Java and, in the end, you saw how to develop cross tabs using Java.

Now that you have read this chapter, you should feel comfortable with the Pentaho Reporting Engine and all the technical details around developing a Pentaho report programmatically. This is an advanced task for developers, creating complex Pentaho reports that are embedded in your custom projects using Java.

As a developer, in the next chapter you will see how to build interactive reports based on events. Event bindings are defined in Pentaho reports, making it possible to receive event notifications from within a report.

14

Building Interactive Reports

In this chapter, you will learn to enable interactive functionality in reports. Interactive reports are less common, but allow for interesting behaviors in various output formats. Each type of interactive approach covered in this chapter is based on a particular layout engine. You will learn about HTML interactive options by creating examples that demonstrate their capabilities. By definition, interactive reports are based on events. Event bindings are defined in the report definition, making it possible to receive event notifications from within a report.

This chapter is highly technical and written as a tutorial for pure Java developers. By the end of this chapter, you would have learnt how to modify report definitions to generate hyperlink events and many different HTML or JavaScript events, and how to modify the report HTML document object model dynamically when events are triggered from the report.

Interactive reports in HTML

With Pentaho Reporting, it is possible to define highly customized interactive reports in the HTML/JavaScript environment. Pentaho Reporting defines a set of properties which, when specified, allow for rich interactivity between the user and the report. In this section, you will get an overview of these properties, along with a rich example that demonstrates potential uses.

In Chapter 5, *Design and Layout in Report Designer*, you have already learnt everything about the HTML properties, but here we would like to again share the details of the properties for better understanding:

Name	Description
class	This property sets the class attribute of the current HTML entity to the specified value.
name	This property sets the name attribute of the current HTML entity to the specified value.
title	This property sets the title attribute of the current HTML entity to the specified value.
xml-id	This property allows the naming of the current HTML entity, setting the id attribute, making it possible to reference in outside scripts.
append-body	This property allows the placement of raw HTML in the body of the HTML document, prior to the rendering of the current element.
append-body-footer	This property allows the placement of raw HTML in the body of the HTML document, after the rendering of the current element.
append-header	Defined only at the master report level, this property allows the inclusion of raw HTML in the header of the generated HTML document. This location is traditionally used to load additional CSS files, as well as external JavaScript files.
on-click	This property renders an onclick HTML attribute on the currently defined element. It is a string of JavaScript that is executed in the browser when a user clicks on the element.
on-double-click	This property renders an ondblclick HTML attribute on the currently defined element. It is a string of JavaScript that is executed in the browser when a user double-clicks on the element.
on-mouse-down	This property renders an onmousedown HTML attribute on the currently defined element. It is a string of JavaScript that is executed in the browser when a user presses a mouse button. This can be used to detect the beginning of a drag operation.

Name	Description
on-mouse-up	This property renders an `onmouseup` HTML attribute on the currently defined element. It is a string of JavaScript that is executed in the browser when a user releases a mouse button.
on-mouse-move	This property renders an `onmousemove` HTML attribute on the currently defined element. It is a string of JavaScript that is executed in the browser when a user moves the mouse.
on-mouse-over	This property renders an `onmouseover` HTML attribute on the currently defined element. It is a string of JavaScript that is executed in the browser when a user moves the mouse over the element.
on-key-down	This property renders an `onkeydown` HTML attribute on the currently defined element. It is a string of JavaScript that is executed in the browser when a user presses down a key.
on-key-pressed	This property renders an `onkeypressed` HTML attribute on the currently defined element. It is a string of JavaScript that is executed in the browser when a user presses a key.
on-key-up	This property renders an `onkeyup` HTML attribute on the currently defined element. It is a string of JavaScript that is executed in the browser when a user releases a key.

Manipulating the reporting HTML DOM

It is possible to alter the HTML **Document Object Model** (**DOM**) dynamically, by combining the `xml-id` property along with the `on-click` event. For instance, by setting a label's `xml-id` to example, and setting the following JavaScript in the `on-click` property, you can toggle between two text values:

```
document.getElementById('example').innerHTML = (document.getElementById
('example').innerHTML == 'Hello') ? 'Goodbye' : 'Hello';
```

Including an external CSS or JavaScript resource

Using the master report object's `append-header` property, it is possible to include CSS or JavaScript in your report. This is useful if you have written a large amount of JavaScript that you would like to keep separate from your report, or if you want to include a useful JavaScript library, as demonstrated in the example that will follow.

An example of the `append-header` value can be:

```
<link type="text/css" rel="stylesheet" href="custom.css" />
```

When implementing the server, it's important to make sure that the relative paths of the files referenced are accessible from the current document.

Example of interactive reports using Java

Thanks to the Pentaho Reporting capabilities, the development of interactive reports is straightforward. As a demonstration of how an interactive report would work, you will see here how to develop different types of interactions. The examples shared here cannot be exhaustive, but will give you an overview of the most relevant features you can use in your future developments.

Opening a static URL from a Pentaho report

The first example we are going to show is about a very basic feature: opening a custom URL by clicking on a report's element. To see in action a working example, a complete project is available in the `https://github.com/fcorti/pentaho-8-reporting-for-java-developers` repository, specifically, in the `interactive-report` project stored in the `Chapter 14 - Building interactive reports` folder.

Looking at the source code of the project, there is something we didn't have the change to see in the previous chapters of the book: how to preview a report in the `.prpt` format using Java. Inside the well known `PentahoServlet` class, you can find the following Java code:

```
// Getting the report.
ResourceManager manager = new ResourceManager();
manager.registerDefaults();
Resource res = manager.createDirectly(
  new URL("file:resources/interactive_report_1.prpt"),
  MasterReport.class);
MasterReport report = (MasterReport) res.getResource();
```

The preceding portion of Java code defines the `MasterReport` object from the `.prpt` file stored in the filesystem. The `.prpt` file is named `interactive_report_1.prpt` and you can find it in the `resources` folder of the project. All the examples described in this section are based on this report, so feel free to open and edit it using Pentaho Report Designer in the way you learned in the previous chapters.

Starting from here, you can decide to preview the content in PDF format, using the following Java code:

```
response.setContentType("application/pdf");
PdfReportUtil.createPDF(report, response.getOutputStream());
```

Else, you can choose to preview the content in HTML format, using the following Java code. As you can expect, for the purpose of this example, you will see the HTML rendering.

```
response.setContentType("text/html");
HtmlReportUtil.createStreamHTML(report, response.getOutputStream());
```

To run the project, open a Terminal, move into the project's folder, and execute the following commands in this sequence:

```
mvn clean install
mvn package
java -jar target/dependency/jetty-runner.jar target/*.war
```

Opening a browser at `http://localhost:8080`, you should see the Pentaho report as in the following screenshot:

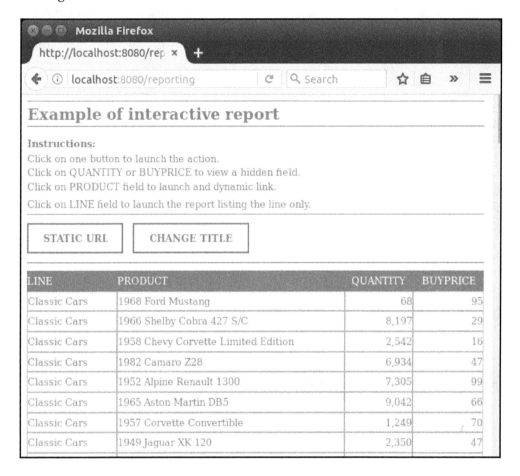

In the report, you can find an easy legend of the available interactions as a reference, but here in this section, you will see them one by one, with descriptions on how to develop them. The first one introduced is related to the **STATIC URL** button. Opening the `interactive_report_1.prpt` file with Pentaho Report Designer, you can see that four properties are customized, as shown in the following screenshot:

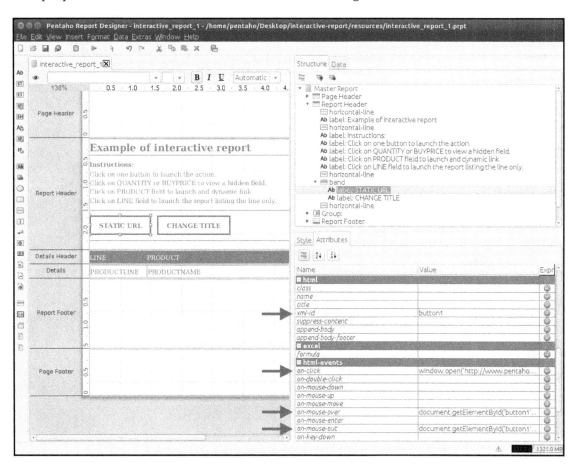

The first property is `xml-id`, to setup the unique identifier of the element (in this case, `button1`), and the second one is `on-click`, containing the static JavaScript source code opening the Google page as a static URL (`window.open('http://www.pentaho.com', '_blank');`). The other two properties (`on-mouse-over` and `on-mouse-out`) contain the JavaScript source code used to color the `label` element representing the button. The following screenshot shows the user experience by clicking on the `label` element:

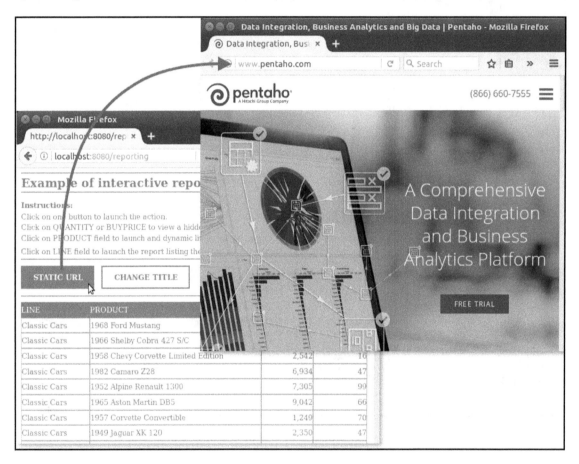

Opening a dynamic URL from a Pentaho report

Another relevant example is an improvement of the static URL you have previously seen. In this section you are going to see two different interactions, opening dynamic URLs by clicking on a report's element. Starting from the previous report, you can click on the QUANTITY field or the BUYPRICE field (of each row). The result is a modal window containing the total cost of the product, calculated by multiplying QUANTITY * BUYPRICE. In the following screenshot, you can see what the user experience looks like:

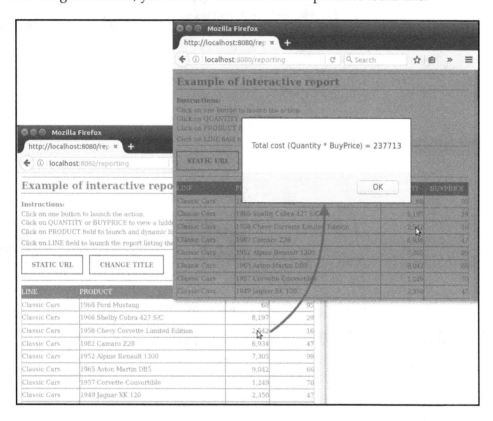

The development of this interaction is very similar to the previous one, thanks to the on-click property. The only difference with the static URL is that the value of the property is dynamically calculated using the following formula:

```
=CONCATENATE(
  "alert('Total cost (Quantity * BuyPrice) = ";
  [QUANTITY]*[BUYPRICE];
  "');")
```

As you can see, the formula is a dynamic calculation of a JavaScript source code, alerting with a string containing the result.

Another interesting example of interaction using dynamic URLs is visible by clicking the PRODUCT field (for each row). In this case, a Google page is opened in a different window, searching for the selected product. In the following screenshot, you can see an example showing the result of clicking the 1958 Chevy Corvette Limited Edition row:

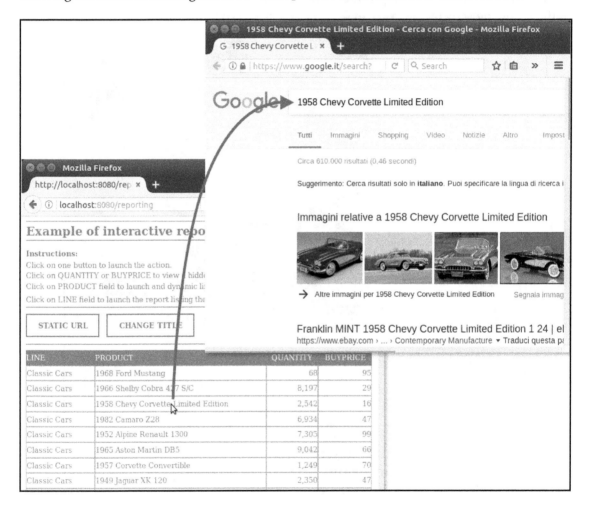

Also in this case, the development of the `on-click` property does the magic. In the following formula, we can see the dynamic portion of the JavaScript code generated from the report element (`text-field` for PRODUCTNAME):

```
= CONCATENATE(
  "window.open(";"'http://www.google.com/search?q=";
  [PRODUCTNAME];
  "','_blank');")
```

Manipulating the content of a Pentaho report

To show an example of element manipulation, in this section you will see how to change the content of a title (a regular `label` element) with a dynamic content showing the current time. Starting again from the same report, click on the **CHANGE TITLE** button and you will get something similar to the following screenshot:

As you can see, the title of the report changes accordingly.

The development of this example follows the same principle with a slightly different application: the xml-id property is defined for the title element and the on-click property of the button element contains the following JavaScript as static text:

```
var currentdate = new Date();
document.getElementById('title').innerHTML = 'Title changed at ' +
  currentdate.getHours() + ':' + currentdate.getMinutes() + ':' +
  currentdate.getSeconds();
```

Example of master/details report interaction

Finally, let's see how to develop one of the most common interactions between reports: the navigation from one report to another, where the content of the target report depends on one parameter. To develop this example, you need a second report, in this case named interactive_report_2.prpt. The second report shows all the products included in one line. As you can expect, the line value is a mandatory parameter.

To develop the interaction, the Java project includes another endpoint called /reporting2, connected to the second report. The implementation is defined in the PentahoServlet2 class containing the following Java code:

```
// Getting the report.
ResourceManager manager = new ResourceManager();
manager.registerDefaults();
Resource res = manager.createDirectly(
  new URL("file:resources/interactive_report_2.prpt"),
  MasterReport.class);
MasterReport report = (MasterReport) res.getResource();

// Mandatory parameter.
report.getParameterValues().put("LINE", request.getParameter("line"));

// Conversion to HTML and rendering.
response.setContentType("text/html");
HtmlReportUtil.createStreamHTML(report, response.getOutputStream());
```

Now that the second report is ready to be called, let's see how the interaction is developed in the first report, `interactive_report_1.prpt`. The requested development in the source report is always the same: a dynamic call to a target URL, defining the `on-click` property of the report's element. In this case, the `on-click` property is defined as following:

```
=CONCATENATE(
    "window.open(";"'/reporting2?line=";
    [PRODUCTLINE];
    "','_self');")
```

In the following screenshot, the user experience shows the interaction between the first report (`interactive_report_1.prpt`) and the second report (`interactive_report_2.prpt`), in case of clicking on the `Classic Cars` row of the `LINE` field:

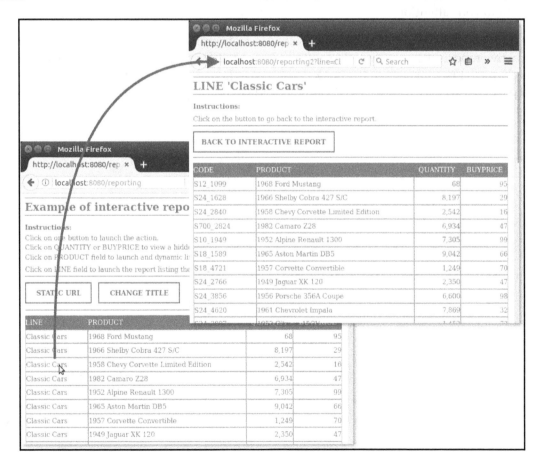

If you plan to develop interactive reports in complex use cases, always remember to consider other solutions more related to dashboard frameworks or OLAP clients. The suggestion is to always remember that the reporting solutions are great, but their main goal is to show detailed or aggregated data in a static or parameterized content. If you force the use of the reporting solutions to develop dashboards or something really dynamic and interactive, the risk of a failure is high. Be aware!

Summary

In this chapter, you learned the basics of developing interactive reports and saw some practical examples that you could use in your future development. After the discovery of the technical solutions, the advice to use the interactive features with moderation has been brought to your attention.

Now that you have read this chapter, you should feel comfortable with the generation of interactive reports using hyperlink events and many different HTML or JavaScript events. This chapter closes the part of the book dedicated to Java development and APIs. In the next part, you will see how to use Pentaho reports in other components of the Pentaho Suite.

15
Using Reports in Pentaho Business Analytics Platform

This chapter is the first one of a short series talking about using Pentaho reports in other components of the Pentaho Suite. In this chapter, in particular, you will learn how to use an existing Pentaho report in the Pentaho Business Analytics Platform. The Pentaho Business Analytics Platform is a web application used as frontend for final users and developers, enabling all of them to use its analytical tools such as dashboards, pivoting sessions, and obviously, reports.

In this chapter, you will be introduced to the basics of the Pentaho Business Analytics Platform, as well as a description of how to install it and upload Pentaho reports. Afterwards, you will learn how to manage permits and preview the report with a direct call or included in a Pentaho dashboard using the Pentaho CTools.

This chapter is written as a tutorial for developers and information technologists. The best way to learn is to follow the instructions on your laptop while reading. By the end of this chapter, you will feel comfortable with the basics of using the Pentaho Business Analytics Platform, together with Pentaho reports. This will be extremely useful for your future projects, enabling you to have a fully featured frontend for your final customers and managers.

Introducing Pentaho Business Analytics Platform

As part of Pentaho's suite of products, Pentaho offers an open source Business Analytics Platform. The Business Analytics Platform is a web application that allows users to publish and manage reports within an enterprise business intelligence system. The Business Analytics Platform offers many capabilities, including the management and execution of Pentaho reports. By combining Pentaho Reporting and Pentaho's Business Analytics Platform, information technologists may utilize Pentaho Reporting in their environment without writing any code. In addition to the publishing and execution of reports, the open source Business Analytics Platform allows for scheduling, background execution, security, and much more.

With Pentaho's Enterprise Business Analytics Platform, additional capabilities are available, but in this book, we prefer to use the Community Edition as it is downloadable and available for everyone without any cost.

Installing the Business Analytics Platform

The installation of the Pentaho Business Analytics Platform is straightforward, following an *unzip and run* task. The prerequisites to run Pentaho Business Analytics Platform are simple; it requires a JRE 8, already installed in your environment. Both Windows-based operating systems and Linux-based operating systems are supported. The screenshots and previews shown in this chapter are done using an Ubuntu 16.04.2 LTS distribution.

Before installing the application, you can download the artifacts distributed in a ZIP file directly from the official Pentaho Community website (`http://community.pentaho.com/`) or the Pentaho SourceForge website (`https://sourceforge.net/projects/pentaho/`). In both cases, you should download a ZIP file named something similar to `pentaho-server-ce-<version>.zip`.

Once the ZIP file has been downloaded into your environment, unzip it into the final path (on a Linux-based operating system, the `/opt` path is suggested), and you will have all the Pentaho Business Analytics Platform data available in the folder `pentaho-server`.

Though you probably cannot believe it, this is all that is needed to install Pentaho Business Analytics Platform into your environment.

Pentaho Business Analytics Platform is mainly a web application deployed in an Apache Tomcat Servlet Container (`https://tomcat.apache.org/`). You can easily run the Pentaho Business Analytics Platform by opening a Terminal and executing the `start-pentaho` script stored in the `pentaho-server` folder (the one with the `.sh` extension for the Linux-based operating systems, and the one with the `.bat` extension for the Windows-based operating systems).

To check what is happening to the web application, you can take a look at the log file at `<pentaho-server>/tomcat/logs/catalina.out`. Once the application has started, you can access the user interface using a supported web browser, at the link `http://<server>:8080/pentaho`. With Pentaho Business Analytics Platform Community Edition, it is suggested to use Mozilla Firefox or Google Chrome, instead of Microsoft Internet Explorer.

To access as administrator, you can use the `admin` user with password `password`. Once accessed, your browser should look like the following screenshot:

By default, the Pentaho Business Analytics Platform distribution comes with an HyperSQL database (`http://hsqldb.org/`) instance to store configurations, data and everything that is requested to run correctly. By its nature, the HyperSQL database is not suggested for a production environment, but for now, it perfectly fits our purpose. If interested, Pentaho Business Analytics Platform can also run using the most common RDBMS and application servers. Refer to the official documentation for further details.

Basics of the Business Analytics Platform

By default, by accessing the home page of a Pentaho Business Analytics Platform installation, you have access to the Pentaho user console. The Pentaho user console serves as the portal for you to access Pentaho tools and features. Home contains easy access buttons, so that you can browse files, create new reports and dashboards, view Pentaho documentation, and quickly open recently viewed or favorite files.

In this book, you will not see all the available features of the Business Analytics Platform. However, what we would like to bring to your attention is the **Browse Files** button, where you can open a window to locate your files using the browsing and files panes, and manage them using the action pane. In the following screenshot, you can see what the Browse Files panel looks likes:

The **Browse Files** page gives you access to the Pentaho repository based on an embedded Apache Jackrabbit (http://jackrabbit.apache.org/) instance, an open source content repository for the Java platform. The Pentaho repository is really relevant for our purpose, because it enables the users to store all the reports, dashboards, and resources in general, in a tree structure with a user experience similar to a filesystem (of course, it is not a real filesystem). The main advantage of using Apache Jackrabbit is that all the content is accessible and manageable through a RESTful API, very easy to consume and integrate. The Pentaho repository is a core feature, widely used in the following sections.

Publishing a report in the Business Analytics Platform

The first task to do to use a Pentaho report in the Business Analytics Platform is uploading it into the Pentaho repository. This is a preliminary task before every action, like previewing, scheduling, and so on. Once uploaded, the Pentaho report is automatically published and can be used to accordance with the Pentaho Business Analytics Platform permits and roles.

A Pentaho report can be uploaded in a Pentaho repository following three main paths: the manual upload, the publication using the Pentaho Report Designer, and the bulk import. In the following sections, you will discover the first two paths, because the bulk import is a suggested way if you have to manage a total or partial restore of the Pentaho repository.

Manually uploading a report

You can directly manually upload a Pentaho report by using the **Browse Files** page of the Pentaho user console. The first thing to do to upload a Pentaho report is to select a folder in the left panel. As you may expect, the folder will contain the report as a regular filesystem (and as a filesystem, you cannot store reports in two different folders simultaneously). On the action panel on the right, you can see the **Upload...** link. Clicking on the link, the upload modal window appears, where you can select the .prpt file from the local filesystem and specify some advanced settings. Once done, select the **OK** button, and the report will be uploaded directly in the Pentaho repository.

In the following image, you can see how the **Browse Files** page looks after the report is uploaded in the Pentaho repository:

Publishing a report using the Pentaho Report Designer

From the Pentaho Report Designer, you can have direct access to a Pentaho Repository, using the standard interface. If you take a look at the **File** item in the upper menu, you can see **Publish...**. Clicking on it, a modal window asks you the basic information to connect to an existing Pentaho repository. Once connected, another modal window shows you the folder structure you can dive into, to find the final location for your report. Once confirmed, the .prpt file is uploaded into its final destination.

In the following screenshot, you can see these three steps:

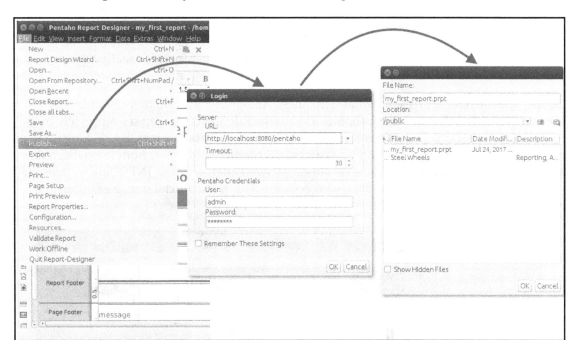

 TIP

If you take a look at the Pentaho Report Designer user interface, you can see the **Open from Repository...** item in **File** of the upper menu. This feature lets you open a report directly from an existing Pentaho repository. The user experience is the same as described previously, and using this feature, together with **Publish...**, you can develop using a centralized Pentaho repository instead of a local filesystem.

Managing data sources

Publishing a Pentaho report into the Business Analytics Platform is not enough to make it work for the final users. As you saw in Chapter 6, *Configuring JDBC and Other Data Sources*, there are several types of possible data sources that a Pentaho report can use. Some of them define the data source directly in the report, but some of them define only a symbolic link to an external definition. If you use a JDBC or JNDI connection to a DBMS (just quoting a common example), you also need to define the data source in Pentaho Business Analytics Platform. Without the same exact definition, your report won't be available and will raise an exception at the first call.

Always remember to double check that the definition of the data source on the Business Analytics Platform is exactly the same as the one used in reporting design, including the same name (case sensitive), type, settings, and parameters. If you miss or misspell something, the report will not work and you will lose a lot of time, even if the report is exactly the same and should work.

To manage the data sources in Pentaho Business Analytics Platform, there is a friendly feature available in the upper menu, included in the **File** item (you can see a preview in the following screenshot). The name of the feature is **Manage Data Sources**. By clicking on it, a simple window will be shown and you can create, modify, and delete both the JDBC data sources and the multidimensional data sources (called analysis). The JNDI data sources are managed in some configuration files, well documented in the official documentation available at `https://help.pentaho.com/Documentation`.

Can you see that the `SampleData (Local)` data source is not available in the default installation of Business Analytics Platform? This is the reason why `my_first_report` will fail if executed. As an exercise, open the report directly from the Pentaho repository using Pentaho Report Designer, and change the data source to `SampleData`. Then publish the report again, replacing it into the Pentaho repository. As an alternative, delete it from the Pentaho repository and replace it with the one you can find in the `https://github.com/fcorti/pentaho-8-reporting-for-java-developers` repository, specifically, in the `Chapter 15 - Using reports in Pentaho Business Analytics Platform/my_reports` folder.

Previewing a report

Now that the Pentaho report is correctly published in the Business Analytics Platform, what you probably expect to do is to start using it. The most simple use we can think of is the preview. The preview of a Pentaho report can be done in two different ways: by manually using the browse files page or through a direct link.

Previewing a report from the browse files page

Previewing a report from the browse files page is as straightforward as clicking on the `.prpt` file and selecting the **Open** item or the **Open in a new window** item. The difference between the two is easy to understand, but the final result is exactly the same, even if the target window will be different.

Previewing a report using a direct link

One of the most powerful features of the Business Analytics Platform is accessing a published report using a public URL. The public URL is defined as follow:

- The base URL. In our example, `http://localhost:8080/pentaho`.
- The endpoint path. In our example, `/api/repos/`.
- The path of the `.prpt` file into the Pentaho repository, where the path separator is the semicolon (`:`). The string is URL-encoded into the URL. In our example, `%3Apublic%3A`.
- The URL-encoded name of the `.prpt` file. In our example, `my_first_report.prpt`.
- The endpoint postfix. In our example, `/viewer`, but you can also use `/generatedContent`, if you'd like to render the report in an IFRAME without the viewer.

In the following URL, you can find the link to the example of this chapter:

```
http://localhost:8080/pentaho/api/repos/%3Apublic%3Amy_first_report.prpt/vi
ewer
```

> The URL accepts parameters to filter the report and the access requires an authentication to show the result. Feel free to read the official documentation at `https://help.pentaho.com/Documentation` for further details.

The bundled report preview

Once a Pentaho report is accessed, the preview is possible using the default output format, defined in the report's settings. According to the output format, the browser will either directly render the preview (for PDF and HTML, mainly) or download it locally (for Excel, CSV, RTF, and plain text).

In case you use the viewer (using the `/viewer` postfix), a toolbar is shown on top of the window. Using the toolbar, you can browse the pages, show/hide the parameters, limit the number of rows, and refresh the report. Below the toolbar, you can find all the report's parameters, if defined, the selector of the output types, and the **Update** button to refresh the preview.

Talking about the output types, by default, you can choose from HTML (paginated, not paginated, and email), PDF, Microsoft Excel (regular and 2007 version), CSV, RTF, and plain text formats. By changing the selection in the drop-down menu, you will see the report updated automatically in the requested format. In the following screenshot, you can see how the preview looks for the PDF output format:

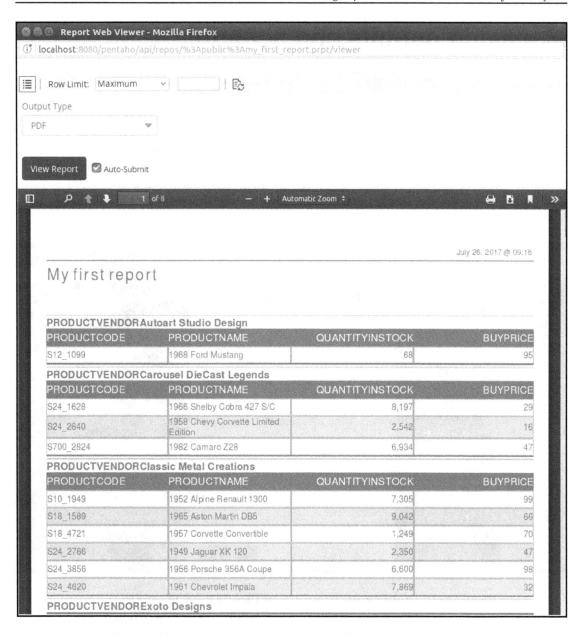

Managing permits and schedule

Using a Pentaho report through the Business Analytics Platform mean also having full control over who can do what. Pentaho Business Analytics Platform has a fine tuning system for permissions and everything is manageable through the browse files page. Starting from there, you can point to a report and you will see the **Share** item on the right panel. Clicking on it, a modal window will be presented, where you can control all the permits. Before moving forward, let's focus on the **Inherits folder permissions** check. This feature in particular enables you to inherit the permits in the repository structure quite easily. If you want to interrupt and customize the inheritance, uncheck this flag and add/remove the roles and single permission according to your needs. In the following screenshot, you can see how this window looks and look at all the possible settings:

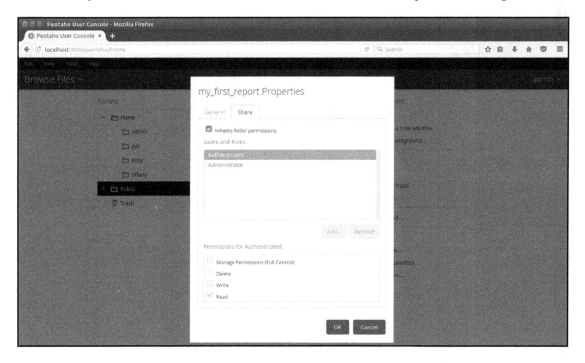

In the same menu (on the right panel of the browse files page), you can see the **Schedule** item. Clicking on it, a modal window will be presented, where some configuration will be asked for. In the following screenshot, you can see all the main settings you can set up: you can decide where the snapshot of the report will be saved, the date/time/frequency of the execution, and the output format. The configuration is asked in three different steps, shown in the following screenshot:

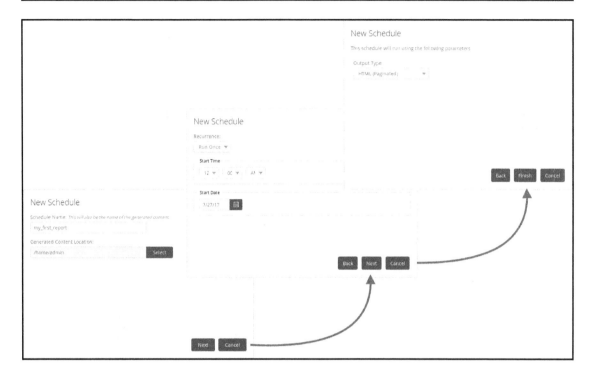

Once done, the report is scheduled, and you can check, change, and control its execution from the **Schedules** page, as shown in the following screenshot:

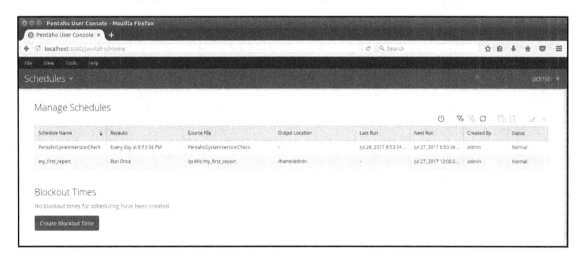

Creating a dashboard with Pentaho reports

In Chapter 14, *Building Interactive Reports*, we discussed limiting the advanced interaction between reports to avoid failing projects. When interactions between visual elements become complex, the dashboards are probably the suggested solution. In the Pentaho suite, the right place to develop dashboards is the Business Analytics Platform, with the support of the CTools. CTools is a set of tools and components created to help you build custom dashboards on top of Pentaho. There are specific CTools for different purposes, but we will only introduce them as an example, considering they need an entire book to describe all the possibilities and nice features. Our goal in this section is to show an example of a dashboard, using the Pentaho reports as elements.

Community dashboard editor basics

A core part of the CTools, the **Community Dashboard Editor** (**CDE**), is included in the Pentaho user console as a graphical tool for creating, editing, and previewing Pentaho dashboards. CDE allows the development and deployment of Pentaho advanced dashboards. It's a very powerful and complete tool, combining frontend with data sources and custom components in a seamless way.

The development of a CDE dashboard is based on a three layer definition. All together, the three layers define the final version of the dashboard. The three layers are: the layout layer, the component layer, and the data source layer.

A dashboard layout layer can be created by a simple combination of rows and columns, along with some HTML blocks and possibly some images. In the layout perspective, you may also provide some look and feel properties. For example, you can set up a background color for a certain element and choose a style for the corners of rows and columns.

Components are the central elements of a dashboard and they are managed in the component layer. The component layer can be defined in a component perspective of the user interface, where you can find all the available components you can choose to include in your Pentaho report.

As you learnt for the reports, the dashboards can also be populated by a variety of different sources. In the data sources perspective, you can set up the origin of the data that will be used to populate your dashboard. Basically, you have to specify where the data comes from and what it looks like.

The creation of a brand new CDE dashboard is straightforward, directly from the Pentaho user console using the **File** | **New** | **CDE Dashboard** item. In the following screenshot, you can see the editing panel of a CDE dashboard, with the three perspective icons on the top right:

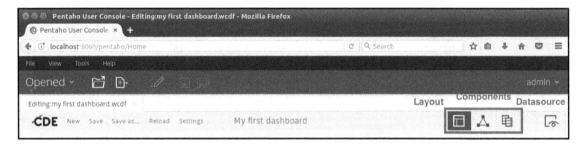

Introduction of the report components

Concering the CDE components, there are three different kinds available: visual components (like charts, textboxes, and so on), parameters representing values that are shared by the components, and scripts that let you customize the look and feel or behavior of other components.

This section is focused on the visual components available to use Pentaho reports. In particular, it will introduce: `PRPT Component`, `Execute Prpt Component`, and `Schedule PRPT Component`.

PRPT Component

The `PRPT Component` enables you to preview a Pentaho report in the `.prpt` format, directly in a portion of the dashboard, driven by the layout layer. The viewer used in the layout is exactly the same as introduced earlier in the chapter. The following screenshot describes the settings of the component and the configuration used in the next example:

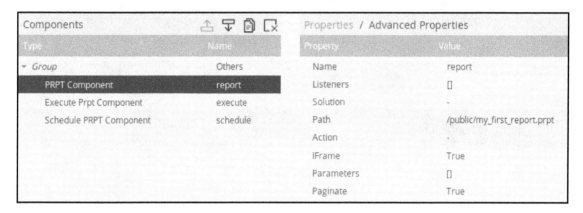

Show parameters	False
Priority	5
Refresh Period	-
HtmlObject	obj1
Execute at start	True
Use Post	False
Pre Execution	...
Post Execution	...
Pre Change	...
Post Change	...
Tooltip	...

Execute Prpt Component

`Execute Prpt Component` is similar to `PRPT Component`, with the difference that the preview is opened in a modal window and it is accessible using a button. The following screenshot describes the settings of the component and the configuration used in the next example:

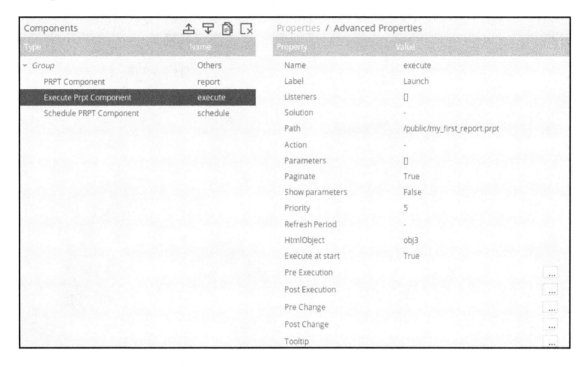

Schedule PRPT Component

`Schedule PRPT component` enables you to schedule a Pentaho report in the `.prpt` format, using a button in the layout layer. By pressing the button, a modal window will be shown with the same settings as introduced previously in the chapter. The following screenshot describes the settings of the component and the configuration used in the next example:

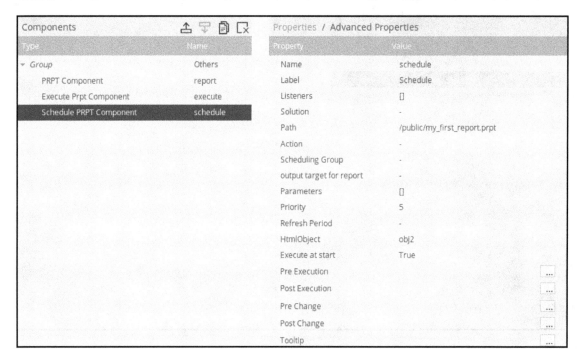

Example of CDE dashboard

Now that you know what a Pentaho dashboard is, and the basics around its development, let's see a concrete example defining a complex preview of the `my_first_report` report. If you followed the examples described earlier in the chapter, you should already have a working `my_first_report.prpt` file available in the `/public` path of the Pentaho repository. If not, you can find it in the `https://github.com/fcorti/pentaho-8-reporting-for-java-developers` repository, specifically, in the `Chapter 15 - Using reports in Pentaho Business Analytics Platform/my_reports` folder.

The example dashboard we are going to build in this section will be composed of a left panel, using most part of the page width, previewing the report using `PRPT Component`, and a right panel, containing two buttons: the **Schedule** button connected to `Schedule PRPT Component` and the **Launch** button connected to `Execute Prpt Component`.

Once you have created a new CDE dashboard using the **File | New | CDE Dashboard** item from the Pentaho user console, in the layout perspective set up the rows and column as shown in the following screenshot:

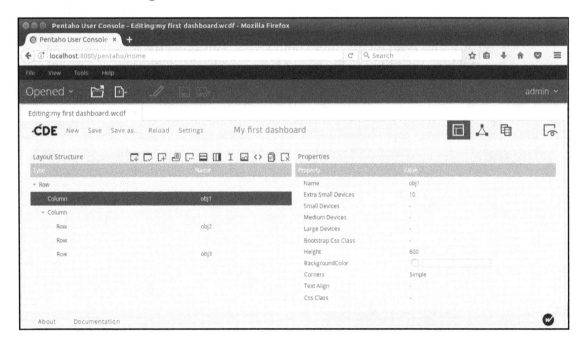

Nothing apart from the nested structure of rows and columns is really relevant, but it is recommended to fill the `Name` property with the correct values (`obj1`, `obj2`, and `obj3`), as it will be used as the link between the components and the layout.

Once done, click on the component perspective and double click on each one of the three components (`PRPT Component`, `Schedule PRPT Component`, and `Execute Prpt Component`) from the right list. This action will automatically add the three to the central panel containing the report components.

Once available as report components, configure them as described in the preceding screenshot. The mandatory and relevant properties to setup are:

- `Name`: This is for all the three components filled with a random but meaningful string.
- `Path`: This is for all the three components filled with the `/public/my_first_report.prpt` string. This property points the components to the correct Pentaho report stored in the repository.
- `Label`: This is for the two buttons (for `Schedule PRPT Component` and `Execute PRPT Component`). This property defines the content to show for each button.
- `HtmlObj`: This is for all the three components. This property is mandatory and relevant because it links to the layout layer specifically, to the layout element where the component will be shown.

After this task is completed, the CDE dashboard can be saved using the **Save** item in the upper menu. Once clicked, a modal window will ask you the path to the Pentaho repository and the name. In this example, the `my first dashboard` name will be used. Since then, two new files are visible in the Pentaho repository. By selecting the one with the CDE blue icon and clicking on the **Open** item in the right panel, a preview similar to the following screenshot will be shown:

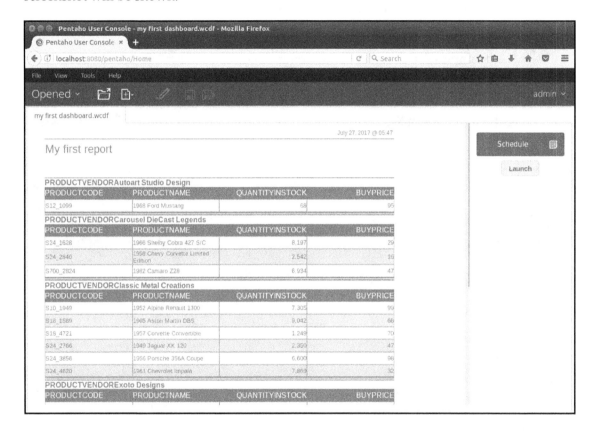

In the CDE dashboard, you should recognize the structure developed with a large column on the left, containing the preview using `PRPT Component`, and a smaller column on the right with three smaller subrows: the first containing the **Schedule** button, the second being only a spacer, and the third containing the **Launch** button.

If you want to play with all the properties of the CDE components to discover their behavior, we strongly recommend that you take your time and do it. As suggested for the Pentaho Report Designer, in case of CDE dashboards also, the best teacher is experimentation through some examples. Don't worry about doing something wrong. You cannot do anything bad to the Pentaho Business Analytics Platform and you can only learn.

To complete the example, in the following screenshot you can see how the browser looks, by clicking on the **Launch** button:

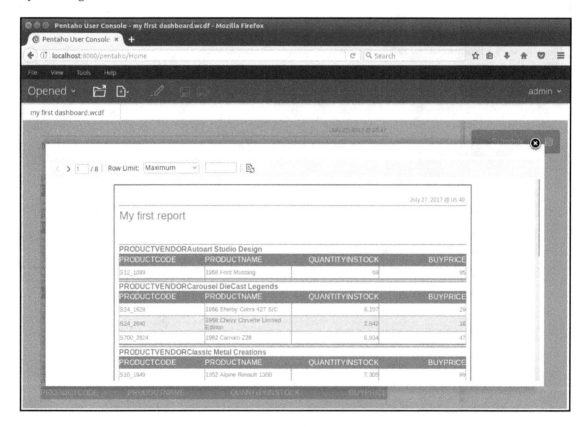

In the following screenshot, you can see how the browser looks, clicking on the **Schedule** button:

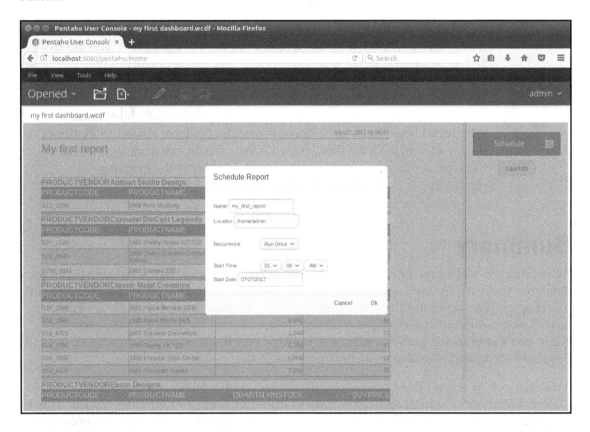

As last topic to share in this section, let's see how a CDE dashboard can be accessed using a public URL. As you saw for Pentaho reports, the public URL for a CDE dashboard is defined as follows:

- The base URL. In our example, `http://localhost:8080/pentaho`.
- The endpoint path. In our example, `/api/repos/`.
- The path of the `.prpt` file into the Pentaho repository, where the path separator is the semicolon (`:`). The string is URL-encoded into the URL. In our example, `%3Apublic%3A`.
- The URL-encoded name of the CDE dashboard. In our example, `my%20first%20dashboard` followed by the `.wcdf` extension.
- The endpoint postfix. In our example, `/generatedContent`.

In the following URL, you can find the link to the example of this chapter:

```
http://http://localhost:8080/pentaho/api/repos/%3Apublic%3Amy%20first%20das
hboard.wcdf/generatedContent
```

 If you have any kind of problem in developing the example or you are too lazy to develop it, in the `https://github.com/fcorti/pentaho-8-reporting-for-java-developers` repository, specifically, in the `Chapter 15 - Using reports in Pentaho Business Analytics Platform/my_dashboards` folder, you can find the CDE dashboard introduced here. To install it into the Pentaho Business Analytics Platform, simply upload both the files (one with the `.cdfde` extension and the other with the `.wcdf` extension) into the `/pubic` folder of the Pentaho repository.

Summary

In this chapter, you learned how to use an existing Pentaho report in the Pentaho Business Analytics Platform, the web application used as frontend for final users and developers. In this chapter, you were introduced to the basics of the Pentaho Business Analytics Platform, as well as provided with a description on how to install it and upload Pentaho reports. After, you learnt how to preview it, how to manage permits, how to schedule it and how to develop a Pentaho dashboard using the Pentaho CTools.

Now that you have read this chapter, you should feel comfortable with the Pentaho Business Analytics Platform and all the basic features for managing Pentaho reports. This is an advanced task for developers and information technologists, to manage the frontend for your final customers and managers.

In the next chapter, you will learn more about using a Pentaho report in ETL jobs (`https://en.wikipedia.org/wiki/Extract,_transform,_load`), using the Pentaho Data Integration (also known as Kettle).

16
Using Reports in Pentaho Data Integration

Having introduced the Pentaho Business Analytics Platform in Chapter 15, *Using Reports in Pentaho Business Analytics Platform*, in this chapter you will learn how to use Pentaho reports in Pentaho Data Integration, also known as Kettle. This will deliver powerful ETL capabilities.

In this chapter, you will be introduced to the basics of the Pentaho Data Integration and ETL tools in general, and be provided with a description of how to install them and use Pentaho reports as an output task. As usual, in this chapter you will see a working example in action. The goal is always the same: to learn by examples.

This chapter is written as a tutorial for developers and information technologists. The best way to learn is to follow the instructions on your laptop while reading. By the end of this chapter, you will feel comfortable with the basics of using the Pentaho Data Integration (also known as Kettle) together with Pentaho reports. This will be extremely useful for your future projects, enabling you to a fully featured ETL tool.

Introducing Pentaho Data Integration

As part of Pentaho's suite of products, Pentaho offers open source data integration. With an intuitive, graphical, drag and drop design environment and a proven, scalable, standards-based architecture, data integration is increasingly the choice for organizations over traditional, proprietary ETL or data integration tools. Pentaho Data Integration in its initial versions was called Kettle, so during your investigations, you may easily find it also named as PDI, DI, or Kettle.

You probably know that ETL refers to the following processes: data extraction is where the data is extracted from homogeneous or heterogeneous data sources, data transformation is where the data is transformed for storing in the proper format or structure for the purposes of querying and analysis, and data loading is where the data is loaded into the final target repository. You will not learn in this book the basics of ETL, but you can easily find lot of literature dedicated to this topic in particular. If you are not aware about ETL principles and best practices, you can think of ETL as batch processes developed specifically to move data from a source to a target.

As we did for the Pentaho Business Analytics Platform, in this chapter also you will use the Community Edition of Pentaho Data Integration, as it is downloadable and available for everyone without any cost. Of course, the description in this chapter is limited to an introduction and a description of what is strictly related to report's management. If interested, a lot of resources are available for you to discover and become an expert of this ETL tool.

Installing Pentaho Data Integration

The installation of the Pentaho Data Integration is straightforward, following an *unzip and run* task. The prerequisites to run Pentaho Data Integration are simple; it requires a **Java Runtime Environment (JRE)** 8, already installed in your environment. Both Windows based operating systems and Linux based operating systems are supported. The screenshots and previews shown in this chapter are done using an Ubuntu 16.04.2 LTS distribution.

Before installing the application, you can download the artifacts distributed in a ZIP file directly from the official Pentaho Community website (`http://community.pentaho.com/`) or from the Pentaho SourceForge website (`https://sourceforge.net/projects/pentaho/`). In both cases, you should download a ZIP file named something similar to `pdi-ce-<version>.zip`.

Once the ZIP file is downloaded into your environment, unzip it into the final path (on a Linux-based operating system, the `/opt` path is suggested), and you will have all the Pentaho Data Integration available in the folder named `data-integration`.

You probably will not believe it, but this is all that is needed to install Pentaho Data Integration into your environment.

Pentaho Data Integration is mainly a Java application running at command-line and embedding the Pentaho Data Integration Engine. Pentaho Data Integration comes with some useful tools: Spoon, a graphical user interface that allows you to design transformations and jobs; Pan and Kitchen, used to run transformations and jobs; and Carte, a simple web server that allows you to execute transformations and jobs remotely. In this chapter, you will see Spoon and Kitchen in a use case example.

Basics of Pentaho Data Integration

As introduced previously, Pentaho Data Integration is an engine with very few graphical tools and interfaces. In accordance with this definition, the following sections describes some basic concepts for understanding its behavior and principles.

Jobs and transformations

Jobs and transformations are probably two of the most important core concepts in Pentaho Data Integration (and ETL in general, but with different naming). Quoting the Pentaho's FAQs:

> *"Transformations are about moving and transforming rows from source to target. Jobs are more about high level flow control: executing transformations, sending mails on failure, transferring files via FTP, and so on. Another key difference is that: all the steps in a transformation execute in parallel, but the steps in a job execute in order."*

As you can read from this FAQ, transformations are based on the concept of streams of data as a potentially huge quantity of data migrating from a generic source to a generic target. A transformation can manage more than one stream, all of them executed in parallel and managed from the Pentaho Data Integration engine.

In the following diagram, you can see a very basic example of transformation, developed using Spoon:

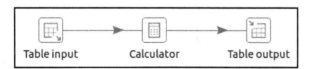

Talking about streams, this is probably one of the most impressive points of strength of an ETL engine. It has the ability to manage huge quantities of data in parallel, in accordance with the limited resources of a server. This is one of the key differences from a regular application a developer can build using the traditional patterns.

Talking about jobs, a job is heavily based on the concept of a sequence of tasks, where it is mandatory to declare the starting point. The ability of the jobs to include other jobs or transformations as subtasks enables them to be a great way to manage complex migrations and reusable actions.

In the following diagram, you can see a very basic example of a job, developed using Spoon:

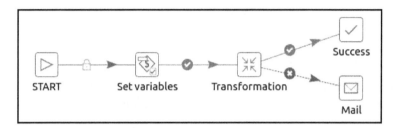

As you can see from the images, a hop connects one transformation step or job entry with another. The direction of the data flow is indicated with an arrow on the graphical view pane. A hop can be enabled or disabled (for testing purposes, for example) and can be conditional (in case of success or failure, for example).

Both jobs and transformations can define parameters and variables. Parameters are defined as input for the execution and can be used to parameterize tasks. Variables are defined into the execution flow and can be used to parameterize tasks, exactly as the parameters.

Steps and entries

Steps and entries are the atomic parts of transformations and jobs, respectively.

A step is one part of a transformation. There are over 140 steps available in Pentaho Data Integration. These steps are categorized according to their main function; for example, input, output, scripting, and so on. In order to perform specific tasks such as reading data from a flat file, filtering rows, and logging to database as shown in the preceding example, each step in the transformation is designed in a specific manner. Steps can be configured to perform the tasks you require. A step can have many connections—some join two steps together while some only serve as input or output for a step. One step named Pentaho Reporting output is available to manage Pentaho reports.

A job entry is one part of a job. Job entries can provide you with a wide range of functionalities, ranging from executing transformations to getting files from a web server. There are over 100 entries available in Pentaho Data Integration and they are grouped according to function, similar to what was described for steps. None of the available entries have direct support for Pentaho reports.

Database connections

As you learned for Pentaho Reporting, in case of Pentaho Data Integration also, the database connections are used to read from a source or to write to a target repository. In case of Pentaho Data Integration, these kinds of data sources are focused on databases, but thanks to steps and entries, you have the opportunity to access different types of sources or targets.

Database connections can be shared between jobs and transformations, and can be reused for better management and maintenance. The list of supported databases is not different from the one you saw for Pentaho Reporting. As you already know, it includes a wide variety of different vendors, types, and costs.

Storage and reuse

Jobs and transformations can be saved on a storage for future reuse. The format used by Pentaho Data Integration to save jobs and transformations is XML, so it can be saved on a file. A job is saved in a file with the `.kjb` extension and a transformation is saved in a file with the `.ktr` extension.

Being files, jobs and transformations can be naturally saved into a filesystem, but this is not the only place where the `.kjb` and `.ktr` files can be stored. Pentaho Data Integration is able to retrieve and store jobs and transformations from the following types of storages:

- **Pentaho repository**: You were introduced to the Pentaho repository in `Chapter 15`, *Using Reports in Pentaho Business Analytics Platform*. From a user perspective, the Penatho repository can be used as a remote filesystem owned by Pentaho Business Analytics Platform. The Pentaho repository is able to store, retrieve, and execute the `.kjb` and `.ktr` files.
- **Database**: This is a regular database with some tables built from Pentaho Data Integration at creation time and managed during retrieving, saving, and execution. Jobs and transformations are not saved in their XML format, but stored as rows in several different custom tables.

- **Filesystem**: You have already learnt that using a filesystem, jobs and transformations are saved in XML format as the `.kjb` and `.ktr` files.

Even if the three different types of storage are supported, the use of Pentaho repository is recommended, because it is standard to use an XML format to store jobs and transformations (database storage is not human readable), and it is centralized and accessible through an API (filesystem is local to a server/machine).

Introduction of Spoon client

PDI client (Spoon) is a desktop application you install on your workstation, enabling you to build transformations and jobs or schedule when jobs should run. Spoon is included in the standard Pentaho Data Integration distribution and can be launched using the `spoon` scripts into the `data-integration` folder (`spoon.sh` is for Linux-based operating system and `spoon.bat` is for Windows-based operating system), as shown as follow:

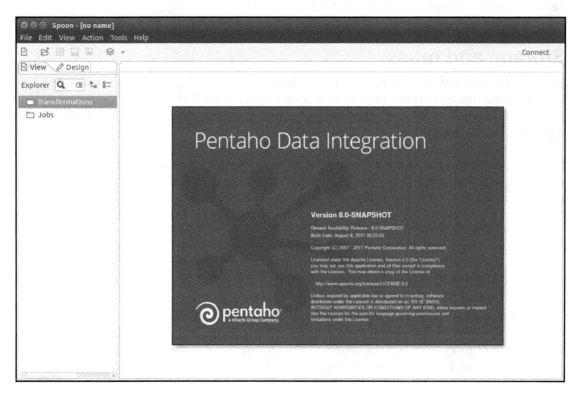

You won't discover all of the details about Spoon in this section, because it definitely needs an entire book for a deep dive. Instead, we would like to share that with a graphical interface, you have a visual representation of flows in transformations and jobs, as well as full control of their execution for debugging purposes. All the images presented in this chapter are done using Spoon, and in the following sections you will see a practical example of its use.

The Pentaho Reporting output step

The Pentaho Reporting Output step is the only Data Integration task completely dedicated to Pentaho Reporting. Being a step, it lives in transformations and it's grouped in the output steps.

The main goal of the step is to generate a Pentaho report, starting from a .prpt file stored locally on the filesystem. As a regular step, it accepts a stream of data as input and performs the task for each row of the flow. Pentaho Reporting output steps can be customized directly from the Spoon interface, by right-clicking on it and selecting the **Edit** item.

In the following screenshot, you can see how the edit window looks in the Spoon interface:

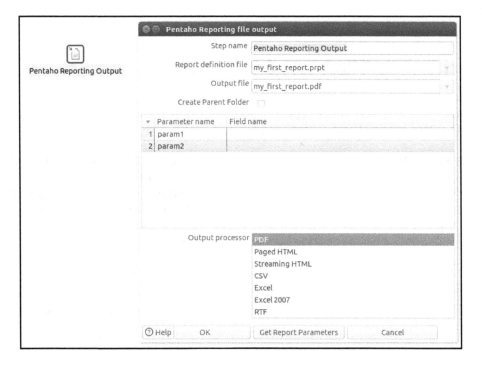

In the following table, you can read brief descriptions for each option, just as introductions of the data integration capabilities to manage Pentaho reports:

Option	Description
Step name	The name of the step. It must be unique in the transformation.
Report definition file	The field of the input stream containing the path (filename included) of the `.prpt` file during execution.
Output file	The field of the input stream containing the path (filename included) of the output file during execution.
Parameter fields	You can pass values from one or more input fields to predefined parameters in the report. To pass data to string arrays, make sure the data is tab-separated. You can use the **Get Report Parameters** button to import parameters from an existing report.
Output processor	The processor used to generate the output file, each one corresponding to a possible output format.

In the example described in this chapter, you will see a concrete use of the Pentaho Reporting output step.

Introducing Pan and Kitchen

To complete the brief introduction of the Pentaho Data Integration main capabilities, let's see how to execute a generic job or transformation from the command line. For this purpose, two Pentaho tools called Pan and Kitchen are available.

Kitchen is a program that can execute jobs designed by Spoon. Pan is a program that can execute transformations designed by Spoon. Usually jobs and transformations are scheduled in batch modes to be run automatically at regular intervals. Kitchen and Pan come bundled in the standard distribution of Pentaho Data Integration and they are available as scripts named `kitchen` and `pan` in the `data-integration` folder (`kitchen.sh` and `pan.sh` are for Linux-based operating system and `kitchen.bat` and `pan.bat` are for Windows-based operating system).

The `kitchen` and `pan` scripts can be launched using several parameters to control and configure their execution. Parameters can be specified at the command line, using the syntax `/param:value` or `-param=value`.

In the following table, you can find the main parameters accepted by `kitchen` and `pan` scripts:

Parameter	Description
rep	Pentaho repository name or database, if you are using one.
user	Username, if you are using a repository or database.
pass	Password, if you are using a repository or database.
trans	Name of the transformation (as it appears in the repository) to launch. Valid for `pan` only.
job	The name of the job (as it appears in the repository) to launch. Valid for `kitchen` only.
dir	Path containing the transformation/job, including the leading slash.
file	If you are calling a local `.ktr`/`.kjb` file, this is the path and filename.
level	Logging level (`Basic`, `Detailed`, `Debug`, `Rowlevel`, `Error`, and `Nothing`).
logfile	Local filename to write log output to.
listdir	Lists the directories in the specified repository.
listtrans	Lists the transformations in the specified repository directory. Valid for `pan` only.
listjob	Lists the transformations in the specified repository directory. Valid for `kitchen` only.
listrep	Lists the available repositories.
exprep	Exports all the repository objects to one XML file. Valid for `pan` only.
export	Exports all the linked resources of the specified job. The argument is the name of a ZIP file. Valid for `kitchen` only.
norep	Prevents from logging into a repository. Environment variables `KETTLE_REPOSITORY`, `KETTLE_USER`, and `KETTLE_PASSWORD` should be setup if you would not like to execute a local `.ktr`/`.kjb` file instead.
safemode	Runs in safe mode, which enables extra checking. Valid for `pan` only.
version	Shows the version, revision, and build date.

param	Sets a named parameter in the `name=value` format. For example, `-param:FOO=bar`
listparam	Lists information about the defined named parameters in the specified transformation.
maxloglines	The maximum number of log lines that are kept internally by Pentaho Data Integration. Set to 0 to keep all the rows (default value).
maxlogtimeout	The maximum age (in minutes) of a log line, while being kept internally by Pentaho Data Integration. Set to 0 to keep all the rows indefinitely (default value).

Creating a transformation with Pentaho reports

Now that you know what a Pentaho transformation is, and the basics around its development, let's see a concrete example, defining an easy ETL generating the PDF output of the well known `my_first_report.prpt` file. The first task to do is to copy the `my_first_report.prpt` file into the `data-integration` folder of your Pentaho Data Integration installation. This is required because it will be used as the current path during the execution of the transformation. If you don't have the `my_first_report.prpt` file available, you can download it from the `https://github.com/fcorti/pentaho-8-reporting-for-java-developers` repository, specifically, from the `Chapter 15 - Using reports in Pentaho Business Analytics Platform/my_reports` folder.

As a first step, let's run the Spoon GUI to start the development: open a Terminal, move to the `data-integration` folder, and run the `spoon` script. From the upper menu, click on the **File | New | Transformation** item to create an empty transformation. Once done, right-click on the empty right panel and select **Properties**. In the opening window, replace the `my first transformation` value with the content of the `Transformation name` field. Then click the **OK** button and press the disk icon (🖫) on the upper toolbar. Ensure that you save the `my first transformation` file in the `data-integration` folder.

Now that the transformation is saved as empty, select the **Design** tab from the left panel and you will find all the available steps to include. Expand the `Input` set, and drag the `Data Grid` step and drop it into the right panel. Double-click on the `Data Grid` step and fill the **Meta** tab of the edit window, as shown in the following screenshot:

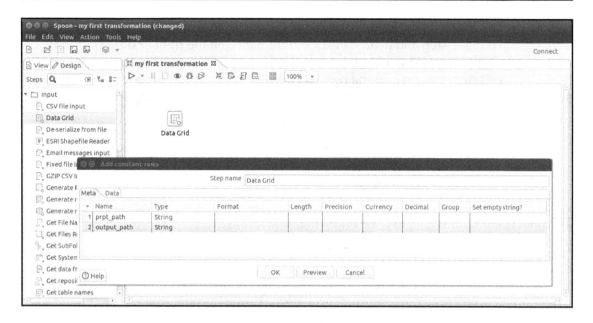

Before leaving the step configuration, select the **Data** tab and fill it as shown in the following screenshot:

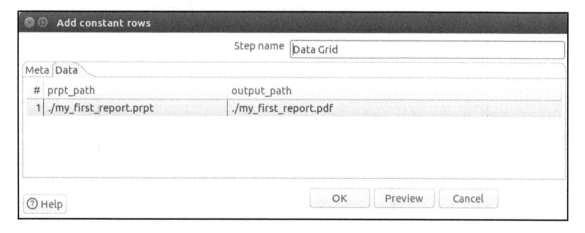

With this action, the first step of the transformation is defined, generating a simple data stream with only one row containing two fields: the prpt_path field with value ./my_first_report.prpt, and the output_path field with value ./my_first_report.pdf. If you want to see how a data stream looks, click on the **Preview** button. Once done, click the **OK** button to confirm the Data Grid setup.

Back to the **Design** tab in the left panel, expand the `Output` set, and drag the `Pentaho Reporting Output` step and drop it into the right panel, on the right of the `Data Grid` step. To instruct the transformation to execute the two steps in the right sequence, click on the `Data Grid` step, and drag on the right connection (⬚) icon and drop it to the `Pentaho Reporting Output` step. The following screenshot shows a visual description of the task:

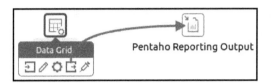

The final result should look like the following:

Now that the data flow is set up, double-click on the `Pentaho Reporting Output` step and fill in the options as shown in the following screenshot:

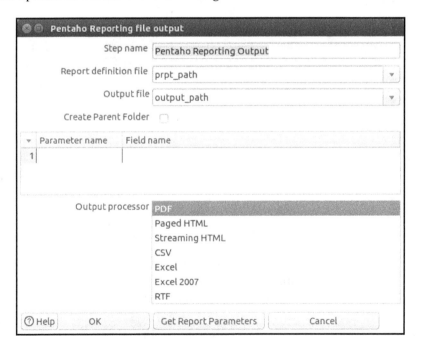

Click on the **OK** button to confirm the step configuration and then click on the save
() icon in the toolbar to save the updated version of the transformation. Now that the
transformation is developed, run it by clicking on the play icon ($\triangleright$) in the transformation
panel; confirm by clicking on the run button. In the following screenshot, you can see how
the execution looks:

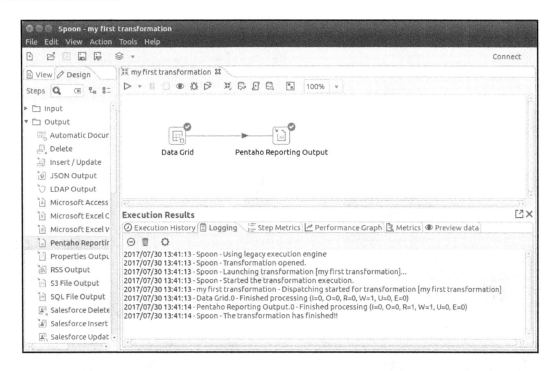

As you can see in the visual representation of the transformation, a green check highlights
the steps executed with success. In the **Logging** panel, a detailed log trail is visible for your
understanding. To confirm that everything has been executed with success, in the `data-`
`integration` folder, you should find the `my_first_report.pdf` file containing the final
rendering of the report.

If you have any kind of problem developing the example or you are too
lazy to develop it, in the `https://github.com/fcorti/pentaho-8-`
`reporting-for-java-developers` repository, specifically, in the `Chapter`
`16 - Using reports in Pentaho Data Integration` folder, you
can find `my first transformation.ktr` introduced here. To install it
in the Pentaho Data Integration, simply download it into the `data-`
`integration` folder and open it as a regular file, using Spoon.

Executing the transformation using Pan

To complete the example, let's see how to run the transformation from the command line using the `pan` script, with the purpose of scheduling the execution regularly using crontab (`https://en.wikipedia.org/wiki/Cron`).

The following the description given earlier in the chapter, open a Terminal and move into the `data-integration` folder, where you should find `my first transformation.ktr`, together with the `my_first_report.prpt` file. Digit the following command and press the *Enter* button to launch its execution:

```
./pan.sh -file:"my first transformation.ktr"
```

In the following screenshot, you can see the result of the execution in the Terminal, as an example:

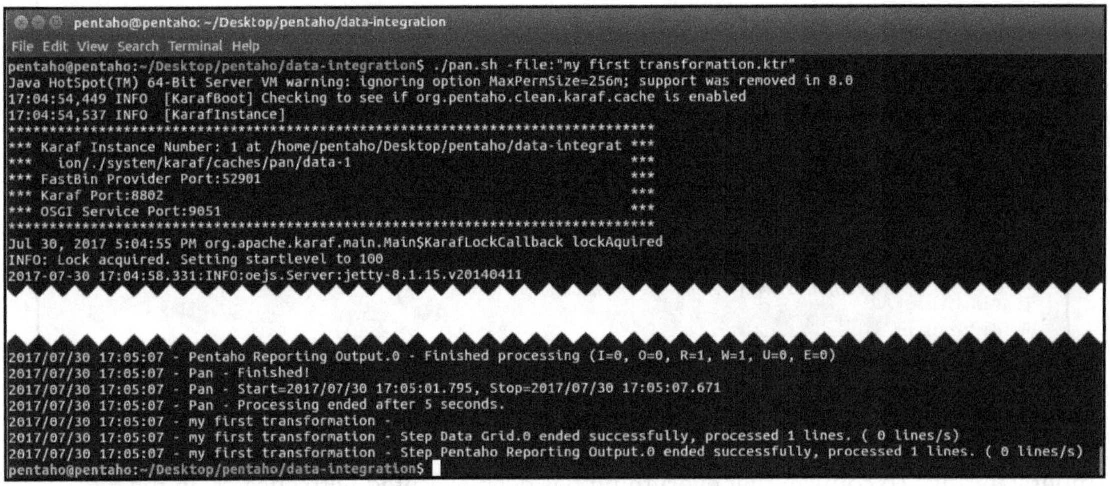

Scheduling the command using crontab or any other scheduler should be straightforward now, in accordance with your operating system.

Summary

In this chapter, you learned how to use an existing Pentaho report within the Pentaho Data Integration, also known as Kettle, delivering powerful ETL capabilities. In this chapter, you were introduced to the basics of the Pentaho Data Integration, as well as provided with a description of how to install it and use Pentaho reports with the Pentaho Reporting output step. Afterwards, you learnt about Spoon client and about how to execute a job/transformation at command line, and you saw how to develop a transformation using Pentaho reports. Finally, you went through the execution of a transformation using Pan.

Now that you have read this chapter, you should feel comfortable with Pentaho Data Integration and all the basic features for managing Pentaho reports. This is an advanced task for developers and information technologists, to manage ETL batches for their future projects.

This chapter closes the section of the book dedicated to the use of Pentaho reports in other components of the Pentaho suite. In the next chapter, you will go through the final topics, just to add the latest details to your expertise.

17
Pentaho Reporting Nightly Build and Support

This last chapter contains two main topics, that will hopefully be useful for completing your expertise in Pentaho Reporting.

The first topic is about downloading, building, installing, and running the latest version of Pentaho Report Designer, usually called **nightly build**. In the same way, you will learn how to use the nightly build in your Java projects; to try the latest version with the latest enhancements. This topic is strictly for developers and will enable you to access the latest version of Pentaho Reporting for evaluation purposes.

In the last topic of this book, you will go through all the ways you may have to find documentation, resources, support, meet the community, and so on as a new developer and expert into Pentaho Reporting. This topic is for developers and information technologists, and should help you to get support and help during your first project and future challenges.

The chapter (and the book) ends by sharing a thought on what to do next, after you have received all the benefits of this open source project and community, and you will become a real expert, with a lot of things to share with all the newbies on Pentaho Reporting.

Pentaho Report Designer nightly build

In the previous chapters, you learnt everything about Pentaho Reporting 8.0 in its stable release. Stable releases can be downloaded as described in Chapter 2, *Getting Started with Report Designer*, but being an open source project, Pentaho Reporting's source code is available on a public repository hosted on GitHub. For future reference, the Pentaho Reporting's project is stored at https://github.com/pentaho/pentaho-reporting.

In the public repository, you can find all the libraries, source code, and everything that is required to understand how Pentaho Reporting works and is developed. Looking at the repository, there are several branches, as usual. The master branch hosts the daily commits of the Pentaho team. Of course, the source code cannot be guaranteed to be stable, but it's definitely the most recent version of the software.

In this section, you are going to learn how to download the latest version of the source code and how to build it, creating the so called nightly build. Using the Pentaho Reporting nightly build can be relevant for two main reasons: if you want to see the latest features in advance, without waiting for the stable release; and if you want to fork it, adding (or customizing) the official source code.

Prerequisites for building the project

Before diving deep into building the artifacts, let's list the prerequisites of the development environment:

- Apache Maven Version 3+.
- Java JDK 1.8.
- The settings.xml file (https://github.com/pentaho/maven-parent-poms/blob/master/maven-support-files/settings.xml) stored in your /.m2 directory (the .m2 folder is used by Apache Maven to host the dependencies). The settings.xml file contains everything that is required to get the libraries and dependencies from the Pentaho's Sonatype Nexus Repository manager (https://public.nexus.pentaho.org/).

Of course, the git client should be available in your development environment to locally clone the repository.

Cloning the GitHub repository

The first task to complete to create your Pentaho Reporting nightly build is to download the entire source code locally. To clone the repository locally, open a Terminal, move into a working folder, and launch the following command:

```
git clone https://github.com/pentaho/pentaho-reporting.git
```

The `git` client will start downloading the whole repository with all the subprojects, and after a few minutes, the complete source code will be available in the `pentaho-reporting` folder. In the `README.md` file of the root folder, you can find detailed descriptions of several topics, like:

- How to build it (in different platforms)
- How to run the tests and the integration tests
- How to import the project on IntelliJ IDE
- How to install it and where to find the documentation

In the following sections, you will focus on the descriptions of building and running the nightly build, to enable you to use the latest (possibly unstable) release for evaluation purpose.

Building the release

Building the release is well described in the `README.md` file. All the required profiles are activated by the presence of a property named `release`. If you are going to build a macOS distribution as well, you must also specify the `mac.jre.path` property, as shown in the following command:

```
mvn clean install -Drelease -Dmac.jre.path=YOUR_MAC_OS_JRE_PATH
(YOUR_MAC_OS_JRE_PATH example jre1.8.0_121.jre\Contents\Home)
```

Once launched, the command will start to download a lot of dependencies, and a very long tail of log messages will appear. Once the subprojects are built, the unit tests will be launched, as well with everything that is requested to build the final package.

 I hope you will not have to complete the build in few minutes. Depending on your connectivity, any failures in downloading the dependencies and several other unexpected behaviors, you may need more than half an hour to complete this task.

At the end of the execution, the final artifact will be generated in the `assemblies/winlinux(mac)/target` folder with the name `prd-ce-<version>.zip`. The ZIP file is everything you will need to run the Pentaho Report Designer, and also to build your personal projects based on Pentaho Reporting.

Installing and running the nightly build

From here on, the installation task is no different from what you learnt in `Chapter 2`, *Getting Started with Report Designer*: uncompressed the ZIP file into the final destination, open a Terminal, move into the `report-designer` folder, and launch the `report-designer` script.

Pentaho Reporting SDK nightly build

Once the Pentaho Reporting artifact has been built, all the Pentaho Reporting libraries will be available in it, as described in `Chapter 1`, *Introduction to Pentaho Reporting*. In this section, you are going to learn how to use the nightly build in your Java projects, using Pentaho Reporting in its latest (and possibly unstable) release for evaluation purpose.

Assuming that you have an existing Java project using Pentaho Reporting, let's see in the following sections how to update it to use the nightly build. As an example, you can use one of the examples available in the GitHub repository at `https://github.com/fcorti/pentaho-8-reporting-for-java-developers`.

To prepare the project, copy it into a working folder. As an example, you could use the project stored in the `Chapter 03 - Getting started with Reporting SDK/pentaho-reporting-web-app` folder.

Updating the pom.xml file

The very first task to prepare the existing project is to change the `pom.xml` file. Opening `pom.xml` with an editor, you will see that all the Pentaho dependencies point to `<version>8.0-SNAPSHOT</version>`. Of course, nothing really changes if your project uses a different version.

For all the Pentaho dependencies, update the version tags to the nightly build version. In our example, you will use `<version>8.1-SNAPSHOT</version>`. Again, nothing really changes if your project uses a different version.

Saving the `pom.xml` file is all that is required to update the Java project.

Adding the nightly build libraries

If you'd run the build of the project now, the Apache Maven client would try to download all the Pentaho dependencies in their newest version, requested from the `pom.xml` file (in our example, `8.1-SNAPSHOT`). Considering that the newest version would not be published yet in the Pentaho's Sonatype Nexus Repository, an error would occur and your build would fail.

To solve this issue, there is a workaround, which is adding the Pentaho newest dependencies into your local Apache Maven repository. In brief, when Apache Maven looks for a dependency, it first looks into the local repository (in the `.m2/repository` folder), and if not found there, it tries to download it from the remote repository. By adding the newest Pentaho dependencies into your local Apache Maven repository, you will skip the need to go to the remote repository, avoiding the failure.

 Be aware that this is a workaround to enable you to use the latest (and possibly unstable) Pentaho Reporting nightly build. Adding libraries to a local Maven repository is not a best practice and should be limited as much as possible.

To install a library or an artifact in general to a local Apache Maven repository, there is a command similar to the following one:

```
mvn
    install:install-file
    -Dfile=path/to/artifact/name.jar
    -DgroupId=...
    -DartifactId=...
    -Dversion=...
    -Dpackaging=jar
```

By using this command for each Pentaho dependency, you can update your local Apache Maven repository with the nightly build. The following is the command list to run, to add all the requested dependencies, to build with success all the examples described in this book:

```
mvn install:install-file -Dfile=./report-designer/lib/classic-core-8.1-
SNAPSHOT.jar -DgroupId=pentaho-reporting-engine -DartifactId=pentaho-
reporting-engine-classic-core -Dversion=8.1-SNAPSHOT -Dpackaging=jar

mvn install:install-file -Dfile=./report-designer/lib/classic-
extensions-8.1-SNAPSHOT.jar -DgroupId=pentaho-reporting-engine -
DartifactId=pentaho-reporting-engine-classic-extensions -Dversion=8.1-
SNAPSHOT -Dpackaging=jar

mvn install:install-file -Dfile=./report-designer/lib/wizard-core-8.1-
SNAPSHOT.jar -DgroupId=pentaho-reporting-engine -DartifactId=pentaho-
reporting-engine-wizard-core -Dversion=8.1-SNAPSHOT -Dpackaging=jar

mvn install:install-file -Dfile=./report-designer/lib/libbase-8.1-
SNAPSHOT.jar -DgroupId=pentaho-library -DartifactId=libbase -Dversion=8.1-
SNAPSHOT -Dpackaging=jar

mvn install:install-file -Dfile=./report-designer/lib/libdocbundle-8.1-
SNAPSHOT.jar -DgroupId=pentaho-library -DartifactId=libdocbundle -
Dversion=8.1-SNAPSHOT -Dpackaging=jar

mvn install:install-file -Dfile=./report-designer/lib/libfonts-8.1-
SNAPSHOT.jar -DgroupId=pentaho-library -DartifactId=libfonts -Dversion=8.1-
SNAPSHOT -Dpackaging=jar

mvn install:install-file -Dfile=./report-designer/lib/libformat-8.1-
SNAPSHOT.jar -DgroupId=pentaho-library -DartifactId=libformat -
Dversion=8.1-SNAPSHOT -Dpackaging=jar

mvn install:install-file -Dfile=./report-designer/lib/libformula-8.1-
SNAPSHOT.jar -DgroupId=pentaho-library -DartifactId=libformula -
Dversion=8.1-SNAPSHOT -Dpackaging=jar

mvn install:install-file -Dfile=./report-designer/lib/libloader-8.1-
SNAPSHOT.jar -DgroupId=pentaho-library -DartifactId=libloader -
Dversion=8.1-SNAPSHOT -Dpackaging=jar

mvn install:install-file -Dfile=./report-designer/lib/librepository-8.1-
SNAPSHOT.jar -DgroupId=pentaho-library -DartifactId=librepository -
Dversion=8.1-SNAPSHOT -Dpackaging=jar

mvn install:install-file -Dfile=./report-designer/lib/libserializer-8.1-
SNAPSHOT.jar -DgroupId=pentaho-library -DartifactId=libserializer -
```

```
Dversion=8.1-SNAPSHOT -Dpackaging=jar

mvn install:install-file -Dfile=./report-designer/lib/libxml-8.1-
SNAPSHOT.jar -DgroupId=pentaho-library -DartifactId=libxml -Dversion=8.1-
SNAPSHOT -Dpackaging=jar

mvn install:install-file -Dfile=./report-designer/lib/legacy-charts-8.1-
SNAPSHOT.jar -DgroupId=pentaho-reporting-engine -DartifactId=pentaho-
reporting-engine-legacy-charts -Dversion=8.1-SNAPSHOT -Dpackaging=jar

mvn install:install-file -Dfile=./report-designer/lib/classic-extensions-
xpath-8.1-SNAPSHOT.jar -DgroupId=pentaho-reporting-engine -
DartifactId=pentaho-reporting-engine-classic-extensions-xpath -
Dversion=8.1-SNAPSHOT -Dpackaging=jar

mvn install:install-file -Dfile=./report-designer/lib/classic-extensions-
pmd-8.1-SNAPSHOT.jar -DgroupId=pentaho-reporting-engine -
DartifactId=pentaho-reporting-engine-classic-extensions-pmd -Dversion=8.1-
SNAPSHOT -Dpackaging=jar

mvn install:install-file -Dfile=./report-designer/lib/classic-extensions-
kettle-8.1-SNAPSHOT.jar -DgroupId=pentaho-reporting-engine -
DartifactId=pentaho-reporting-engine-classic-extensions-kettle -
Dversion=8.1-SNAPSHOT -Dpackaging=jar

mvn install:install-file -Dfile=./report-designer/lib/classic-extensions-
mondrian-8.1-SNAPSHOT.jar -DgroupId=pentaho-reporting-engine -
DartifactId=pentaho-reporting-engine-classic-extensions-mondrian -
Dversion=8.1-SNAPSHOT -Dpackaging=jar

mvn install:install-file -Dfile=./report-designer/lib/classic-extensions-
olap4j-8.1-SNAPSHOT.jar -DgroupId=pentaho-reporting-engine -
DartifactId=pentaho-reporting-engine-classic-extensions-olap4j -
Dversion=8.1-SNAPSHOT -Dpackaging=jar
```

Compiling and running the project

Now that your Java project is updated to the newest Pentaho Reporting version, and the local Apache Maven repository contains the available nightly build, you can build it as usual, running the `mvn clean package` command from a Terminal. Using this workaround, you will be able to try the very last version of Pentaho Reporting in its nightly build containing the latest enhancements and features.

Getting help from the community

As an open source project, Pentaho Reporting has a community of people and organizations who contribute by answering questions, providing translations, filing and fixing bugs, writing documentation, and of course, by contributing code. To make sure you can find what you need to engage the Pentaho Reporting community, the following is a list of online places and tools to help you get started.

Asking questions and helping others

Today, there are two primary methods of communication in the Pentaho Reporting community. The first and most widely used method is Pentaho Reporting forums. These forums are located at `http://forums.pentaho.org/` under the main category **Pentaho Reporting**. You can search and read forum discussions, or sign up for an account and ask your own questions.

Another main method of communication is Pentaho's IRC channel, set up by Pentaho community members. This channel is located on the FreeNode IRC (`https://freenode.net/`), as channel `##pentaho`. If you don't have an IRC client, feel free to join the channel using the FreeNode WebChat (`http://webchat.freenode.net`). A large number of active Pentaho community members are available to answer technical questions.

Online documentation

While the reading this book, you have already seen that Pentaho has a website dedicated to documentation and it is available at `https://help.pentaho.com/`. In the documentation's website, you will find all the available content about the latest version, and also the content related to the previous versions.

Pentaho hosts a wiki, which contains community documentation for Pentaho's various projects. You can find the wiki at `http://wiki.pentaho.com`, which contains links to Pentaho Reporting documentation, as well as tech tips that walk you through specific use cases. As a wiki, community members may contribute their own tech tips or documentation around any of the Pentaho projects.

Pentaho also hosts a sub-domain dedicated to the Pentaho Reporting community at `http://reporting.pentaho.org`, which contains information about the latest releases and download links. Also, Javadoc for the latest versions of Pentaho's open source projects is hosted online at `http://javadoc.pentaho.com`. Pentaho Reporting Javadoc can be found at `http://javadoc.pentaho.com/reporting/`.

Submitting bugs and viewing backlogs

To submit a bug, or view Pentaho Reporting's backlog, you can visit Pentaho's JIRA bug tracking system at `http://jira.pentaho.com`. Pentaho Reporting is broken into two main projects: the Pentaho Reporting Engine and the Pentaho Report Designer. Each project contains a road map link, containing a list of prioritized activities that Pentaho and the open source community are working on.

Contributing code

If you'd like to add a new feature to Pentaho Reporting or fix a bug, the source code for the Reporting Engine and Report Designer is easily accessible. Pentaho maintains the reporting project in a GitHub repository at `https://github.com/pentaho/pentaho-reporting`. The reporting engine's core source code is located in the `engine` subfolder, and the Report Designer is located in the `designer` subfolder. By going to `https://github.com/pentaho/pentaho-reporting/releases`, you can browse the dozens of releases and version changes, using your browser.

One of the many types of contributions Pentaho receives is translated message bundles. These message bundles are located in the reporting projects, and can be found by searching for the `messages.properties` files in each project. For instance, there are many of these files in the `engine` project.

Enterprise support

Pentaho offers an enterprise edition of Pentaho Reporting, which includes direct customer support, as well as additional functionality, such as enterprise auditing within Pentaho's Business Analytics Platform. If you are working in an enterprise and would like to purchase an enterprise license, you can contact Pentaho directly by visiting `http://www.pentaho.com`. Subscription customers have access to Pentaho which contains many articles and enterprise documentation on all of Pentaho's products. Pentaho works with a large set of partners to offer consulting, which may include everything from setting up your reporting server to writing custom functionality that your business requires.

What to do once you become an expert

Did you see how powerful Pentaho Reporting is? And it is still given for free after several years. Can you imagine how much effort has been invested from a bunch of developers to reach this level of maturity? How much of your precious time has been saved, thanks to the use of tools like Pentaho Reporting? How many things you will learn attending the forums, the chat, learning from the public documentation or the blog posts written from real experts?

Now it's probably your time to benefit from all of this, but don't forget to give something to the others, once you reach the point where you are a Pentaho Reporting expert.

Help the others in the same way as someone else helped you. This makes the community valuable.

Summary

In this chapter, you learnt how to build and use the Pentaho Reporting nightly build, with Pentaho Report Designer and the Pentaho dependencies in your Java projects. In the last topic of this book, you went through all the ways to find documentation, resources, support, meet the community, and so on, as a new developer and expert in Pentaho Reporting.

Thank you for taking the time to read this book. My hope is that now you feel comfortable with Pentaho Reporting and feel excited to try new projects using it. Enjoy!

Index